lonely planet

POCKET

NEW YORK CITY

TOP EXPERIENCES • LOCAL LIFE

JOHN GARRY, ZORA O'NEILL

Welcome to New York City

Glass towers and artists lofts, stock deals and sleek galleries, hallowed publishers and buzzing media hubs. NYC offers a million opportunities for people who've immigrated from next door or the other side of the globe: the beauty of New York is that it is virtually everything to seemingly everyone. What will it be for you?

New York City's Top Experiences

Ramble Through Central Park (p204)

VERGIE AZEVEDO/SHUTTERSTOCK ©

SUSANNE POMMER/SHUTTERSTOCK ©

Dive into World Culture at the Metropolitan Museum of Art (p184)

OSCITY/SHUTTERSTOCK ©

Visit the Statue of Liberty & Ellis Island (p44)

MONICA CARLSON/SHUTTERSTOCK ©

Scale the Heights of the Empire State Building (p154)

Light up the Night in Times Square (p152)

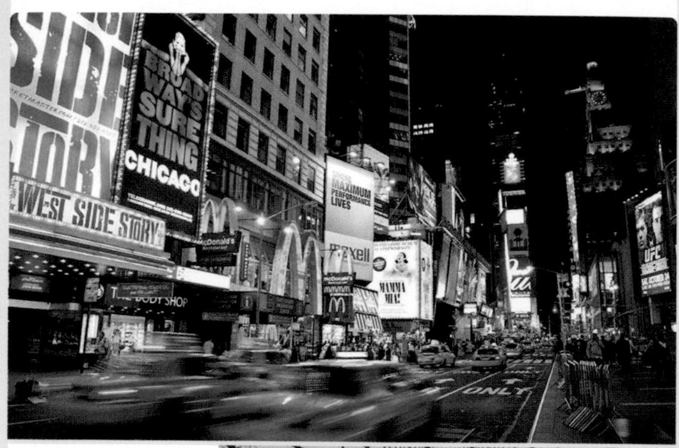

SONGQUAN DENG/SHUTTERSTOCK ©

Stroll Brooklyn Bridge (p48)

MAPMAN/SHUTTERSTOCK ©

SHUTTERSTOCK / GAGLIARDI PHOTOGRAPHY © / ARCHITECT: DAVID CHILDS

See NYC from One World Observatory (p50)

Discover the Museum of Modern Art (p156)

ERIKA CROSS/SHUTTERSTOCK ©

Wander Along the High Line (p110)

ASIASTOCK/SHUTTERSTOCK ©

GUILLAUME GAUDET/LONELY PLANET ©

Sail Away to Governors Island (p66)

Spend a Day at Coney Island (p236)

LAZYLLAMA/SHUTTERSTOCK ©

CY AUZEN/500PX ©

Experiment with Art at MoMA PS1 (p178)

Dining Out

New York City's dining scene is seemingly infinite and all-consuming, a testament to its kaleidoscope of citizens, made all the better as COVID-era outdoor dining seems here to stay. Unlike some foodie cities, though, it can be too easy to wander into a pricey, mediocre meal. Research and planning pay off.

Food Trucks & Carts

Standard food-cart options: pretzels, candied nuts and 'dirty-water dogs' (boiled hot dogs, good with sauerkraut). In the past decade, the scene has diversified, and even the 'halal carts' (spiced meat over rice) have developed distinct styles. For several years, the Vendy Awards honored the best; check online (www.vendyawards.streetvendor.org) for past champs. Trucks park in designated zones throughout Manhattan, particularly near Madison Square Park and in Midtown and the Financial District.

Hot Tables

Some of the finest restaurants require reservations (check about four to six weeks ahead); some even require prepayment. Small trendy places often do first come, first served: put your name on the list and wait. You won't be seated until your whole group is present. And you'll probably be served fast and moved out, to make room for the next diners.

Best Fine Dining

Eleven Madison Park Cutting-edge cuisine that just happens to be veggie. (p141)

Le Bernardin A holy grail of NYC fine dining, starring a seafood menu. (p165)

Bâtard Classic, beautifully balanced continental cuisine in Lower Manhattan. (p57)

Modern Mouthwatering Michelin-starred morsels beside MoMA's sculpture garden. (p165)

Cosme Expanding New Yorkers' ideas of Mexican food since 2014. (p142)

RBLFMR/SHUTTERSTOCK ©

Best Vegetarian

Bunna Cafe All-vegan Ethiopian in Bushwick. (p228)

HanGawi Meat-free (and shoe-free) Korean restaurant in Koreatown. (p165)

Cadence Proof that Southern soul food can be done without pork. (p96)

Best Counter Service

Grand Central Oyster Bar Efficient waiters and excellent seafood. (p164)

Thai Diner Retro Bangkok flair and plenty of spice. (p77)

Golden Diner Asian meets everything else in this comfort-food mashup. (p77)

Best Food Halls

Chelsea Market The first gourmet food hall, and still one of the best. (pictured; p117)

Tin Building In the old wholesale fish market, expertly curated by chef Jean-Georges Vongerichten. (p59)

Essex Market A great mix of functional produce and chic food shops. (p98)

Smorgasburg A cool weekly outdoor food fest. (p228)

Best Quick Bites

Prince Street Pizza Classic NYC pizza. (p80)

Papaya King Hot dogs and papaya juice. (p193)

Taïm Possibly the city's best falafel, fresh and healthy. (p121)

Tacombi An always-reliable Mexican minichain. (p78)

Restaurant 'Week'

Actually about a month in summer (July to August) and winter (January), this promo sees the city's finer restaurants offering prix-fixe meals for as little as $30. See www.nycgo.com/restaurant-week.

New York City on a Plate

The Best Pastrami Sandwich

Purists agree: rye bread (preferably seeded) is best.
Top the pastrami with spicy brown mustard.
Toast the bread so it doesn't fall apart.
A dill pickle on the side adds complexity.

★ Five Top Places for Pastrami Sandwiches

Katz's Delicatessen (p97) The NYC deli of your dreams.

Pastrami Queen (p192) Nice and fatty, and piled high.

Zabar's (p214) King of the gourmet deli-supermarkets.

Barney Greengrass (p213) The Sturgeon King also knows pastrami.

Ess-a-Bagel (p167) Humble but classic.

LEONARD ZHUKOVSKY/SHUTTERSTOCK ©

The Pastrami-Sandwich Experience

Biting into a pastrami sandwich is a classic New York City experience. It's best eaten in one of the city's old-school Jewish delis: neon signs out front, counter seating inside and gruff but kind-hearted staff. The sandwich comes piled high with thick, succulent slices of lightly spiced and smoked meat, which contrast with the crunch of toasted rye bread. Zingy brown mustard binds it all into a delectable work of art.

Katz's Delicatessen

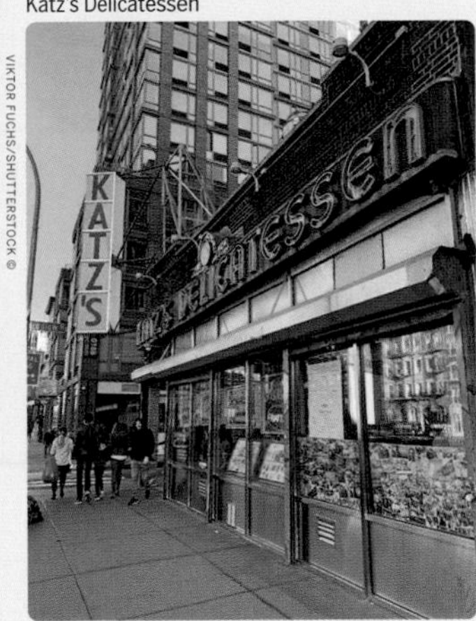

VIKTOR FUCHS/SHUTTERSTOCK ©

Bar Open

New York satisfies nearly every niche, so whether you crave banjos, vintage booze or perfectly hopped brews, you'll find them. The city's nightclubs are legendary, but also oddly limited due to Prohibition-era rules. That should finally shift in 2023, with a proposed zoning change that permits dancing in small bars and clubs.

Cart Coffee

The city's humblest form of caffeine is the cheap, not-too-strong coffee in an iconic 'We Are Happy to Serve You' paper cup, bought on the go from a shiny silver sidewalk cart. Even if you prefer fair-trade single-origin beans (NYC has all that too), try the cart coffee once, in solidarity: say 'regular,' and it comes with milk and sugar.

Cocktail City

In NYC, where the term 'cocktail' is claimed to have been born, mixed drinks are still stirred with the utmost gravitas, often based on Prohibition recipes and always featuring flawless ice. A good cocktail bar now also dedicates a chunk of its menu to low- and no-alcohol options as well.

Best Coffee & Tea

SEY Coffee The latest in Nordic-style coffee connoisseurship. (p231)

Plowshares Coffee They've been pulling espresso here since the aughts. (p216)

Té Company Utterly refined teas from Taiwan, along with lovely cakes. (p128)

Best Cocktails

Bar Goto Japanese *izakaya* on the Lower East Side with exquisitely precise drinks. (p100)

Employees Only Fantastic barkeeps and arresting libations in the West Village. (p123)

Dead Rabbit Consistently on world's-best lists, with a notable low-alcohol menu. (p60)

Maison Premiere Absinthe, atmosphere and oysters in Williamsburg. (p229)

Best Old Style

Fraunces Tavern George Washington drank here – say no more. (p62)

PATTI MCCONVILLE/ALAMY STOCK PHOTO ©

Campbell A robber baron's offices, tucked away in Grand Central. (p168)

Bemelmans Bar Vintage hotel bar, now an Instagram phenomenon. (p195)

Best Roofs & Views

Overstory The 64th-floor view justifies the pricey cocktails. (p62)

Top of the Standard Swanky jazz, nice nibbles and river views above the High Line. (p125)

Cantor Roof Garden Bar Survey all of Central Park from the top of the Met. (p195)

Empire Rooftop There's plenty of space at this Upper West Side hotel bar. (p216)

Best Themes

Gallow Green Theater people put their all into this rooftop spot where *Sleep No More* is staged. (p123)

Serra The decor changes with the seasons, but it's always transporting. (p144)

PDT Of all NYC's modern speakeasies, this one, leans into it hardest. (p100)

Best Wine & Beer

Four Horsemen A leader in the natural-wine trend, in Williamsburg. (p229)

Proletariat Craft beer and vegan food: a winning East Village combo. (p100)

La Compagnie des Vins Surnaturels French wine rules here (it's a branch of a Paris bar). (p82)

As Is A sunny corner spot to taste craft beers, with satisfying food too. (p170)

Best Small Clubs & Stages

Joe's Pub Comfortable, affordable and an interesting roster of cabaret, country, jazz and comedy. (p81)

City Vineyard Big-name singers are a draw; the wine and the water view are bonuses. (p63)

Arlene's Grocery A destination for indie rock since the 1990s. (p104)

House of Yes One of Brooklyn's best, for super-creative themed dance nights. (p229)

New York City in a Glass

The Egg Cream

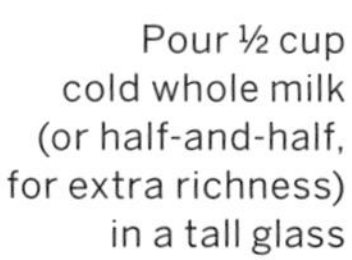

Pour ½ cup
cold whole milk
(or half-and-half,
for extra richness)
in a tall glass

Add 3 Tbsps

syrup and stir
Fill glass with
seltzer (never
club soda) and
stir to make a
frothy head

be bottled so are
always made fresh

★ Five Top Places for Egg Creams

Yonah Schimmel Knish Bakery (p99) Great way to wash down your knish.

Russ & Daughters (p97) Make an egg cream a part of your nutritious smoked-fish brunch.

Veselka (p97)
Also serves vanilla egg creams.

Lexington Candy Shop (p194) The old-school-diner atmosphere is key.

Ray's Candy Store (www.rayscandystore.com) The proprietor is as famous as his egg creams.

HORTIMAGES/SHUTTERSTOCK ©

A Delicious Paradox

The egg cream: no eggs, no cream. This refreshing made-to-order chocolate-milk soda was invented in the 1900s by Louis Auster, a Jewish candy-store owner who served them from his shop at Second Ave and E 7th St, in the heart of the old Yiddish theater district. Today it's a dwindling part of the NYC diet, but a treasure nonetheless. Seek one out and drink it fast, before it loses its fizz.

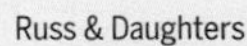
Russ & Daughters

DANIEL M SILVA/SHUTTERSTOCK ©

Treasure Hunt

Unsurprisingly for a capital of commercialism, creativity and fashion, this is one of the world's best shopping destinations. From indie designer-driven boutiques to landmark department stores, from zines to signed first editions, it's all somewhere in the city – though little is outright cheap.

Vintage Adventures

As much as New York chases after the new, it's also a repository for cool old stuff. The most popular flea market is the **Brooklyn Flea** (www.brooklynflea.com), in Dumbo April through December, and in Chelsea year-round.

The East Village is the city's go-to neighborhood for secondhand and vintage stores.

Sample Sales

Beyond the usual seasonal sales, sample sales are how high-end labels get rid of overstock. They're held in designated spaces, with wonderfully deep discounts but minimal service and an 'all sales final' policy. One major organizer is 260 Sample Sale (www.260samplesale.com), which runs daily sales at three locations.

Best Fashion & Accessories

Bergdorf Goodman The most magical of NYC's department stores, with stellar store displays, pictured. (pictured; p175)

R Swiader Gender-free fashion and all-around clubhouse, with a salon in the back. (p84)

Fine & Dandy Spats, suspenders, pocket squares – all that a dapper man requires. (p176)

Only NY Deeply normcore NYC-themed streetwear, such as the Greek-cup bucket hat. (p106)

LEONARD ZHUKOVSKY/SHUTTERSTOCK ©

Best Secondhand

Screaming Mimis Lots of appealing clothes from decades past. (p132)

Beacon's Closet Get a new outfit without breaking the bank at this great vintage shop. (p134)

Michael's Upper East Side ladies resell their couture here. (p199)

Best Bookshops

Strand Book Store Hands-down NYC's best used bookstore. (p132)

Housing Works Bookstore Used books and a cafe in an atmospheric setting in Nolita. (p86)

McNally Jackson Great SoHo spot for book browsing and author readings. (p84)

Printed Matter, Inc Zines and other printed oddities are the specialty here. (p134)

Best Only in NYC

Fishs Eddy Fun NYC-themed plates and glasses, among other things. (p147)

M&J Trimming Warning: this Garment District shop will induce sequin overload. (p176)

B&H Every techy gadget is in stock and sold by smart sales staff – and an odd mechanized bin system. (p176)

ABC Carpet & Home Every New Yorker comes here to fantasize over furniture that won't fit in their apartment. (p147)

Top Tip

Individual items of clothing and footwear that cost less than $110 are exempt from sales tax. For everything else, you'll pay 8.875% retail sales tax on every purchase.

Top Souvenirs

JEFF GREENBERG/UNIVERSAL IMAGES GROUP VIA GETTY IMAGES ©

New York Public Lions

Bibliophiles can get a New York Public Library lion paperweight and other bookish gifts at the main library gift shop (p161).

I ♥ NY Anything

Milton Glaser's 1976 design (intended for the whole state of New York) has never gone out of style. Get the classic logo, plus many variants, on T-shirts, mugs, baby onesies and more at CityStore (p65).

LEONARD ZHUKOVSKY/SHUTTERSTOCK ©

BOKEHBOO STUDIOS/SHUTTERSTOCK ©

Clever Coffee Cup

A ceramic version of the classic paper 'Anthora' coffee cup – one of NYC's most enduring, and endearing, symbols – can be found at the Moma Design Store (p175).

RACHEL MOON/SHUTTERSTOCK ©

Black-and-White Cookies

The oddly satisfying black-and-white cookie, usually spotted shrink-wrapped on bodega counters, is made elegant at William Greenberg Desserts (p193).

SAN FRANCISCO CHRONICLE/HEARTS IMAGES VIA GETTY IMAGES ©

Scents of the City

Perfumers DS & Durga (p233) capture the city in scented candles such as Wild Brooklyn Lavender and Concrete After Lightning. (No Mid-July Garbage...yet!)

Under the Radar

DAN HERRICK/LONELY PLANET ©

Manhattan's bucket-list favorites like Times Square and the Broadway blockbusters are spectacular, but they don't give much sense of how New Yorkers really live. For experiences you won't see on postcards, hop on a train to less famous parts of town, and seek out shows at smaller venues.

Best Neighborhoods & Subway Lines

Astoria Dip your toe in Queens' international pool with this suggested walk. (p180)

7 Train The so-called 'International Express' runs through Jackson Heights (where the Himalayas meet Colombia) and ends in Flushing, the city's biggest Chinatown.

Q Train Admire Brooklyn brownstone grandeur in Fort Greene and Park Slope.

Brooklyn Heights The promenade gives a classic view of Manhattan, and the history here runs deep. (p235)

Harlem Lively with African American and West African culture and shops, historic jazz clubs and mouthwatering food. Like the song says, take the A train. (p200)

L Train Connecting the East Village, Williamsburg and Bushwick, this train draws artistic energy (and great street fashion).

Best Places to See the Next Big Thing

Apollo Theater This famous stage has launched the careers of countless Black musical legends. (pictured; p201)

Public Theater Why pay Broadway prices, when so many hits have gotten their start here? (p84)

Smalls This basement jazz club is indeed tiny, but big in atmosphere. (p129)

92nd Street Y This bastion of uptown culture hosts fascinating lectures and concerts, many of which are family friendly. (p198)

Brooklyn Academy of Music (www.bam.org) This avant-garde-but-accessible venue is worth the trip to downtown Brooklyn, especially during its Next Wave Festival every fall.

Museums

MARCIA CRAYTON/SHUTTERSTOCK ©

The Met and MoMA are essential, but don't overlook some of the city's smaller (and sometimes stranger) collections. You can spend a day or even a lifetime in the giants, or just feast your eyes for 15 minutes in the smallest.

Best Classic Museums

Museum of Modern Art Brilliantly curated galleries feature no shortage of iconic modern works. (p156)

Metropolitan Museum of Art Simply huge. Don't even try to see it all. (p184)

Frick Collection A Gilded Age mansion sparkling with Vermeers, El Grecos and Goyas. (p189)

Brooklyn Museum Worth a trip to the Prospect Park area, this excellent collection rivals the Met, with fewer crowds. The First Saturday series is a monthly free party (pictured; www.brooklynmuseum.org).

Best Contemporary Art

Whitney Museum of American Art Especially great during the Biennial, which runs in even years. (p116)

New Museum of Contemporary Art A cutting-edge temple to contemporary art in all its forms. (p94)

MoMA PS1 An adapted schoolhouse that always has something edgy. (p102)

Best Historical Museums

Lower East Side Tenement Museum Life as an immigrant in the 19th and early 20th centuries. (p94)

Ellis Island Moving exhibits on American immigration history. (p47)

Museum of the City of New York New angles on the city culture and lore. (p191)

Best Quirky Collections

City Reliquary An artists' love letter to NYC, featuring individuals' weird city-themed collections. (p226)

Mmuseumm Tiny objects in the tiny space of a freight elevator. (p76)

Donald Judd Home Studio Enter the mind of the minimalist sculptor. (p74)

With Kids

New York City has loads of activities for young ones, including imaginative playgrounds and leafy parks where kids can run free, plus lots of kid-friendly museums and sights. Other highs include carousel rides and noshing at markets around town.

Eating Out

In the most touristed areas, restaurants stand ready with high chairs and kiddie menus. But most popular spots are cramped and can be a hassle with little ones; dining early (before 7:30pm) can help take the pressure off. Food halls offer excellent casual dining with options to please nearly everyone, and parks are another option: in good weather, grab groceries and picnic.

Resources

Check for kid-friendly events at Time Out New York Kids (www.timeoutnewyorkkids.com) and at Mommy Poppins (www.mommypoppins.com).

For kids eight and up, Lonely Planet's *Not for Parents: New York* shares fascinating facts and intriguing stories about the city's people, places, history and culture.

For a date night out, hire a sitter to come to your hotel from a service such as Baby Sitters' Guild (www.babysittersguild.com), in operation since 1940.

Best Family Outings

American Museum of Natural History The dioramas are works of art and the dinosaur skeletons never fail to impress. (p210)

Metropolitan Museum of Art Are the kids going through an Ancient Egypt phase? Make a beeline to the mummies. (p184)

New York City Fire Museum Kids (and parents) can live out their firefighting dreams at this historical museum. (p75)

Coney Island The tattoos-and-sideshows element here skews more adult, but thrill-seeking teens will love the wooden coaster, the Cyclone. (pictured; p236)

LEV RADIN/SHUTTERSTOCK ©

Museum of the Moving Image Head to Queens for edutainment: DIY flipbooks, a Tut-theme silent-movie palace and the history of the Muppets. (p181)

Best Parks

Central Park Row a boat, visit the zoo and hit Heckscher playground, the best of the park's 21 playgrounds. (p204)

Hudson River Park All along the lower west side of Manhattan, with mini-golf, water features and science-themed play, among other entertainments. (p117)

Little Island Opened in 2021, this artificial island (part of larger Hudson River Park) was built for exploring. (p116)

Governors Island Fun slides, hammocks, even camping – plus you can drop kids for an hour at The Yard (www.play-ground.nyc), a wild junkyard/playground. (p66)

Best Shopping

Books of Wonder Storybooks, teen novels, NYC-themed gifts and storytime make this rainy-day perfection. (p148)

Economy Candy No frills, just bulk-candy goodness – and a place to introduce your kids to your generation's faves. (p107)

FAO Schwarz The city's oldest toy store (in a newish location), complete with dance-on floor piano. (p175)

Tiny Doll House Every little thing you could possibly need for your miniature projects. (p198)

Worth a Trip

The 265-acre **Bronx Zoo** (www.bronxzoo.com) is one of the USA's oldest and largest. It features over 6000 animals and habitats ranging from African plains to Asian rainforests. Wednesday tickets are discounted ($18).

Festivals

ANOOP BALAKRISHNAN REMA/SHUTTERSTOCK ©

Any given week in NYC, you can bet something notable is happening. These events are the biggest public parties, annual celebrations of local pride or dazzling creativity. If you like a big public party, plan your trip around one – or just take note of when you might encounter more crowds than usual.

Lunar (Chinese) New Year Festival (http://betterchinatown.com; late Jan/early Feb) Fireworks and dancing dragons – one of the USA's biggest fests.

St Patrick's Day Parade (www.nycstpatricksparade.org; Mar 17) A city institution: kitschy, boozy and historical.

Tribeca Film Festival (www.tribecafilm.com; Apr-May) A major star of the indie movie circuit.

SummerStage (www.cityparksfoundation.org/summerstage; May-Oct;) The city's best free summer-concert series.

Celebrate Brooklyn! (www.bricartsmedia.org; Jun–mid-Aug) More excellent free summer concerts.

Shakespeare in the Park (www.publictheater.org; Jun-Aug) Star actors shine in these free productions.

Bryant Park Summer Film Festival (www.bryantpark.org; Mon mid-Jun–Aug) Classic films on a huge outdoor screen on the park lawn.

Mermaid Parade (www.coneyisland.com; late Jun; pictured) Coney Island at its creative best.

July 4 Fireworks (www.macys.com; Jul 4) Watch the Independence Day light show over the East River.

Village Halloween Parade (www.halloween-nyc.com; Oct 31) A costumed combo of Mardi Gras and wild art project.

NYC Marathon (www.nycmarathon.org; 1st Sun Nov) Cheer on runners through all five boroughs.

Thanksgiving Day Parade (www.macys.com; 4th Thu Nov) Massive cartoon character balloons soar overhead.

Rockefeller Center Christmas Tree Lighting (www.rockefellercenter.com; Wed after Thanksgiving) The official start of the holiday season.

New Year's Eve (www.timessquarenyc.org/nye; Dec 31) A raucous, freezing party in Times Sq.

For Free

JIAWANGKUN/SHUTTERSTOCK ©

The Big Apple is seldom a bargain, but there are ways to crack the treasure chest for free or nearly so – especially in summer, when free festivals abound and park life flourishes. Save year round by visiting museums on discount days. In general, life is cheaper beyond Manhattan.

Big Apple Greeter (www.bigapplegreeter.org) Let a local volunteer show you around their neighborhood.

Staten Island Ferry Wave at the Statue of Liberty and take postcard-worthy photos of Lower Manhattan. (p244)

Chelsea Galleries More than 300 spaces in Manhattan's West 20s; go to Thursday-night openings for drinks and snacks. (p112)

Christie's Hobnob with assorted treasures before they're sold at auction. (p177)

Barnes & Noble Author readings often feature big names and are nearly always free. (p149)

TV Show Tapings See how TV gets made, while laughing it up in the audience. (p172)

New York Public Library Sumptuous architecture, interesting exhibits and simply a nice place to sit. (pictured; p161)

National Museum of the American Indian Beautiful textiles, objects and art. (p55)

African Burial Ground National Monument A memorial to the legacy of enslaved Africans in colonial New York. (p55)

American Folk Art Museum Where handicrafts like quilts reach the level of art. (p210)

Nicholas Roerich Museum Gorgeous paintings by a Russian poet-painter in an old town house. (p210)

Museum of the City of New York Pay what you wish to learn city culture and history. (p191)

Museum Discounts

Many big museums have a weekly or monthly afternoon or evening that's free or pay-what-you-wish.

Timed tickets are usually still required; plan ahead.

When admission is 'suggested,' don't be shy: you're welcome to pay far less.

LGBTIQ+ Travelers

LAZYLLAMA/SHUTTERSTOCK ©

The city 'where pride began' (at the Stonewall riot in 1969) nurtures almost every LGBTIQ+ subculture. Folx go out every night of the week, and June is jammed with Pride events. Don't stop at the Manhattan gayborhoods of the West Village, Chelsea and Hell's Kitchen: a strong scene grows in Brooklyn too.

Resources

For info on parties and more, see, among many other websites, ***Get Out*** (www.getoutmag.com). Also follow promoters on social, and, for face-to-face advice in real life, stop by West Village institution **The Center** (LGBT Community Center; www.gaycenter.org; 208 W 13th St, West Village; 9am-10pm Mon-Sat, to 9pm Sun; S 1/2/3 to 14th St, A/C/E, L to 8th Ave-14th St).

Best Promoters

Ty Sunderland (www.instagram.com/tysunderland) Pop-loving parties in Manhattan and Brooklyn – and on boats.

Hot Rabbit (www.hotrabbit.com) Regular women-friendly parties in Manhattan and Brooklyn.

Horse Meat Disco (www.instagram.com/yougivemethelight) Quarterly pop-ups – worth the trek to Maspeth, Queens.

LadyFag (www.instagram.com/ladyfag) The excellent monthly Battle Hymn party, usually in Chelsea.

Best Classic Hangouts

Stonewall Inn Friendly and informal, this veritable pilgrimage site wears its history well. (p127)

Marie's Crisis Sing your show-tune-loving heart out at this chummy piano bar. (p125)

Cubbyhole A veteran Village lesbian bar with jukebox tunes, chatty regulars and no attitude. (p124)

Julius' A long-established and refreshingly unsceney gay bar. (p124)

Best for Dancing Queens

Q Sweat it out at this multilevel space in Hell's Kitchen. (p169)

3 Dollar Bill Head to Brooklyn for 10,000 sq ft to werk. (p229)

Active New York City

For both New Yorkers and for visitors, the city itself, with flights of subway stairs and a strong walking culture, can be an ample workout. But you'll also find various opportunities for more structured fitness – or sit back and root for the home teams.

MATT DUTILE/GETTY IMAGES ©

Running & Cycling

Join a group run on the weekend with ***New York Road Runners Club*** (www.nyrr.org). Bike lanes crisscross NYC, but for a more placid ride, head for car-free Central Park, Brooklyn's Prospect Park or the riverside greenway around Manhattan.

Fitness

Yoga and Pilates studios dot the city; Soul Cycle (www.soul-cycle.com) got its start here. Parks host free or donation-based classes; see www.nycgovparks.org. Major gym chains offer day passes (sometimes free). To recover from a workout, head for the Russian & Turkish Baths (p91).

Spectator Sports

For baseball, it's all about the Yankees (in the Bronx) or the Mets (in Queens) – or check out minor-league teams in Coney and Staten Islands; see www.mlb.com. Basketball is the Knicks (Manhattan) and the Nets (Brooklyn). The Rangers cover hockey. All tickets via www.ticketmaster.com.

Best Outdoor Activities

Unlimited Biking (www.unlimitedbiking.com/new-york) Well-organized bike tours around the city, from two to seven hours.

Jacqueline Kennedy Onassis Reservoir Run this scenic 1.6-mile loop in Central Park. (p206)

Downtown Boathouse Part of Hudson River Park, this place rents kayaks. (p57)

Wollman Skating Rink Zip on the ice in winter; roller-boogie in summer. (p211)

Responsible Travel

Follow these tips when you're in New York City to leave a lighter footprint, support local and have a positive impact on local communities.

Leave a Small Footprint

Drink tap water – NYC is rightly proud of its quality.

BYO bag, as the city's plastic-bag ban means you have to pay for them at stores.

BYO coffee cup, even though this trend is still getting a foothold in the city.

Turn off air-conditioning in your hotel room when you leave.

Don't flush stuff. No wipes, no tampons – it all gums up the sewage system.

Learn More

Take a class with League of Kitchens (www.leagueofkitchens.com), a group of immigrant women who teach cooking in their own homes.

Attend a cultural festival such as the West Indian Day Parade (September) or the Puerto Rican Day Parade (June). See www.nycgo.com for events.

Visit the Schomburg Center for Research in Black Culture (www.nypl.org/locations/schomburg) to learn about Black people who helped shape the city.

Identify NYC's birds and how to protect them with NYC Audubon Society (www.nycaudubon.org).

Give Back

Help feed low-income families and homebound New Yorkers with City Harvest (www.cityharvest.org) and Citymeals on Wheels (www.citymeals.org).

Support homeless people by making backpacks with food and essentials at Backpacks for the Street (www.backpacksforthestreet.org).

Get your hands in the dirt volunteering with NYC Parks (www.nycgovparks.org) to keep green space clean.

Support Local

Skip the chains. Favor local shop-owners as much as possible. See curated lists at Made in NYC (www.madeinnyc.org) and Black-Owned Brooklyn (www.blackownedbrooklyn.com).

Visit a greenmarket for fresh produce and other area farm products. Check schedule and locations at www.grownyc.org

LITTLENYSTOCK/SHUTTERSTOCK ©

Enjoy Nature

Relax in a community garden such as the vacant lots made lush while also reflecting the neighborhood character. See more than 150 locations at www.grownyc.org.

New York Botanical Garden (www.nybg.org) is worth the trip to the Bronx for its wide variety of plant species.

Tour the green roof at Jacob Javits Center (www.javitscenter.com), home to 17 bird species and 300,000 honeybees.

Forage in city parks on a tour with Wildman Steve Brill (www.wildmanstevebrill.com).

Take quiet time at the Central Park Conservatory Garden or the tiny Elizabeth Street Garden. (p206; p74)

Climate Change & Travel

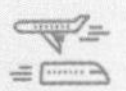

It's impossible to ignore the impact we have when traveling, and the importance of making changes where we can. Lonely Planet urges all travelers to engage with their travel carbon footprint. There are many carbon calculators online that allow travelers to estimate the carbon emissions generated by their journey; try resurgence.org/resources/carbon-calculator.html. Many airlines and booking sites offer travellers the option of offsetting the impact of greenhouse gas emissions by contributing to climate-friendly initiatives around the world. We continue to offset the carbon footprint of all Lonely Planet staff travel, while recognising this is a mitigation more than a solution.

Four Perfect Days

Day 1

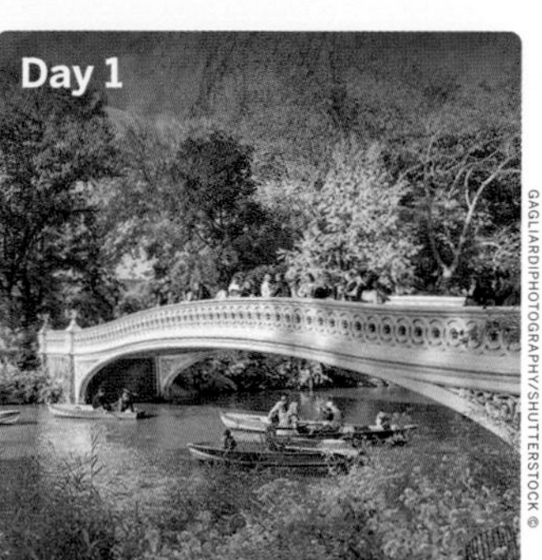

GAGLIARDIPHOTOGRAPHY/SHUTTERSTOCK ©

Start your day at the **Metropolitan Museum of Art** (p184), admiring the Egyptian, Roman and European masterpieces; in summer head to the roof for a view over Central Park. Nearby **Neue Galerie** (p190) offers a feast of German and Austrian art in a 1914 mansion.

Spend the afternoon in **Central Park** (pictured; p204), visiting **Bethesda Fountain** (p205), **Belvedere Castle** (p206) and **Strawberry Fields** (p205).

Pick up tickets for a **Broadway** show or check out something ahead of the curve at **Playwrights Horizons** (p173). After the show, dine at classic **Barbetta** (p166), quaff cocktails at **Lantern's Keep** (p169) or just soak up the light show at **Times Square** (p152).

Day 2

DAVE Z/SHUTTERSTOCK ©

Start your morning amid the commuter bustle of **Grand Central Terminal** (p160), admire the **Chrysler Building** (p160) from the street and from the observation deck at the **Empire State Building** (pictured; p154).

Back on the ground, stroll through the **New York Public Library** (p161) or spend a bit longer at the **Museum of Modern Art** (p156). Then head downtown, grabbing lunch around **Madison Square Park** (p139) and admiring the classic **Flatiron Building** (p140).

Do some **shopping** (p86) in SoHo and Chinatown. Have dinner, maybe at a Chinatown classic like **Nom Wah Tea Parlor** (p77), then catch a show at **Joe's Pub** (p81).

Day 3

CAITLIN RIDELL/LONELY PLANET ©

Walk over the **Brooklyn Bridge** (p48) and up to the **Brooklyn Heights Promenade** (p235), to admire how far you've come. Stroll **Brooklyn Heights** (p234) and treat yourself to pastries at **L'Appartement 4F** (p235).

Walk down to the river and catch the **NYC Ferry** (p244) to north **Williamsburg,** passing under **Williamsburg Bridge** (pictured; p226). Stroll Bedford Ave, browsing interesting shops like **Spoonbill & Sugartown** (p232), and nab unique souvenirs at **Artists & Fleas** (p232, pictured). Metropolitan Ave offers more eclectic attractions, such as the **City Reliquary** (p226). Hit **Maison Premiere** (p229) for dinner and cocktails, then take a stroll back to the waterfront, to admire magnificent views of Manhattan.

Day 4

PISAPHOTOGRAPHY/SHUTTERSTOCK ©

Catch an early **Staten Island Ferry** (p244) and watch the morning sun glitter on Lower Manhattan's glass towers, then take another boat to **Ellis Island** (p47).

Head to the Meatpacking District to visit the gorgeous **Whitney Museum of American Art** (p116). The **High Line** (pictured; p110) offers a wander along a once-abandoned elevated rail line; stop for snacks, coffee and intriguing streetscapes.

For dinner, head back downtown to the lovely streets of Greenwich Village, perhaps followed by live jazz at **Smalls** (p129) or the **Village Vanguard** (p131). End up at basement bar **Tippler** (p127) for craft beer or cocktails.

Need to Know

For detailed information, see Survival Guide (p238)

Currency
US dollar (US$)

Language
English

Visas
Nationals of 38 countries can enter the US without a visa, but must fill out an ESTA application.

Money
ATMs ubiquitous; credit cards accepted widely.

Mobile Phones
International travelers can use local SIM cards in an unlocked phone (or buy a cheap US phone and load with prepaid minutes).

Time
Eastern Standard Time (GMT/UTC minus five hours)

Tipping
Not optional. Restaurant servers 18–20%; bartenders $1 per beer or $2 per cocktail; taxi drivers 10–15%; hotel cleaners $3–5 per night.

Daily Budget

Budget: Less than $300

Dorm bed: $60–80

Slice of pizza: around $4

Food-truck tacos: from $6

Happy-hour glass of wine: $12

Bus or subway ride: less than $3

Midrange: $300–500

Double room in a midrange hotel: from $200

Empire State Building ticket: $45

Midrange restaurant dinner for two: $160

Craft cocktail: $20

Discount Broadway tickets: around $80

Top end: More than $500

One night at opulent Bowery Hotel: from $650

Upscale tasting menu: $200–365

Metropolitan Opera orchestra seats: $85–445

Advance Planning

Two months before Reserve accommodation. Book tickets to Broadway shows or other performances. Request a free Big Apple Greeters tour.

One month before Make restaurant reservations, especially if you're planning a very high-end meal. Book timed tickets for museums.

One week before Check city listings magazines such as *New Yorker* and *New York* for events of interest, such as author readings or art openings.

Arriving in New York City

John F Kennedy International Airport (JFK)

AirTrain ($8) links to the subway ($2.75); it's one hour into Manhattan. Taxis cost a flat $52, excluding tolls, tip and rush-hour surcharge.

LaGuardia Airport (LGA)

Q70 express bus (free) runs to the 74th St–Broadway for subway ($2.75), or M60 bus ($2.75) to upper Manhattan and free subway transfer. Taxis $35 to $55, excluding tolls and tip.

Newark Liberty International Airport (EWR)

AirTrain to Newark Airport train station, then NJ Transit train to New York's Penn Station ($15.50 combined ticket). Taxis range from $50 to $70 (plus $15 toll and tip).

Getting Around

Subway

Cheap, efficient and operates 24/7. One ride is $2.75; pay with credit card or stored-value OMNY card.

Bus

Convenient between Manhattan's east and west sides. Per ride $2.75, paid same as subway.

Taxi

Hail on the street or use Curb app (for about 30% more). Sample fare: $15 across Manhattan. See www.nyc.gov/taxi.

Ferry

Makes waterside stops in all five boroughs. See www.ferry.nyc.

Bicycle

Citi Bike (www.citibikenyc.com) bike-share system. A 24-hour pass is $15, with additional fees for electric bikes.

Grand Central Terminal (p160)

New York City Neighborhoods

Upper West Side & Central Park (p203)
Home to Lincoln Center and Central Park – the city's antidote to the endless stretches of concrete.

West Village, Chelsea & the Meatpacking District (p109)
Quaint streets and well-preserved brick townhouses lead to neighborhood cafes mixed with trendy nightlife options.

SoHo & Chinatown (p69)
Hidden temples and steaming dumpling houses dot Chinatown. Next door are SoHo's streamlined streets and high-end shopping.

One World Observatory

Ellis Island

Brooklyn Bridge

Statue of Liberty

Governors Island

Financial District & Lower Manhattan (p43)
Home to the National September 11 Memorial & Museum, the Brooklyn Bridge and the Statue of Liberty.

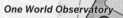

Upper East Side (p183)
High-end boutiques and sophisticated mansions culminate in the architectural flourish of Museum Mile.

Midtown (p151)
This is the NYC you're thinking of: Times Square, Broadway theaters, canyons of skyscrapers and bustling crowds.

Union Square, Flatiron District & Gramercy (p137)
The tie that binds the colorful menagerie of surrounding areas. It's short on sights but big on buzz-worthy restaurants.

Brooklyn: Williamstown & Bushwick (p223)
Two of NYC's most popular residential areas and home to one of its best parks. Hidden treasure Green-Wood Cemetery is nearby.

East Village & the Lower East Side (p89)
Old meets new on every block of this downtown duo – two of the city's hottest 'hoods for nightlife and cheap eats.

Explore New York City

Worth a Trip

Walking Tours

Bryant Park (p164) GAGLIARDIPHOTOGRAPHY/SHUTTERSTOCK ©

Explore

Financial District & Lower Manhattan

White-collar Wall Streeters may reign supreme, but Manhattan's southern tip isn't strictly business. Navigate the skyscraper-shadowed sidewalks of 'FiDi' to see architectural icons like One World Trade Center, then sail offshore for Ellis Island and Lady Liberty herself. North of FiDi is Tribeca, with upmarket restaurants, bars and retail.

The Short List

- ***Statue of Liberty (p44)*** *Marveling at America's most famous statue, a beguiling green goddess guarding the world's greatest city.*
- ***Ellis Island (p47)*** *Standing in the shoes of American immigrants at the USA's historically significant and personally poignant point of entry.*
- ***One World Observatory (p50)*** *Zipping up to the top of the Western Hemisphere's tallest building for a knockout metropolitan panorama.*
- ***Staten Island Ferry (p54)*** *Taking in sunset-blazing skyscrapers while crossing the harbor on one of NYC's fantastic – and free – floating icons.*
- ***South Street Seaport (p58)*** *Exploring cobblestone streets and stunning new complexes along the East River.*

Getting There & Around

S The Financial District is well serviced by subway lines; main hub Fulton St connects the A/C, J/Z, 2/3 and 4/5 lines. Take the 1 train to South Ferry for ferries to Staten Island or the Statue of Liberty and Ellis Island.

Neighborhood Map on p52

One World Trade Center COSMIN COITA/SHUTTERSTOCK ©

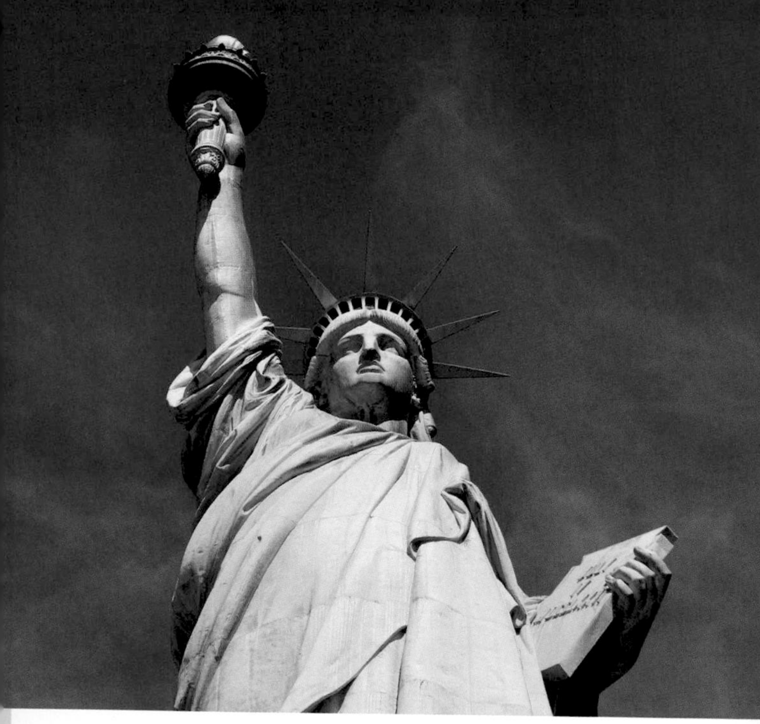

Top Experience

Visit the Statue of Liberty & Ellis Island

Lady Liberty has been gazing sternly toward 'unenlightened Europe' since 1886. Dubbed the 'Mother of Exiles,' she's often interpreted as a symbolic admonishment to an unjust Old World. Emma Lazarus' 1883 poem 'The New Colossus' reads: 'Give me your tired, your poor, your huddled masses yearning to breathe free, the wretched refuse of your teeming shore.'

MAP P52, C8

www.nps.gov/stli

Liberty Island adult/child incl Ellis Island $24/12

8:30am-6pm, hours vary by season

to Liberty Island

From the Suez to the City

It comes as a surprise to many that France's jumbo-size gift to America was not originally conceived with the US in mind. Indeed, when sculptor Frédéric-Auguste Bartholdi began planning the piece, his vision was for a colossal sculpture to guard the entrance to the Suez Canal in Egypt, one of France's greatest 19th-century engineering achievements. But the ambitious monument failed to attract serious funding from either France or Egypt, and Bartholdi's dream seemed destined for the scrap heap. A French politician and writer, Édouard de Laboulaye, proposed a gift to America as a symbol of the democratic values that underpinned both France and the US. Bartholdi tweaked his vision and turned his Suez flop into 'Liberty Enlightening the World' – an immortal gift to commemorate America's centennial of the Declaration of Independence.

Creating the Statue

Bartholdi spent almost 20 years turning his dream – to create the hollow copper colossus and mount it in New York Harbor – into reality. Hindered by serious financial problems, the statue's creation was helped by the fund-raising efforts of newspaper publisher Joseph Pulitzer and poet Emma Lazarus, whose ode to Lady Liberty is now inscribed on the statue's pedestal, designed by American architect Richard Morris Hunt. Bartholdi's work on the statue was also delayed by structural challenges – a problem resolved by the metal-framework mastery of railway engineer Gustave Eiffel (yes, of the famous tower).

Finally completed in 1884 (a bit behind schedule for the centennial), it was shipped to NYC as 350 pieces packed into 214 crates, then reassembled over a span of four months and placed on the US-made granite pedestal. Its spectacular October 1886 dedication included

★ Top Tips

- To see both the Statue of Liberty and Ellis Island, get a ferry before 2pm.
- Security at the ferry terminal is tight, with airport-style screening. Allow for 30- to 90-minute waits in high season.
- Don't believe any street sellers who tell you otherwise – official tickets are sold only through **Statue Cruises** (Map P52, C8; www.statuecruises.com). Buying tickets in advance online is recommended.

✕ Take a Break

Skip the mediocre cafeteria fare on Liberty Island and pack a picnic lunch. Or visit early and return to Lower Manhattan for the gastronomic delights of French food emporium Le District, located in Brookfield Place (p60).

New York's first ticker-tape parade and a flotilla of almost 300 vessels. The Lady was placed under the administration of the National Park Service in 1933; a restoration of her oxidized copper began in 1984, the same year she made it onto the UN's list of World Heritage Sites.

Liberty Today

Folks who reserve their tickets in advance can climb the 215 steps to the top of Lady Liberty's pedestal for commanding city and harbor views. As of this writing, the 162-step ascent to the statue's crown, which delivers the island's most impressive panorama, was closed to visitors. Check www.nps.gov/stli for up-to-date information and availability.

Due to their popularity, timed pedestal tickets are limited and should be reserved in advance, either online or by phone. Only pedestal ticket holders can access the old Statue of Liberty museum within the monument.

If you don't have pedestal tickets, don't fret. All ferry tickets to Liberty and Ellis Islands offer access to the grounds, including the new (and significantly more illuminating) **Statue of Liberty museum** — a $100-million complex completed in 2019. The 26,000-sq-ft space features three galleries, highlighting the statue's history and America's complicated relationship to the ideals she represents. The original torch, removed in 1984, shimmers as the museum's centerpiece.

Ellis Island National Museum of Immigration

Ellis Island

America's most famous and historically important gateway, **Ellis Island** (www.nps.gov/elis) is where Old World despair met New World promise. Between 1892 and 1924, over 12 million immigrants passed through this processing station, dreams in tow; an estimated 40% of Americans today have at least one ancestor who was processed here. The journey from Ellis Island led straight to the Lower East Side, where streets reflected these myriad origins with shop signs in Yiddish, Italian, German and Chinese. Buy tickets online in advance (at www.statuecruises.com) to avoid the soul-crushingly long ferry queues.

An Irish Debut

Ellis Island's very first immigrant was 17-year-old Anna 'Annie' Moore. After a 12-day journey in steerage from County Cork, Ireland, Annie arrived on January 1, 1892, accompanied by her brothers Phillip and Anthony; the three were headed to America to join their parents, who had migrated to New York City four years earlier.

She later married German immigrant Joseph Augustus Schayer and gave birth to at least 11 children, only five of whom survived. Annie died on December 6, 1924, and was laid to rest at Calvary Cemetery, Queens.

The Main Building

After the original wooden building burnt down in 1897, architects Edward Lippincott Tilton and William A Boring created a suitably impressive and imposing 'prologue' to America. The beaux-arts Main Building has majestic triple-arched entrances, decorative Flemish bond brickwork, and granite cornerstones and belvederes.

Under the beautiful vaulted herringbone-tiled ceiling of the 338ft-long **Registry Room**, the newly arrived lined up to have their documents checked (polygamists, paupers, criminals and anarchists were turned back).

A Modern Restoration

After a $160 million restoration, the island's Main Building was reopened to the public in 1990 and renamed the Ellis Island National Museum of Immigration in 2015, delivering a poignant tribute to the immigrant experience: narratives from historians, immigrants themselves and other sources animate a fascinating collection of personal objects, official documents, photographs and film footage.

Top Experience

Stroll the Brooklyn Bridge

A New York icon, the Brooklyn Bridge was the world's first steel suspension bridge, with an unequaled span of almost 1596ft when it opened in 1883. The bridge's neo-Gothic towers have endured as city emblems, inspiring poets, writers and painters — even today, it never fails to dazzle. Take the breeze-buffeted journey for soul-stirring views of Manhattan, the East River and the waterfront.

MAP P52, F4

S 4/5/6 to Brooklyn Bridge-City Hall, J/Z to Chambers St, R/W to City Hall, 2/3 to Clark St; A/F to High St-Brooklyn Bridge Station

The Bridge's Heavy Toll

German-born engineer John Roebling designed the bridge, but after contracting tetanus when his foot was crushed by a ferry at Fulton Landing, he died before construction even began. His son, Washington Roebling, assumed responsibility for the project, which lasted 14 years. However, Roebling junior also became a victim, contracting 'the bends' from working underwater in a pressurized *caisson*. Bedridden within sight of the bridge for many years, he relied on his wife, Emily Warren Roebling, herself a mathematician and engineer, to oversee construction in his stead. She had to deal with budget overruns and unhappy politicians. At least 27 workers died during the bridge's construction. And there was one final tragedy to come: in 1883, six days after the official opening, a massive crowd of pedestrians was bottlenecked at a stairway when rumors of a collapse, possibly started in jest, set off a stampede in which dozens were injured and 12 were crushed to death.

Crossing the Bridge

The mile-plus journey across the Brooklyn Bridge usually figures quite high on 'must-do' lists for NYC visitors. The pedestrian walkway affords wonderful views of Lower Manhattan and Governors Island, while observation points under the support towers offer brass 'panorama' histories of the waterfront. The trip can take 20 to 40 minutes to walk, depending on how often you stop to admire the view.

The Manhattan entrance is directly off the eastern edge of City Hall Park, and the Brooklyn side has two exits. The first leads to hip shopping and dining destination Dumbo, while the second ends where leafy, residential Brooklyn Heights meets gritty Downtown Brooklyn.

★ Top Tips

- To beat the crowds, come early in the morning (before 7am) or after sundown, when you'll have the views largely to yourself.
- If cycling the bridge, use the protected bike path beneath the elevated pedestrian platform. The views aren't as awe-worthy and there's no place to pause, but it's faster and more efficient than walking across the East River.

Take a Break

- Fuel up postwalk at the ***TimeOut* Market** (timeoutmarket.com/newyork), an upscale food hall in a 19th-century warehouse near the Brooklyn Bridge in Dumbo.
- Twirl underneath the Brooklyn Bridge on **Jane's Carousel** (janescarousel.com), a merry-go-round from 1922 housed in a glass pavilion near the TimeOut Market.

Top Experience

See NYC from One World Observatory

Filling what was a sore and glaring gap in the Lower Manhattan skyline, One World Trade Center symbolizes rebirth, determination and resilience. More than just another supertall skyscraper, it's a richly symbolic giant, well aware of the past yet firmly focused on the future. For lovers of New York, it's also one of the city's highest stops for dizzying, unforgettable urban views.

MAP P52, B4

www.oneworld observatory.com

285 Fulton St, cnr West & Vesey Sts, Lwr Manhattan

9am-9pm Sep-Apr, from 8am May-Aug

The Building

Leaping from the northwestern corner of the World Trade Center site, the 104-floor tower completed in 2014 is architect David M Childs' redesign of Daniel Libeskind's original 2002 concept. The tapered giant is currently the Western Hemisphere's tallest building – not to mention the seventh-tallest in the world. The tower soars skywards with chamfered edges, resulting in a series of isosceles triangles that, seen from the building's base, reach to infinity. Crowning the structure is a 408ft cable-stayed spire. Codesigned by sculptor Kenneth Snelson, it brings the building's total height to 1776ft, a symbolic reference to the year of American independence.

It's also one of the world's most sustainable buildings, winning LEED Gold certification for its various ecofriendly features. Almost half of the construction materials were made from postindustrial recycled content, and rainwater is harvested for cooling machinery and irrigating greenery. Natural light and low-consumption electrical and HVAC systems reduce electrical requirements.

From the Heights

The city's loftiest observation deck spans levels 100 to 102, reached by five Sky Pod elevators, where riders zoom through 500 years of NYC history in 47 seconds. On level 100 is an epic 360-degree panorama guaranteed to keep you busy searching for landmarks, from the Brooklyn and Manhattan Bridges to Lady Liberty and the Woolworth, Empire State and Chrysler Buildings. For insight into what you're seeing, interactive mobile tablets programmed in multiple languages are available for hire (included with the combo ticket for $10 more). The view is extraordinary, taking in all five boroughs and three adjoining states. Go on a clear day for the best experience.

★ Top Tips

- Prepurchase your tickets online (www.oneworldobservatory.com/tickets) to avoid the longest queues.
- When purchasing your ticket, you'll select a specific visiting time; head in by 9:15am for short waiting periods and thin crowds. Sunset is often busiest.
- If you're really pressed for time (or just impatient), you can skip *all* the lines with a Priority Reserve ticket.

✕ Take a Break

There are dining options on level 101, but, being aimed at tourists, they're wildly overpriced. You're better off holding on to your appetite until you're down, then heading west to grab a bite at the food courts inside Brookfield Place (p60).

For reviews see

Top Experiences	p44
Sights	p54
Eating	p57
Drinking	p60
Entertainment	p63
Shopping	p64

0 — 200 m
0 — 0.1 miles

A B C D E F
1 2 3 4

Downtown Boathouse 11
34
Pier 26
Pier 25
16
Rockefeller Park
North End Ave
West St (West Side Hwy)
One World Observatory
Desbrosses St
Vestry St
Laight St
Hubert St
Collister St
Holland Tunnel
Canal St
Beach St
26
TRIBECA
27
12
N Moore St
Franklin St
30
Harrison St
Greenwich St
Jay St
Hudson St
Duane St
Washington Market Park
Reade St
Chambers St
Warren St
Murray St
Barclay St
Vesey St
Varick St
St Johns La
(Avenue of the Americas)
Sixth Ave
14
15
22
24
W Broadway
17
13
35
39
Church St
Canal St
Lispenard St
33
Walker St
White St
18
Leonard St
Worth St (Ave of the Strongest)
Thomas St
Duane St
African Burial Ground National Monument 5
40
City Hall
Park Place
Park Pl
Woolworth Building 8
St Paul's Chapel
9
Broadway
Howard St
Cortlandt Al
Lafayette St
Centre St
Federal Plaza
Thomas Paine Park
Foley Square
Elk St
City Hall Park
Park Row
Broadway-Nassau St
Nassau St
Ann St
Beekman St
Spruce St
Gold St
Chambers St/Brooklyn Bridge City Hall
38
Police Plaza
St Andrews Plaza
Ave of the Finest
Frankfort St
Baxter St
Mulberry St
Mott St
CHINATOWN
Bayard St
Columbus Park
Hogan Pl
Mosco St
Chatham Square
Pearl St
Park Row
James St
Oliver St
Madison St
Catherine St
Henry St
St James Pl
TWO BRIDGES
Dover St
Pearl St
Water St
Front St
31
South St
Brooklyn Bridge

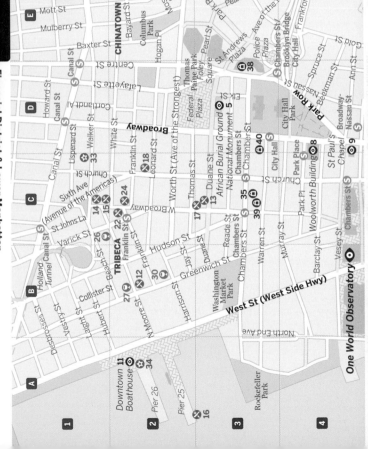

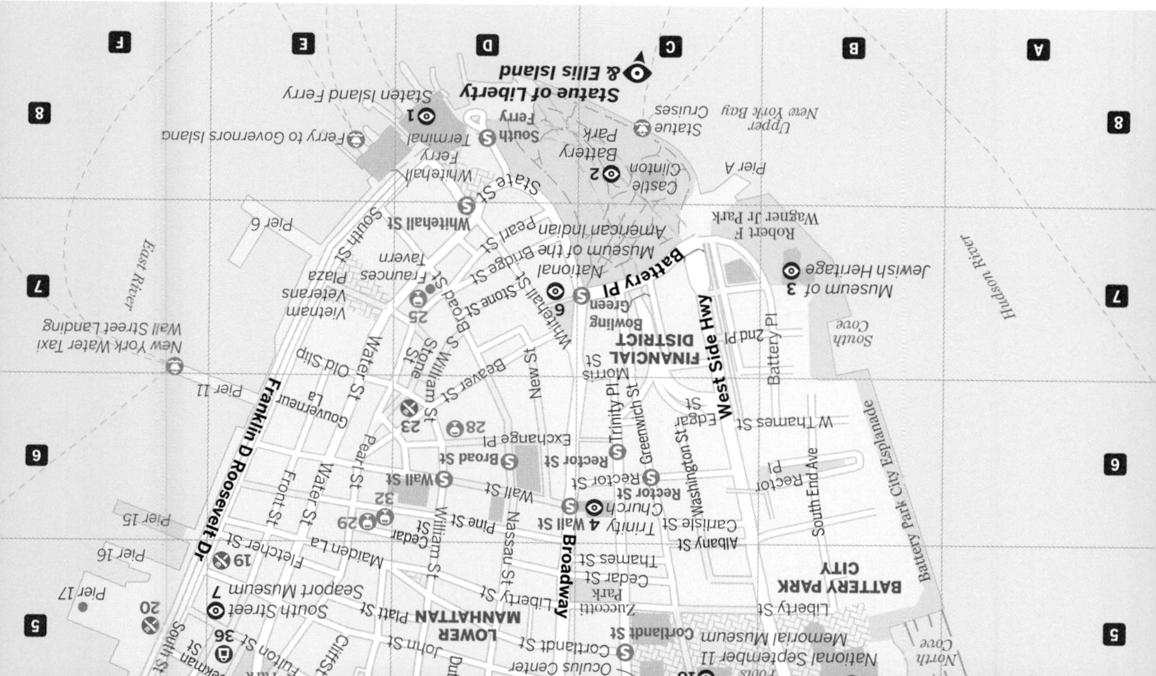
Statue of Liberty & Ellis Island
Staten Island Ferry
Ferry to Governors Island
South Ferry
Whitehall Ferry Terminal
Battery Park
Castle Clinton
Statue Cruises
Upper New York Bay
Pier A
Robert F Wagner Jr Park
Museum of Jewish Heritage
Hudson River
South Cove
Battery Park City Esplanade
BATTERY PARK CITY
North Cove
National September 11 Memorial Museum
Pools
Oculus Center
FINANCIAL DISTRICT
LOWER MANHATTAN
National Museum of the American Indian
Bowling Green
Battery Pl
West Side Hwy
Broadway
Franklin D Roosevelt Dr
Trinity Church
Fraunces Tavern
Vietnam Veterans Plaza
South Street Seaport Museum
New York Water Taxi Wall Street Landing
East River
Pier 6
Pier 11
Pier 15
Pier 16
Pier 17
Zuccotti Park
State St
Whitehall St
Pearl St
Water St
Front St
South St
Broad St
Stone St
S William St
Beaver St
New St
Exchange Pl
Wall St
Rector St
Trinity Pl
Greenwich St
Washington St
Carlisle St
Albany St
Thames St
Cedar St
Liberty St
Cortlandt St
John St
Fulton St
Beekman St
Cliff St
Platt St
Maiden La
Fletcher St
Pine St
William St
Nassau St
Gouverneur La
Old Slip
Morris St
Edgar St
2nd Pl
Battery Pl
W Thames St
Rector Pl
South End Ave
Whitehall St
Bridge St
1
2
3
4
6
7
10
19
20
23
25
28
29
32
36
A
B
C
D
E
F
5
6
7
8

Sights

Staten Island Ferry CRUISE

1 MAP P52, D8

Staten Islanders know these hulking orange ferries as commuter vehicles, while Manhattanites think of them as their secret, romantic vessels for a spring-day escape. Yet many tourists are also wise to the charms of the Staten Island Ferry, whose 25-minute, 5.2-mile journey between Lower Manhattan and the Staten Island neighborhood of St George is one of NYC's finest free adventures. (www.siferry.com)

Battery Park PARK

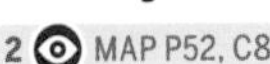

Skirting the southern edge of Manhattan, this 12-acre oasis lures visitors with public artworks, meandering walkways and perennial gardens. Its memorials include tributes to those who died in the Korean War and Italian navigator Giovanni da Verrazzano. The first Dutch settlement on Manhattan was founded here in 1625, and the city's first battery was later erected in its defense. You'll also find the lovely **SeaGlass Carousel** (www.seaglasscarousel.nyc), historic **Castle Clinton** (www.nps.gov/cacl) and the ferry service to Ellis Island and the Statue of Liberty. (www.nycgovparks.org)

Museum of Jewish Heritage MUSEUM

3 MAP P52, B7

This evocative waterfront museum explores all aspects of modern Jewish identity and culture, from religious traditions to artistic accomplishments. The museum's core exhibition covers three themed floors: *Jewish Life a Century Ago*, *Jewish Renewal* and *The War Against the Jews* – a detailed exploration of the Holocaust through thousands of personal artifacts, photographs, documentary films and survivor testimony. Also commemorating Holocaust victims is the external installation **Garden of Stones**, a narrow pathway of 18 boulders supporting living trees. (www.mjhnyc.org)

Trinity Church CHURCH

4 MAP P52, C6

New York City's tallest building upon consecration in 1846, Trinity Church features a 280ft-high bell tower and a richly colored stained-glass window over the altar.

Famous residents of its serene cemetery include Founding Father and first secretary of the Treasury (and now Broadway superstar) Alexander Hamilton, while its excellent musical program includes organ-recital series Pipes at One (1pm Friday), evening choral performances including new works co-commissioned by Trinity, and an annual December rendition of

Handel's *Messiah*. (www.trinitywallstreet.org)

African Burial Ground National Monument MEMORIAL

5 MAP P52, D3

In 1991, construction workers here uncovered a large number of stacked wooden caskets, just 16ft to 28ft below street level. The boxes contained the remains of both enslaved and free African Americans from the 17th and 18th centuries (from 1697, nearby Trinity Church refused them burial in its graveyard). Today, a poignant **memorial site** and a **visitor center** with four rooms of educational displays honor the estimated 15,000 men, women and children buried in America's largest and oldest African cemetery. (www.nps.gov/afbg/index.htm)

National Museum of the American Indian MUSEUM

6 MAP P52, D7

An affiliate of the Smithsonian Institution, this elegant tribute to Native American culture occupies Cass Gilbert's spectacular 1907 **Custom House**, one of NYC's finest beaux-arts buildings. Beyond a vast elliptical rotunda capped by a 140-ton skylight, sleek galleries play host to changing exhibitions featuring Indigenous American art, culture, life and beliefs.

The museum's permanent collection includes stunning decorative arts, textiles and ceremonial objects that document

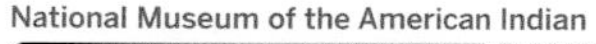

National Museum of the American Indian

the diverse native cultures across the Americas, while the interactive **imagiNATIONS Activity Center** explores their technologies. (www.nmai.si.edu)

South Street Seaport Museum MUSEUM

7 MAP P52, E5

Opened in 1967, this museum dispersed amid the cobblestone streets of the **seaport district** (www.seaportdistrict.nyc) consists of fascinating exhibitions relating to the city's maritime history, an 18th-century printing press and shop (p64), and a handful of mighty sailing ships to explore on Pier 16. Besides touring the moored 1885 *Wavertree* and the 1907 lightship *Ambrose*, in warmer months you can take a harbor cruise on the 1885 **Pioneer** (www.southstreetseaportmuseum.org) and the 1930 wooden tugboat **WO Decker** (www.southstreetseaportmuseum.org).

Woolworth Building NOTABLE BUILDING

8 MAP P52, D4

The world's tallest building upon completion in 1913 (it was surpassed in height by the Chrysler Building in 1930), Cass Gilbert's 792ft-tall masterpiece is a neo-Gothic marvel, elegantly clad in masonry and terra-cotta. Entry to the breathtaking lobby is only accessible on prebooked guided tours, which were on pause as of this writing. Instead, find a seat across the street in **City Hall Park** and crane your neck toward the sky to eye the 60-story structure's exceptional stonework.

St Paul's Chapel CHURCH

9 MAP P52, D4

After his inauguration in 1789, George Washington worshipped at this Classical Revival brownstone chapel, built in 1766 and narrowly avoiding destruction in the fire of 1776.

It avoided disaster again on September 11, 2001, when the destruction of the World Trade Center a mere block away left the chapel untouched. Now famous as 'The Little Chapel That Stood,' St Paul's offered round-the-clock refuge, spiritual and emotional support, and food service to first responders and rescue workers. (www.trinitywallstreet.org)

National September 11 Memorial Museum MUSEUM

10 MAP P52, C5

Beyond the reflective pools of the September 11 Memorial sits this striking and solemn museum, incorporating part of the site and a few remnants from the Twin Towers.

The exploration of the tragic day is visceral, if not emotionally overwhelming, and the museum has received criticism for failing to provoke thoughtful dialogue about controversial sociopolitical events preceding and following 9/11. Still, the memorial provides a powerful look at stories of grief, resilience and the hope that followed. (www.911memorial.org/museum)

Downtown Boathouse

KAYAKING

11 MAP P52, A2

See NYC from a cormorant's point of view while floating on the Hudson River.

This active, volunteer-run public boathouse on Pier 26 offers free, walk-up, 20-minute kayaking sessions (including equipment) on weekends and some weekday evenings. For more activities here and at Piers 84 and 96 – kayaking trips, stand-up paddleboarding and classes – check www.hudson-riverpark.org. (www.downtownboathouse.org)

Eating

Locanda Verde

ITALIAN $$$

12 MAP P52, B2

Curbside at the **Greenwich Hotel** (www.thegreenwichhotel.com) is this Italian fine diner by Andrew Carmellini, where velvet curtains part onto a scene of loosened button-downs, black dresses and slick bar staff.

A see-and-be-seen spot in 2009, the restaurant has graduated to neighborhood stalwart thanks to its food – perhaps the *pappardelle*, lobster *oreganata*, or lamb meatball sliders – which still steals the show. (www.locandaverdenyc.com)

Tiny's & the Bar Upstairs

AMERICAN $$$

13 MAP P52, C3

The rustic interior of this blushing pink Tribeca town house from 1810 – antique wallpaper, salvaged wood paneling, original tin ceilings and handmade tiles – makes it worth a visit, but you won't regret staying for a meal or a cocktail. Food is modern American with French accents: go small with a kale salad or hit the big-time with filet mignon. (www.tinysnyc.com)

Frenchette

FRENCH $$$

14 MAP P52, C1

Mahogany-red banquettes, warm lighting and worn wood floors lend this Parisian eatery old-world charm, and the ever-changing menu surprises with contemporary takes on French bistro classics. An entire meal could be made out of the 'Amuses' menu alone — and amused you will be, particularly if you order the razor clams with fennel. (www.frenchettenyc.com)

Bâtard

EUROPEAN $$$

15 MAP P52, C1

Chef Doug Brixton heads this warm, *Michelin*-starred spot, where a pared-back interior puts the focus squarely on the food. Brixton's seasonal dishes are precise examples of classical French and Italian cooking: the prix-fixe menus hold rich delights like roasted pork loin with peaches,

South Street Seaport

Before Hurricane Sandy flooded this enclave of cobbled streets, maritime warehouses and tourist-oriented shops in 2012, locals tended to leave this area to the tourists. Its nautical and historic importance was thought diluted by the manufactured 'Main Street' feel, with street performers and poor-quality restaurants. Revitalization and redevelopment have been slow, but recently, momentum has picked up.

The glossy **Pier 17** (Map P52, F5; www.pier17ny.com), which opened in 2018, caters to postwork Wall Streeters with its upscale eateries, street-level riverdeck and rooftop bar-and-performance space; the Tin Building, a 53,000-sq-ft food hall for high-end market fare and fine dining, opened next door in 2022. As development continues, supertall buildings may be on the horizon.

Like elsewhere in the city, the new and the novel are threatening historic preservation, but a few holdout bars and restaurants have maintained their atmospheric authenticity and are worth a look.

peking duck with beets and cardamom and a cauliflower side dish you shouldn't pass up. (www.batardtribeca.com)

Grand Banks SEAFOOD $$

16 MAP P52, A3

Chef Kerry Heffernan's menu features sustainably harvested seafood at this seasonal restaurant on the *Sherman Zwicker,* a 1942 schooner moored on the Hudson, with the spotlight on Atlantic Ocean oysters. Alternatively, try the ceviche, lobster rolls or sea scallops with succotash. It's mobbed with dressy crowds after work and on weekends; come for a late-dinner sundowner and enjoy the stupendous sunset views. (www.grandbanks.nyc)

Odeon BISTRO $$$

17 MAP P52, C3

The red neon sign glowing above this bistro since 1980 is almost as iconic as the restaurant itself. This is where the Cosmo was invented; where NYC tastemakers Warhol and Scorsese dined on favorites like steak tartare and oysters. Basquiat even dated one of the waitresses. It might not be a trendsetter today, but it's a Tribeca classic, and brunch remains top tier. (www.theodeonrestaurant.com)

Two Hands AUSTRALIAN $$

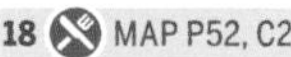

18 MAP P52, C2

An interior of whitewashed brick gives this modern 'Australian-style' cafe-restaurant chain an airy feel

– and the local crowds love it. The menu offers light breakfast and lunch dishes such as a fully loaded acai bowl with berries and granola or a fried chicken burger with spicy aioli. The coffee's top-notch, and there's happy hour from 3pm to 7pm. (www.twohandsnyc.com)

Luchadores NYC

MEXICAN **$**

19 MAP P52, E5

On a nice day grab a seat in the tiny courtyard of this corner joint featuring fresh-made burritos, tacos and quesadillas made with short ribs, *carne asada* (charred beef), *pollo asado* (roasted chicken) or cajun shrimp. With a happy hour from 3pm to 6pm (nachos free with any two beers), it's a welcome alternative to less down-to-earth options around South Street Seaport.

Tin Building

MARKET **$$**

20 MAP P52, F5

Acclaimed chef and restaurateur Jean-Georges Vongerichten attracts curious taste buds to the South Street Seaport with this expertly curated 53,000-sq-ft marketplace, which opened in 2022. Impressive 1st-floor displays of seafood, charcuterie, cheeses and pastries make a strong case for picnicking along the waterfront, while 2nd-floor sit-downs, including the Chinese-inspired House of the Red Pearl, draw posh crowds for more refined dining. (www.tinbuilding.com)

South Street Seaport

Brookfield Place

FOOD HALL $$

21 MAP P52, B5

This high-end retail complex along the Hudson River offers two fancy food courts. Francophile foodies should hit **Le District** (www.ledistrict.com), a gourmet marketplace with several stand-alone restaurants and counters selling tartines, stinky cheese, steak frites and more. One floor above is **Hudson Eats** (https://bfplny.com/directory/food), a fashionable mess hall for Wall Street's worker bees, including fast bites from popular chains like **Blue Ribbon Sushi**, **Dig** and **Dos Toros Taqueria**. (www.brookfieldplaceny.com)

Gotan

CAFE $

22 MAP P52, C2

This buzzy, light-filled corner cafe is frequented by the downtown digerati, who make ample use of free wi-fi, thoughtfully placed power outlets and tabletop charging pads.

The menu is light but filling, featuring sandwiches, salads and breakfast dishes with Mediterranean and Middle Eastern accents. Counter Culture coffee provides the beans; the skilled baristas do the rest. (www.gotannyc.com)

Leo's Bagels

BAGELS $

23 MAP P52, D6

Hand-rolled and boiled to gooey-dough perfection, Leo's Bagels started attracting long morning lines in 2007 thanks to its need-not-be-toasted torus of gluten joy. Add scrambled eggs, smoked fish, pastrami or lox, but with lightly crisped bottoms and chewy interiors, a cream-cheese schmear does these bagels just fine. Take your goods to go and nosh streetside like a true New Yorker. (www.leosbagels.com)

Maman

CAFE $

24 MAP P52, C2

With faded white paint, skylight windows and dried lavender in jars, this beloved cafe chain combines the air of a Provençal farmhouse with an industrial-hip downtown space. The French-inflected menu features a host of richly designed salads, omelettes and sandwiches, as well as luscious nectarine buttermilk waffles and a daily quiche. A front counter offers coffee and pastries to go. (www.mamannyc.com)

Drinking

Dead Rabbit

BAR

25 MAP P52, D7

Named for a feared 19th-century Irish American gang, this three-story drinking den is regularly voted one of the world's best bars. Hit the sawdust-sprinkled Taproom for specialty beers, historic punches and pop-inns (lightly soured ale spiked with different flavors).

On the next floor there's the cozy Parlor, serving meticulously researched cocktails and creamy Irish coffees, and above that the reservation-only Occasional Room, ideal for private tastings of the substantial whiskey list. (www.deadrabbitnyc.com)

Brandy Library

COCKTAIL BAR

26 MAP P52, C1

This brandy-hued bastion of brown spirits is the place to go for top-shelf cognac, whiskey and brandy. Settle into handsome club chairs facing floor-to-ceiling, bottle-lined shelves and sip your tipple of choice, paired with nibbles such as Gruyère-cheese puffs, salmon ceviche and raw oysters.

Saturday nights are generally quieter than weeknights, making it a civilized spot for a conversational weekend tête-à-tête. (www.brandylibrary.com)

Smith & Mills

COCKTAIL BAR

27 MAP P52, B2

Petite Smith & Mills ticks all the cool boxes: unmarked exterior, design-conscious industrial interior, and expertly crafted cocktails with a penchant for the classics. Space is limited, so head in early if you fancy kicking back on a plush banquette. A seasonal menu spans light snacks to a particularly notable burger bedecked with caramelized onions. (www.smithandmills.com)

Split Eights

COFFEE, COCKTAIL BAR

28 MAP P52, D6

You can have it both ways at this slick bi-level cafe, which serves as barista and bartender for Wall St's buttoned-up crowd.

Le District

A Toast to History

Raise a glass to America's forefathers at **Fraunces Tavern** (Map P52, D7; www.fraunces tavern.com), which opened as a saloon in 1762 and served as both parlor and political hangout for the likes of George Washington and Alexander Hamilton. (Washington famously bid his officers farewell here in 1783, following the British evacuation of New York.)

These days, visitors drink and dine downstairs, then head upstairs to peep at 18th-century relics in an adjoining museum.

Stop by until 3pm for Brooklyn-based Parlor Coffee, then return at 4:30pm, when business folks liquor up and loosen their neckties. Can't decide between caffeine or cocktail? The espresso martini is the best of both worlds. (www.spliteightsnyc.com)

Overstory ROOFTOP BAR

29 MAP P52, E6

Perched on the terrace-wrapped 64th floor of an art-deco skyscraper from 1932, this lofty lounge is best for marveling at the city's sunsets and sparkling lights. Reserve a table for outdoor seating ($50) — the burgundy-trimmed interior is classy, but the exterior views are jaw-dropping. Cocktails will set you back $24 (included in the reservation fee), a price worth the panoramas. (www.overstory-nyc.com)

Terroir Tribeca WINE BAR

30 MAP P52, B2

This unpretentious wine bar gratifies wine lovers with its well-versed, well-priced selection, including drops from the Old World and the New, among them natural wines and niche tipples from smaller producers. It has good knowledge behind the bar, a generous selection of wines by the glass, and a menu ranging from bread-and-butter pickles to *wiener schnitzel* (mains $15 to $29). Offers early *and* late happy hours. (www.wineisterroir.com)

Cowgirl SeaHorse BAR

31 MAP P52, F4

In an ocean of more serious bars and restaurants, Cowgirl SeaHorse is a party ship. Its ranch-meets-sea theme (wagon wheels and seahorses on the walls) and Southern home cooking (blackened fish tacos, pulled pork sliders, creamy coleslaw etc) make it irresistibly fun. Live music on Monday, happy hour Monday through Friday and great frozen margaritas don't hurt, either. (www.cowgirlseahorse.com)

Black Fox Coffee CAFE

32 MAP P52, E6

Internationally sourced beans have drawn coffee connoisseurs to the original location of this NYC mini-chain since 2016. Order a flat white (opt for the house-made nut milk) and a chocolate chip cookie fresh from the oven, then join the laptop crew working away in this spacious cafe. (https://blackfoxcoffee.com)

Entertainment

Soho Rep

THEATER

33 MAP P52, C1

This is one of New York's finest off-Broadway companies, wowing audiences and critics with its annual trio of sharp, innovative new works. Kathleen Turner, Allison Janney, Ed O'Neill and John C Reilly all made their professional debuts in this 65-seat theater, and the company's productions have garnered more than 20 Obie (Off-Broadway Theater) Awards. Check the website for current or upcoming shows. (www.sohorep.org)

City Vineyard

LIVE MUSIC

34 MAP P52, A2

Known for its vino and rooftop views in spring and summer, this waterside bar-restaurant also makes a splash between November and March with its intimate, 233-seat cabaret-style theater featuring the Voices on the Hudson concert series.

The calendar tends toward emerging singer-songwriters, folk superstars and indie rock bands; past performers include notables like Suzanne Vega, Squirrel Nut Zippers and Billy Bragg. (www.citywinery.com)

Fraunces Tavern

MARIUSZ LOPUSIEWICZ/SHUTTERSTOCK ©

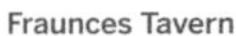

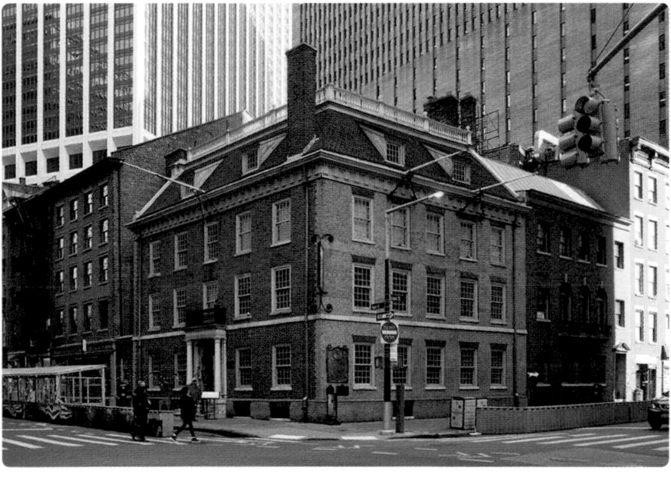

The Architecture of Shopping

New Yorkers may lament Manhattan's mall-ification – where chain stores turn streets into sanitized commercial strips – but there's an occasional awe-worthy aspect to the corporate land grab: intriguing architecture. Descending into **Westfield World Trade Center**, a mall-and-transit hub inside Santiago Calatrava's gleaming cream **Oculus** (Map P52, C5; www.officialworldtradecenter.com), feels like entering a dinosaur's polished rib cage. Walk its bony underground passage to arrive at **Brookfield Place** (p60), a lux office-and-retail complex where 40ft-tall *Washingtonia robusta* palms shoot to the heavens in a glassy atrium overlooking the Hudson. As for the shops, don't expect anything uniquely New York — it's the buildings here that shine.

Shopping

Philip Williams Posters

VINTAGE

35 MAP P52, C3

You'll find more than 100,000 posters dating back to 1870 in this cavernous treasure trove, from oversized French advertisements for perfume and cognac to Eastern European film ads and decorative Chinese *nianhua* (New Year) prints. Prices range from $20 for small reproductions to thousands of dollars for rare, showpiece originals. Advertising ephemera, poster books and paintings are also on display. (www.postermuseum.com)

Bowne & Co Stationers

GIFTS & SOUVENIRS

36 MAP P52, E5

Suitably set in cobbled South Street Seaport and affiliated with the South Street Seaport Museum (p56), this 18th-century veteran stocks reproduction-vintage New York posters and NYC-themed notepads, pencil cases, cards, stamps and even wrapping paper. At the printing workshop you can order customized business cards or hone your printing skills in monthly classes (see the museum website's events page).

Pasanella & Son

WINE

37 MAP P52, F5

Once a 19th-century brothel, this savvy wine shop now attracts oenophiles with its 400-plus drops both inspired and affordably priced.

The focus is on small producers, with a number of biodynamic and organic winemakers all deep in the mix. Come for the free wine tastings on Saturdays, 5:30pm to 7:30pm. (www.pasanellaandson.com)

CityStore

GIFTS & SOUVENIRS

38 MAP P52, D3

Score all manner of officially produced New York City memorabilia here, from authentic-looking taxi medallions, sewer-hole-cover coasters and borough-themed T-shirts to NYPD baseball caps, subway-station signs and books about NYC. Curious, though less relevant for the average visitor, are the municipal building codes and other regulatory guides for sale. (www.nyc.gov/citystore)

Mysterious Bookshop

BOOKS

39 MAP P52, C3

With more crime per square inch than any other corner of the city, this mystery-themed bookstore peddles everything from classic espionage and thrillers to contemporary Nordic crime fiction and literary criticism. You'll find both new and secondhand titles, including rare first editions, signed copies, obscure magazines and picture books for budding sleuths. Check the website for in-store events. (www.mysteriousbookshop.com)

Fountain Pen Hospital

GIFTS & SOUVENIRS

40 MAP P52, D3

Some things never go out of style. For over 70 years this family business has specialized in beautifully crafted fountain pens, with several thousand in stock, including luxe brands such as Mont Blanc. You can also buy regular pens (if you must) and high-end stationery items – it carries a large line of Rhodia notebooks and journals. (www.fountainpenhospital.com)

Oculus

Worth a Trip

Sail Away to Governors Island

Car-free, glamping-friendly, and threaded with trails for outdoor adventures: it's hard to believe Governors Island is a five-minute ferry ride from Lower Manhattan. This military-fortress-turned-maritime-park is New York Harbor's recreational darling thanks to 172 acres of hilly playgrounds, historic architecture and outdoor art installations. Leave the city bustle behind to enjoy life in the slow lane.

www.govisland.com

admission free

10am-6pm Mon-Fri, to 7pm Sat & Sun May-Oct, later hours Fri Jun-Aug

S 4/5 to Bowling Green; 1 to South Ferry

Changing Landscapes

Governors Island has altered dramatically since indigenous Lenape people fished here in the 1500s. It's now 100 acres larger (bulked up in 1912 with debris from the Lexington Ave subway excavation) and sprinkled with architectural ghosts from two centuries as an American military outpost, which ended in 1996. **Fort Jay** and **Castle Williams**, completed in the early 19th century, are the most imposing of these structures; both served as prisons for Confederate soldiers during the Civil War. Wander their brick walls on weekends for a look at the island's legacy.

Public Playgrounds

Today, it's hard to imagine this urban escape was ever a prison. Aesthetes ponder contemporary art housed within former officers' residences at **Colonel Row**, and children glide down the city's highest slide (57ft) at the aptly named **Slide Hill**. Locavores get their fill at **Ligget Terrace**, an open-air food court with spots like Brooklyn beer-maker **Threes Brewing** (https://shop.threesbrewing.com), and cyclists spin around the island's 2.2-mile perimeter for arresting panoramas of bridges, skyscrapers and a Lady Liberty close-up. To do it all justice, allow a few hours.

Island Upgrades

If you're willing to spend a pretty penny, it's possible to turn this people's park into a luxury Elysium. Glamping tents by **Collective Retreats** (www.collectiveretreats.com) allow visitors to fall asleep to the Financial District's twinkling lights, and at QC NY's Roman-style **spa** (www.qcny.com/en) you can soak up city views from a heated infinity pool. Add to that the saunas, steam rooms and other well-appointed on-site amenities, and city-life stresses are bound to melt away.

★ Top Tips

- Walking is excellent, but biking is best for seeing the sites. Rent wheels from **Blazing Saddles** (www.blazing-saddles.com) or use one of three Citi Bike stations around the island.
- If you want access to most on-site eateries, plan a weekend day trip between April and October.
- Weekend ferries from Lower Manhattan are free from 7am to 11:20am; all others cost $4 round trip.
- Check www.govisland.com for year-round events, which have included everything from the annual **Jazz Age Lawn Party** to LGBTIQ+ **Pride Island**.

Take a Break

- Bring your lunch to **Picnic Point** and eat with views of Liberty Island and the Verrazano-Narrows Bridge.
- Head to tree-fringed **Hammock Grove** and lie back in one of 50 red-latticed swings – ideal for a midday cat nap.

60
號怡豐商場
66

Explore SoHo & Chinatown

Trendy neighborhoods SoHo (South of Houston), NoHo (North of Houston) and Nolita (North of Little Italy) are known for their boutiques, bars and eateries. Bustling Chinatown and a nostalgic sliver of Little Italy lure with idiosyncratic street life. Together, these areas offer a delicious hodgepodge of cast-iron architecture, strutting fashionistas, sacred temples and hook-hung salami.

The Short List

- **Shopping** *Maxing out credit cards on big-name fashion streets in SoHo, Nolita and NoHo.*
- ***Chinatown (p74)*** *Exploring vibrant streets, slurping soup dumplings and admiring a high-stakes game of mah-jongg.*
- ***Little Italy (p82)*** *Savoring a pizza slice while observing grandfathers sipping grappa and speaking in the mother tongue.*
- ***Merchant's House Museum (p74)*** *Exploring this time-jarred, possibly haunted museum, imagining NYC life in the 1800s.*
- ***Thai Diner (p77)*** *Feasting on disco fries at this Southeast Asian restaurant with New York-diner chutzpah.*

Getting There & Around

S The subway lines service various points of Canal St (J/Z, N/Q/R/W and 6). Once here, explore on foot.

Avoid taking cabs or buses here – especially in Chinatown, as the traffic is full-on.

Neighborhood Map on p72

Chinatown (p74) F11PHOTO/SHUTTERSTOCK ©

Walking Tour

Spend an Artisanal Afternoon in SoHo

Shopaholics across the world lust for SoHo and its sharp, chic whirlwind of flagship stores, coveted labels and sartorial trendsetters. Look beyond the giant global brands, however, and you'll discover that talented artisans and independent, one-off enterprises keep things local, unique and utterly inspiring.

Walk Facts

Start Café Integral; S Spring St

End IF Boutique; S Canal St

Length 1.5 miles; three hours

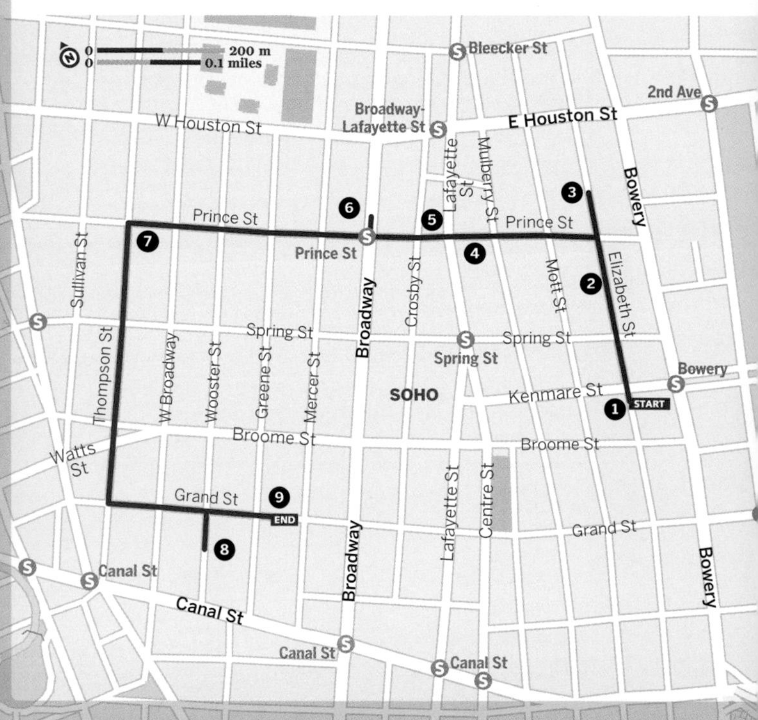

❶ Café Integral

Charge up with a cup of Nicaraguan coffee (best with a dash of house-made nut milk) from this airy **cafe** (www.cafeintegral.com) on Elizabeth St.

❷ Elizabeth Street Garden

Pause inside this verdant **sculpture garden** (p74) for a moment of calm amid SoHo's chaos.

❸ Corridor

Search for sophisticated urban threads at this **menswear store** (p86), created by a former FBI employee who decided to switch careers and started sewing shirts out of his East Village apartment.

❹ McNally Jackson

Browse the shelves inside one of the city's best-loved independent **bookstores** (p84), stocked with hard-to-find titles, cognoscenti magazines, and an in-house cafe for quality downtime and conversation.

❺ Alexis Bittar

Brooklyn-born Bittar started selling his signature Lucite jewelry on the streets of SoHo in the 1980s. Now, customers from Kendal Jenner to Michelle Obama sport his accessories. Browse his stunning A-lister **boutique** (www.alexisbittar.com) imagined by Tony Award–winning set designer Scott Pask.

❻ Sidewalk Art

Watch where you step – the sidewalk engraving on the northwest corner of Prince St and Broadway (outside Prada) is the work of Japanese-born sculptor Ken Hiratsuka, who carved roughly 40 sidewalks since moving to NYC in 1982. While this took about five hours of actual work, its completion took two years (1983–84), as Hiratsuka's illegal nighttime chiseling was often disrupted by pesky police patrols.

❼ The Hat Shop

This **haberdashery** (www.thehatshopnyc.com) has held onto its SoHo storefront since 1995 thanks to an enticing mix of high-art headwear ranging from *Great Gatsby* glam to regal royal wedding.

❽ Jeffrey Deitch Gallery

Avant-garde art is the raison d'être at the Wooster St outpost of this bicoastal **gallery** (https://deitch.com), founded by its namesake art dealer, who helped foster careers of contemporary greats like Kehinde Wiley and Shepard Fairey.

❾ IF Boutique

IF (www.ifsohonewyork.com) started selling high-end clothing in 1978, when SoHo was still a gritty up-and-comer. The neighborhood might've changed, but IF has stayed the same – a pioneer on the front lines of fashion.

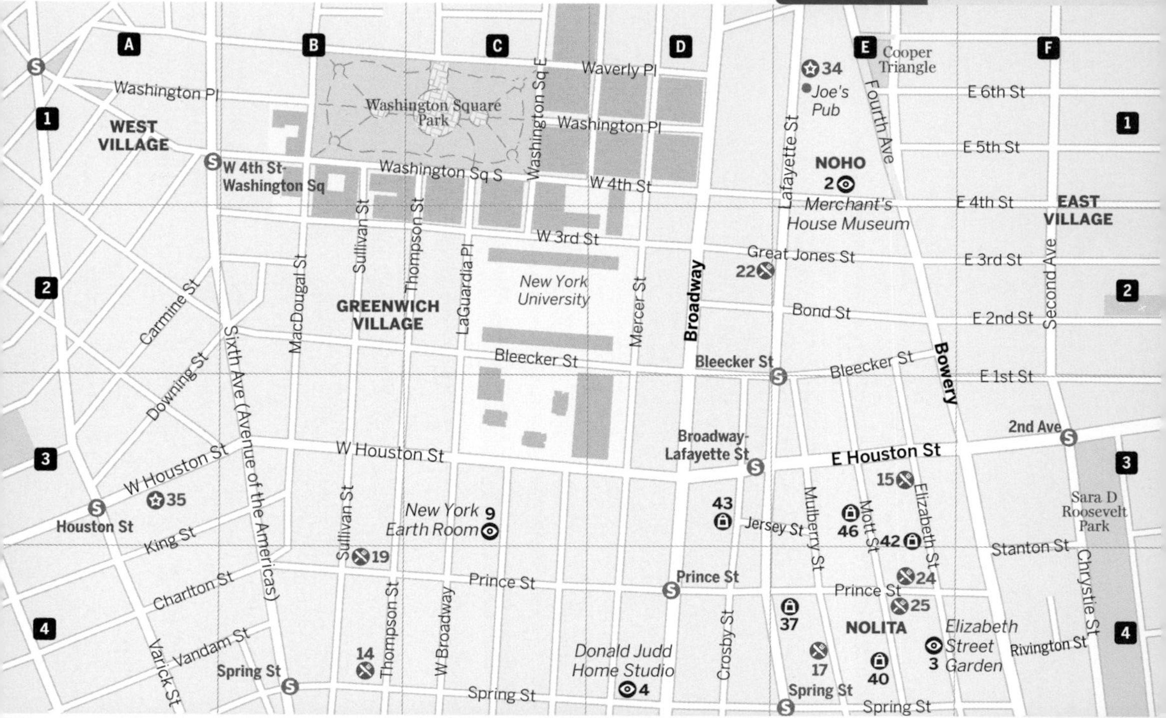

A B C D E F
1 2 3 4

WEST VILLAGE
GREENWICH VILLAGE
EAST VILLAGE
NOHO
NOLITA

Washington Square Park
New York University
Sara D Roosevelt Park
Cooper Triangle

2 Merchant's House Museum
3 Elizabeth Street Garden
4 Donald Judd Home Studio
9 New York Earth Room
14
15
17
19
22
24
25
34 Joe's Pub
35
37
40
42
43
46

W 4th St-Washington Sq
Broadway-Lafayette St
Bleecker St
Prince St
Spring St
Houston St
2nd Ave

Fourth Ave
Bowery
Second Ave
Chrystie St
Elizabeth St
Mott St
Mulberry St
Lafayette St
Crosby St
Broadway
Mercer St
LaGuardia Pl
W Broadway
Thompson St
Sullivan St
MacDougal St
Sixth Ave (Avenue of the Americas)
Varick St
Vandam St
Charlton St
King St
Washington Pl
Waverly Pl
Washington Sq E
Washington Sq S
W 4th St
W 3rd St
E 6th St
E 5th St
E 4th St
E 3rd St
E 2nd St
E 1st St
Great Jones St
Bond St
Bleecker St
E Houston St
W Houston St
Jersey St
Prince St
Spring St
Stanton St
Rivington St
Downing St
Carmine St

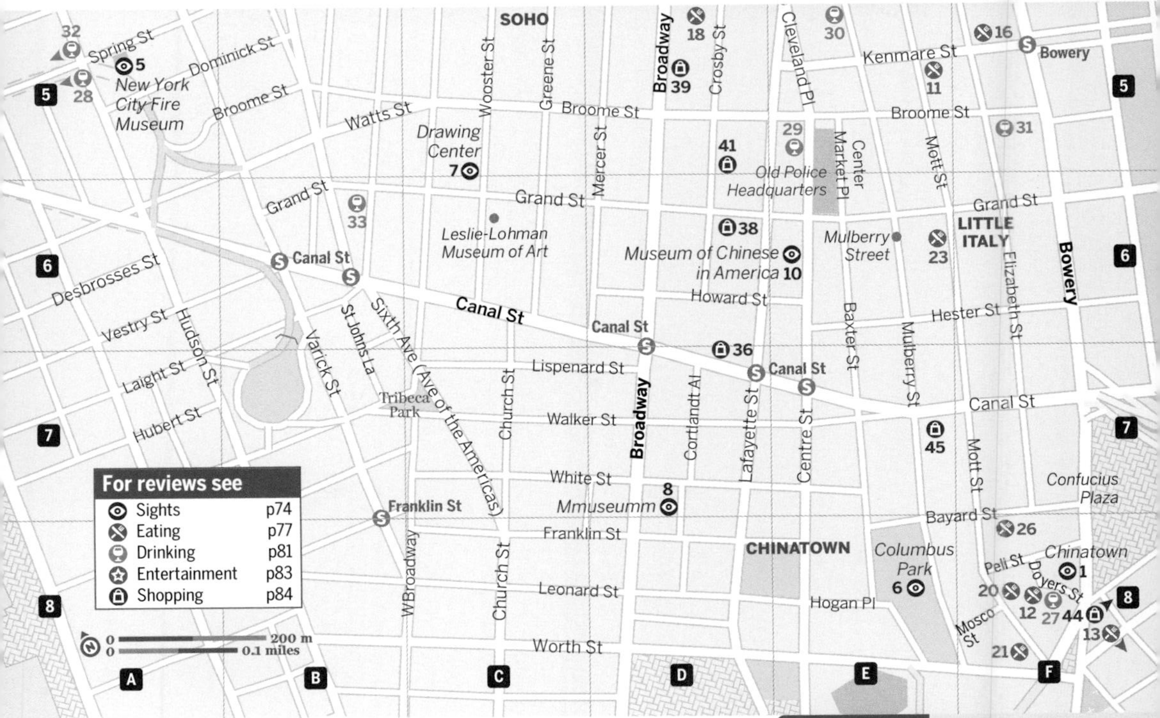

For reviews see

Sights	p74
Eating	p77
Drinking	p81
Entertainment	p83
Shopping	p84

0 200 m
0 0.1 miles

SOHO
LITTLE ITALY
CHINATOWN
Bowery
Elizabeth St
Mott St
Mulberry St
Baxter St
Centre St
Lafayette St
Cortlandt Al
Broadway
Church St
Sixth Ave (Ave of the Americas)
WBroadway
Varick St
Hudson St
Canal St
Hester St
Howard St
Grand St
Broome St
Kenmare St
Cleveland Pl
Crosby St
Mercer St
Greene St
Wooster St
Watts St
Dominick St
Spring St
Desbrosses St
Vestry St
Laight St
Hubert St
St Johns La
Lispenard St
Walker St
White St
Franklin St
Leonard St
Worth St
Hogan Pl
Bayard St
Pell St
Doyers St
Mosco St
Columbus Park
Confucius Plaza
Chinatown
Center Market Pl
Old Police Headquarters
Mulberry Street
Museum of Chinese in America
Leslie-Lohman Museum of Art
Drawing Center
Mmuseumm
Tribeca Park
New York City Fire Museum

Sights

Chinatown

AREA

1 MAP P72, F8

A walk through Manhattan's most colorful, cramped neighborhood is never the same, no matter how many times you hit the pavement. Peek inside temples and exotic storefronts. Catch the whiff of ripe persimmons, hear the clacking of mah-jongg tiles on makeshift tables, eye dangling duck roasts swinging in store windows and shop for anything from rice-paper lanterns and 'faux-lex' watches to tire irons and a pound of pressed nutmeg. America's largest congregation of Chinese immigrants is your oyster. (www.explorechinatown.com)

Merchant's House Museum

MUSEUM

2 MAP P72, E1

Built in 1832 and purchased by merchant Seabury Tredwell three years later, this red-brick mansion remains the most authentic Federal house in town. It's as much about the city's mercantile past as it is a showcase of 19th-century high-end domestic furnishings, from the bronze gasoliers and marble mantelpieces to the elegant parlor chairs, attributed to noted furniture designer Duncan Phyfe. Even the multilevel call bells for the servants work to this day. (www.merchantshouse.org)

Elizabeth Street Garden

PARK

3 MAP P72, E4

Cement-smacked SoHo is largely devoid of green space, save for this hidden gem between Prince and Spring Sts. It started in 1991, when an antiques dealer leased the abandoned lot from the city, added landscaping and sprinkled the acre of property with outdoor sculptures. Now, this whimsical garden is a public oasis guarded by limestone-carved lions. Visit while you can – the city has spent years battling with the garden's grassroots community to pave paradise and put up an apartment building. (www.elizabethstreetgarden.com)

Donald Judd Home Studio

GALLERY

4 MAP P72, D4

Enter this five-story, cast-iron building from 1870 for a fascinating glimpse into the life of the late American artist Donald Judd. The minimalist maverick's former home and studio, which he bought in 1968 for a now-unthinkable $68,000, is more art installation than crash pad, with modern works by Dan Flavin, Marcel Duchamp, Frank Stella and more on every floor.

Guided tours run for roughly 90 minutes and must be booked online (tours often sell out a month in advance). (www.juddfoundation.org)

New York City Fire Museum

MUSEUM

5 MAP P72, A5

In a grand old firehouse dating from 1904, this ode to firefighters includes a fantastic collection of historic equipment and artifacts. Eye up everything from horse-drawn firefighting carriages and early stovepipe firefighter hats to Chief, a four-legged firefighting hero from Brooklyn.

Exhibits trace the development of the NYC firefighting system, and the museum's heavy equipment and friendly staff make this a great spot for kids. (www.nycfiremuseum.org)

Columbus Park

PARK

6 MAP P72, E8

Mah-jongg meisters, slow-motion tai-chi practitioners and old aunties gossiping over home-made dumplings: it might feel like Shanghai, but this leafy oasis is core to NYC history. In the 19th century, this was part of the infamous Five Points neighborhood, the city's first tenement slums and the inspiration for Martin Scorsese's *Gangs of New York*.

Drawing Center

GALLERY

7  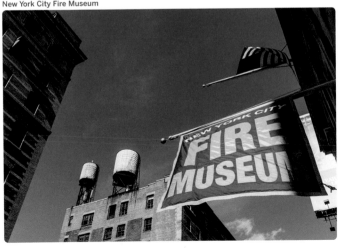 MAP P72, C5

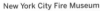

America's only nonprofit institute focused solely on drawings, the Drawing Center uses work by masters as well as unknowns to

New York City Fire Museum

Leslie-Lohman Museum of Art

Charles Leslie and the late Fritz Lohman started showcasing their gay-themed art collection from a SoHo loft in 1969 – an assemblage that rapidly expanded as they rescued works by dying artists during the 1980s AIDs pandemic.

Today, they're best known for founding the world's first LGBTIQ+ **museum** (Map p72, C6; www.leslielohman.org) with over 25,000 pieces that span three centuries and includes notable names like Keith Haring and Robert Mapplethorpe.

Exhibitions take place year-round, with themed shows and solo-art retrospectives.

juxtapose the medium's various styles. Historical exhibitions have included work by Michelangelo, James Ensor and Marcel Duchamp, while contemporary shows have showcased heavyweights such as Richard Serra, Ellsworth Kelly and Richard Tuttle. As to the themes themselves, expect anything from playful to the politically controversial. (www.drawingcenter.org)

Mmuseumm MUSEUM

8 MAP P72, D7

Once a freight elevator that opened to the street, this 36-sq-ft space is now a white-walled museum highlighting tiny objects with big stories. Crafts made by US prisoners, imagined world-leader-used tissues and children's posters from an NYC climate march: these pieces might get overlooked in a larger museum, but instead, they shine as provocative visual poems about the lived human experience. Hours are limited to Fridays and Saturdays between spring and winter, but small windows allow visitors to see the room 24/7. (www.mmuseumm.com)

New York Earth Room GALLERY

9 MAP P72, C3

Since 1980 the oddity of the New York Earth Room, the work of artist Walter De Maria, has been wooing the curious with something not easily found in the city: dirt (250 cu yd – or 280,000lb – of it, to be exact). Walking into the small space is a heady experience, as the scent will make you feel like you've entered a wet forest; the sight of such beautiful, pure earth amid this crazy city is surprisingly moving. (www.earthroom.org)

Museum of Chinese in America MUSEUM

10 MAP P72, E6

In this space designed by architect Maya Lin (designer of the famed

Vietnam Memorial in Washington DC) is a multifaceted museum with engaging permanent and temporary exhibitions that shed light on Chinese American life, both past and present.

Browse through interactive multimedia exhibits, maps, timelines, photos, letters, films and artifacts. The museum's anchor exhibit, *With a Single Step: Stories in the Making of America,* provides an often-intimate glimpse into topics that include immigration, cultural identity and racial stereotyping.

At the end of 2023, the site will close temporarily for renovations. (www.mocanyc.org)

Eating

Thai Diner

THAI $$

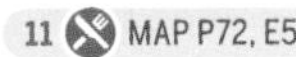

Big Apple goes Bangkok at this quirky tiki temple. Think classic NY diner – chrome bar stools, spacious booths and kitschy ephemera clutter the space, but everything sparkles with Southeast Asian pizzazz.

Pop-music covers in Thai bounce off bamboo-woven walls, and the menu delivers wok-made wonders.

Crab fried rice and *phat see eiw* (rice, noodle, stirfry) are fan favorites, and the vegan *baan* salad is a spicy sensation. The place is perpetually packed for good reason. (www.thaidiner.com)

Nom Wah Tea Parlor

CHINESE $

Hidden down a narrow lane, 1920s Nom Wah Tea Parlor might look like an American diner, but it's actually the oldest dim sum place in town. Grab a seat at one of the red banquettes or counter stools and simply tick off what you want on the menu provided. Roast pork buns, Shanghainese soup dumplings, shrimp *siu mai (open dumplings)* ...it's all finger-licking good. Expect to wait for seats on weekends. (www.nomwah.com)

Golden Diner

AMERICAN $$

Surprising takes on greasy-spoon grub make it worth trekking to this hip haunt underneath the Manhattan Bridge. Most of the excitement comes from Asian influences, like the refreshing Yuzu Palmer, Korean fried chicken, and a decadent Thai tea tres leches – but there's also the pastrami-spiced portobello stuffed in a Reuben-style quesadilla, proving this spot's knack for versatility and innovation. (www.goldendinerny.com)

Dominique Ansel Bakery

BAKERY $

One of New York City's best and most well-known patisseries has more to offer than just cronuts (its world-famous doughnut-croissant hybrid), including buttery

Eating in Chinatown

The most rewarding experience for Chinatown visitors is to access this wild and wonderful world through their taste buds. More than any other area of Manhattan, Chinatown's menus sport wonderfully low prices, uninflated by ambience, hype or reputation. But more than cheap eats, the neighborhood is rife with family recipes passed across generations and continents. Food displays and preparation remain unchanged and untempered by American norms; it's not unusual to walk by storefronts sporting a tangled array of lacquered animals – chickens, rabbit and duck, in particular – ready to be chopped up and served at a family banquet. Steaming street stalls serve pork buns and other finger-friendly food. Wander down the back alleys for a Technicolor assortment of spices and herbs to perfect your own Eastern dishes.

kouign-amman (Breton cake), gleaming berry tarts, and the Paris–New York, a chocolate/caramel/peanut twist on the traditional Paris-Brest. If you insist on a cronut, queue up before opening (8am Monday to Saturday, 9am Sunday) to beat the 'sold out' sign. (www.dominiqueansel.com)

Tacombi Fonda Nolita MEXICAN $

15 MAP P72, E3

Festively strung lights, foldaway chairs and Mexican men flipping tacos in an old VW Kombi: if you can't make it to the Yucatan shore, here's your Plan B. Casual, convivial and ever-popular, the original location of this New York–based chain serves some of the tastiest tacos and burritos in town.

Wash down the goodness with a pitcher of sangria and start plotting that south-of-the-border getaway. (www.tacombi.com)

Butcher's Daughter VEGETARIAN $$

16 MAP P72, F5

The butcher's daughter certainly has rebelled, peddling nothing but fresh herbivorous fare in her whitewashed cafe.

While healthy it is, boring it's not: everything from the 'crab' cakes made with jackfruit and sweet potato to the spicy kale Caesar salad with almond Parmesan or the dinnertime Butcher's burger (vegetable and black-bean patty) is devilishly delish. (www.thebutchersdaughter.com)

Rubirosa PIZZA $$

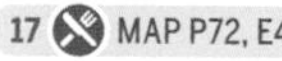

Rubirosa's infallible family recipe for its whisper-thin pie crust lures a steady stream of patrons from all over the city.

Shovel slices from the bar stools or grab a table amid cozy surrounds and make room for savory appetizers and antipasti.

Other options include bowls of pasta (the 'small' portion should fill most bellies). Gluten-free diners have their own menu. (www.rubirosanyc.com)

Balthazar

FRENCH **$$$**

18 MAP P72, D5

Still the king of bistros after more than 20 years, bustling (OK, *loud*) Balthazar is never short of a mob. That's all thanks to three winning details: its location in SoHo's shopping heartland; the uplifting Paris-meets-NYC ambience; and the something-for-everyone menu. Highlights include the outstanding raw bar, steak *frites*, Niçoise salad, and the goat cheese and caramelized onion tart. (www.balthazarny.com)

The Dutch

AMERICAN **$$$**

19  MAP P72, B4

Whether perched at the lively bar or dining snugly in the back room, you can always expect smart, farm-to-table comfort grub at this see-and-be-seen stalwart. Flavors traverse the globe, from wagyu steak tartare with béarnaise aioli to an Israeli mezze plate with sesame eggplant and falafel.

Reservations are recommended, especially for dinner reservations and all day on weekends. (www.thedutchnyc.com)

Balthazar

LEONARD ZHUKOVSKY/SHUTTERSTOCK ©

Peking Duck House

CHINESE **$$$**

20 MAP P72, F8

Offering arguably the best Peking duck in the region, the eponymous restaurant has a variety of set menus that include the house specialty.

The space is fancier than some Chinatown spots, making it great for a special occasion. Do have the duck: perfectly crispy skin and moist meat make the slices ideal for a pancake, scallion strips and sauce. (www.pekingduckhousenyc.com)

Buddha Bodai

CHINESE **$**

21 MAP P72, F8

Chinatown's go-to for vegetarian and certified-kosher cuisine serves classic Cantonese flavors in dishes like vegetarian duck noodle soup, spinach rice rolls and vegetarian 'roast pork' buns.

Since another restaurant with the same name and similar menu opened nearby in 2015, this restaurant (which opened in 2004) is referred to as the 'Original Buddha Bodai'. Dim sum is served until 4pm; BYOB. (www.buddha-bodai.com)

ATLA

MEXICAN **$$**

22 MAP P72, D2

The Mexican dishes on this menu – flautas, quesadillas, tacos, huevos rancheros – might sound like standard fare, but ATLA elevates them to the echelon of fine dining.

Settle into the striking black-and-white restaurant with a mezcal negroni, and order a banquet of sharing dishes like guacamole, *aguachile verde* striped bass or flaxseed *chilaquiles*. (www.atlanyc.com)

The Golden Steamer

CHINESE **$**

23 MAP P72, E6

Squeeze into this hole-in-the-wall for some of Chinatown's fluffiest, tastiest *bao* (steamed buns), made on-site by bellowing Chinese cooks. Fillings include succulent roast pork, Chinese sausage, salted egg and the crowd favorite – pumpkin.

For something a little sweeter, try the egg custard tart. Come early for the best choice.

Prince Street Pizza

PIZZA **$**

24 MAP P72, E4

While waiting in line inside this standing-room-only pie place, you'll likely spot a caricature of Marlon Brando in *The Godfather* saying, "I'm gonna make you a pizza you can't refuse."

And he's right – the slightly sweet red sauce, crispy bottom, and doughy crust make it worth a slice, particularly if you get pepperoni. But is it worth the long line? Perhaps not.

Little Cupcake Bakeshop

DESSERTS $

25 MAP P72, E4

Famed for its Brooklyn Blackout Cake (a chocolate confection invented by former chain Ebinger's, honoring citywide blackouts to protect the Brooklyn Navy Yard during World War II), this retro bakehouse has plenty of treats worth a taste: moist mini cupcakes, homemade ice cream, and cookies galore. The Brooklyn brothers who run the shop are trying to ruin your waistline. (www.littlecupcakebakeshop.com)

Original Chinatown Ice Cream Factory

ICE CREAM $

26 MAP P72, F8

Chinatown's favorite ice-cream peddler keeps it local with flavors such as green tea, pandan, durian and lychee sorbet, all written on a whiteboard. The Factory also sells ridiculously cute, trademark T-shirts with an ice-cream-slurping happy dragon on them. (www.chinatownicecreamfactory.com)

Drinking

Apothéke

COCKTAIL BAR

27 MAP P72, F8

It takes a little effort to track down this former opium-den-turned-apothecary bar on Doyers St (look for the 'chemist' sign with a beaker illustration hanging above the doorway). Inside, skilled barkeeps work like careful chemists, using local, seasonal produce from greenmarkets to concoct intense, flavorful 'prescriptions.' The pineapple-cilantro-spiced Sitting Buddha is one of the best drinks on the menu. (www.apothekenyc.com)

Joe's Pub

Part bar, part cabaret and performance venue, intimate **Joe's Pub** (Map p72, E1; www.joespub.com; Public Theater, 425 Lafayette St, NoHo), named for Public Theater founder Joseph Papp, serves up emerging acts and top-shelf entertainers, ranging from downtown icon Joey Arias to Broadway's biggest divas and even Adele.

Take a chance on lesser-known names. They're generally great and – who knows? – they might be New York's next big thing.

Ear Inn

PUB

28 MAP P72, A5

Want to see what SoHo was like before the trendsetters and fashionistas? Come to the creaking old Ear Inn, proudly billed as one of the oldest drinking establishments in NYC. The house it occupies was built in the late 18th century for James Brown, an African aide to George Washington. Drinks are cheap and the crowd's eclectic. (www.theearinn.com)

Little Italy

In the last 50 years, New York's Little Italy has shrunk from a big, brash boot to an ultraslim sandal. A mid-century exodus to the suburbs of Brooklyn and beyond would see this once-strong Italian neighborhood turn into a micro pastiche of its former self, with the most authentic Italian restaurants now found along Arthur Ave, up in the Bronx.

These days Little Italy is little more than **Mulberry Street** (Map p72), a kitsch strip of gingham-tablecloths, mandolin muzak and nostalgia for the old country. But a stroll around the area still offers up 19th-century tenement architecture, fresh pizza by the slice, gelato by the cone and some of the best tiramisu in town. Come late September, Mulberry St turns into a raucous, 11-day block party for the **San Gennaro Festival** (https://sangennaronyc.org), a celebration honoring the patron saint of Naples. It's a loud, convivial affair, with food and carnival stalls, free entertainment and more big hair than Jersey Shore.

La Compagnie des Vins Surnaturels WINE BAR

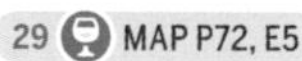

A snug melange of Gallic-themed decor, svelte armchairs and tea lights, La Compagnie des Vins Surnaturels is an offshoot of a Paris bar by the same name. A team of sommeliers can help you navigate an impressive, French-heavy wine list, with some 600 drops and no shortage of arresting labels by the glass. A short, sophisticated menu includes housemade charcuterie and duck buns. (www.compagnienyc.com)

Spring Lounge BAR

This decades-old dive has never let anything get in the way of a good time. In Prohibition days, it peddled buckets of beer. In the '60s its basement was a gambling den. These days, it's best known for its kooky stuffed sharks, early-start regulars and come-one, come-all late-night revelry.

It's a perfect last stop on a bar-hopping tour of the neighborhood. (www.thespringlounge.com)

Garret Cocteleria COCKTAIL BAR

31 MAP P72, F5

It isn't only the jungle-green walls and plant-lined bar that give this stylish cocktail lounge its coastal Latin flair. The menu – including mezcal flights, seafood bites and alcoholic slushies ($13 to $20) – is one mouthful away from a

Caribbean vacation. Arrive early in the evening to snag a spot in the spacious wood booths; seats fill up fast on weekends. (www.thegarretcocteleria.com)

Felix Roasting Company

CAFE

32 MAP P72, A5

Cafe culture gets a Gilded Age glow-up at this airy cafe fit for a modern-day Astor. Floral wallpaper, velvet seats, and a delft-tile mural make every seat seem princely, but the atrium tucked in back – outfitted with a skylight and live plant wall – is the most regal place to hold court. Espresso service stops at 3pm. (www.felixroastingco.com)

Jimmy

COCKTAIL BAR

33 MAP P72, B6

Atop the ModernHaus Soho hotel, Jimmy is a sky-high hangout with sweeping views of the city. The summer months teem with tipsy patrons who spill out onto the open deck; in cooler weather drinks are slung indoors from the centrally anchored bar. An outdoor pool adds to the fun. (www.jimmysoho.com)

Entertainment

Public Theater

LIVE PERFORMANCE

34 MAP P72, E1

This legendary theater was founded as the Shakespeare Workshop back in 1954 and has launched some of New York's big

Mulberry Street

Shopping in SoHo & Chinatown

SoHo bursts at its fashionable seams with stores big and small. Hit Broadway for Main Street chains, shoe shops and jeans outlets, or the streets to the west for higher-end fashion and accessories. On Lafayette, shops cater to the DJ and skate crowds with indie labels and vintage thrown into the mix. Style fiends hyperventilate over SoHo's fashion-conscious streets, but serious shopaholics should consult the city's in-the-know retail blogs before hitting SoHo and surrounds – there's always some sort of 'sample sale' or offer going on, or a new boutique showcasing fresh talent. Use https://thestylishcity.com and www.thecut.com as a resource for what's hot.

If indie-chic is your thing, continue east to Nolita, home of tiny jewel-box boutiques selling unique threads, kicks and fragrances. Mott St is best for browsing, followed by Mulberry and Elizabeth.

For medicinal herbs, exotic fruits, woks and Chinese teapots, scour the frenetic streets of Chinatown.

hits, including *Hamilton* in 2015. Today, you'll find a lineup of innovative new works and reimagined classics, with Shakespeare in heavy rotation.

Speaking of the bard, the Public also stages star-studded Shakespeare in the Park (p220) performances during the summer. (www.publictheater.org/programs/joes-pub)

Film Forum CINEMA

35 MAP P72,A3

This nonprofit cinema shows an astounding array of independent films, revivals and career retrospectives for greats such as Orson Welles. Showings often include director talks or other film-themed discussions for hardcore cinephiles.

Expect to find yourself seated between NYU undergrads and octogenarians who started coming here in 1970. (www.filmforum.org)

Shopping

Canal St Market MARKET

36 MAP P72, D7

In the borderlands where Chinatown morphs into SoHo, this lively retail and food market unavoidably turns heads.

Korean shaved ice from **Lazy Sundaes** is a sweet-tooth must-have, but don't linger too long in the warehouse-like dining area – the retail section is where the real action happens.

Vintage wares, K-pop clothes and locally made jewelry. (www.canalstreet.market)

McNally Jackson

BOOKS

37 MAP P72, E4

Bustling indie MJ stocks an excellent selection of magazines and books, covering contemporary fiction, food writing, architecture and design, art and history. If you can score a seat, the in-store **cafe** is a fine spot to settle in with some reading material or to catch one of the frequent readings and book signings held here. (www.mcnallyjackson.com)

R Swiader

FASHION

38 MAP P72, D6

New York–based designer Raf Swiader creates his collection of gender-optional clothing in the basement below this uber-versatile boutique. Thumb racks of urban-chic threads, peep at fine art from rotating exhibits or get a haircut at the sleek salon in back.

With so much on offer, this SoHo establishment feels more like a 'community clubhouse' than a 'clothing store.' (www.rswiader.com)

Galeria Melissa

SHOES

39 MAP P72, D5

This Brazilian designer specializes in downpour-friendly plastic footwear, reminiscent of the 1980s jellies craze.

Women's shoes are the main focus, but men and children can also choose from the recyclable, sustainable and stylish selection of sandals, brogues and boots. (www.melissa.com.br/us/galerias/ny)

Kevin Smith Kirkwood performs at Joe's Pub at the Public Theater (p83)

Oroboro

FASHION & ACCESSORIES

40 MAP P72, E4

If you're a fan of Free People, try this womenswear boutique with a global roster of designers. Essential oils fill the air, fashionable threads line the walls, and tables sprinkled with handmade jewelry, pottery and a colorful assortment of home goods make this tiny space feel like an art gallery. (www.oroborostore.com)

Saturdays NYC

FASHION & ACCESSORIES

41 MAP P72, D5

SoHo's version of a surf shop sees boards and wax paired up with designer grooming products, graphic art and surf tomes, and Saturdays' own line of high-quality, fashion-literate threads. Once you're styled up, grab a coffee from the in-house espresso bar, hang in the back garden and fish for some crazy, shark-dodging tales. (www.saturdaysnyc.com)

Corridor

CLOTHING

42 MAP P72, E3

Designer Dan Snyder is a remarkable New York City success story. He started his career as an intelligence contractor with the FBI, made shirts for fellow students to put himself through grad school, and now he's selling casual-cool menswear alongside big-name brands in Nolita, Los Angeles and beyond. Thick plaid button-downs, crocheted cardigans, draw-string shorts and Italian-made denim ($265) attract laid-back urbanites

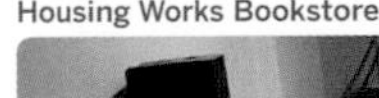

Housing Works Bookstore

CNMAGES/ALAMY STOCK PHOTO ©

with fashionable flair to his tiny flagship shop on popular Elizabeth Street. (www.corridornyc.com)

Housing Works Bookstore

BOOKS

43 MAP P72, D3

Relaxed, earthy and featuring a great selection of secondhand books, vinyl, comics and more that you can buy for a good cause (proceeds go to New York's low-income population affected by HIV and AIDS), this creaky hideaway is ideal for whiling away a few afternoon hours browsing, sitting in the on-site cafe, or rummaging in its adjoining thrift store. (www.housingworks.org/locations/bookstore-cafe)

Fong On

FOOD

44 MAP P72, F8

In 2019, Paul Eng opened this soy-stocked food counter in honor of his family, who sold fresh tofu and noodles out of the same location from 1933 to 2017.

The new shop attracts both longtime locals and tofu newbies with beloved Eng family recipes for homemade tofu, soy milk, *bai tang gao* (a sweet, steamed rice cake) *dau fu fa* (a syrupy tofu pudding) and more.

New Kam Man

HOMEWARES

45 MAP P72, E7

Head past hanging ducks to the basement of this classic Canal St food store for cheap Chinese and Japanese tea sets, plus kitchen products like chopsticks, bowls, stir-frying utensils and rice cookers. Upstairs is a wide selection of Asian foods and other products that are hard to find in the US

Olfactory NYC

PERFUME

46 MAP P72, E3

Unlike most perfumeries in Nolita's unofficial fragrance district, this bespoke scent shop gives visitors the option to craft a signature style ($85).

The DIY process starts by choosing from a series of 'core' concoctions, then mixing in new notes (lavender, cedarwood, geranium and more) with the help of a 'Scentologist.' Choose a label, create a name, and leave perfectly perfumed. (www.olfactorynyc.com)

Explore East Village & Lower East Side

Generations of immigrants began their American adventure in this low-rent landing place. Today, these areas buzz with bohemian energy, offering some of the city's finest bars and indie boutiques. New development poses an inevitable threat, but there are still plenty of remnants of the 'authentic' Lower East Side.

The Short List

- ***Lower East Side Tenement Museum (p94)*** *Witnessing the shockingly cramped conditions of 19th-century immigrants.*
- ***New Museum of Contemporary Art (p94)*** *Appreciating the mind-bending iterations of art across myriad media.*
- ***St Marks Place (p95)*** *Walking the storied strip to stumble upon dumpling shops and drinking dens.*
- ***Alphabet City (p94)*** *Hitting up cocktail lounges and peeking into lush community gardens.*
- ***Essex Market (p98)*** *Hunting this spacious food hall and market for international cuisines and locally made threads.*

Getting There & Around

S For the East Village, take the L to First or Third Aves, the 6 to Astor Pl or the F to Second Ave. For the Lower East Side, take the B/D to Grand St or the F or J/M/Z to Delancey-Essex Sts.

The M14, M21 and B39 buses run along 14th, Houston and Delancey Sts, respectively.

Neighborhood Map on p92

The Museum at Eldridge Street (p95) FELIX LIPOV/SHUTTERSTOCK ©

Walking Tour

Uncover East Village History

The East Village has a long history as part of NYC's multicultural melting pot, which saw it become home to successive waves of immigrant communities, remnants of which still haunt its streets.

Walk Facts

Start St Marks Pl & Second Ave; S Astor Pl

End Tompkins Square Park; S 1st Ave

Length 1 mile; 1½ hours

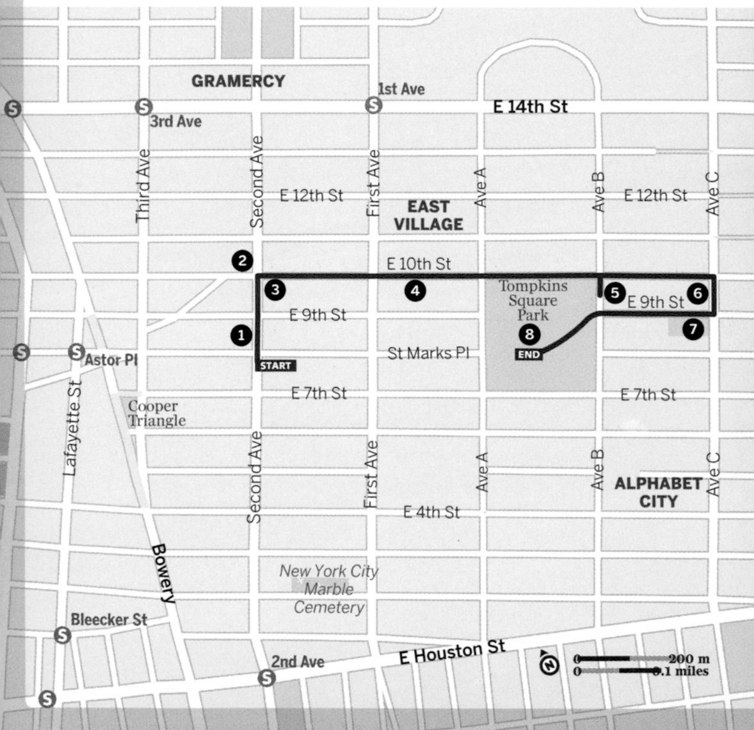

❶ Mosaic Trail

Look for a piece of the **Mosaic Trail** (www.mosaicmannyc.com) on the southeast corner of St Marks Pl and Second Ave, a series of tile artworks adorning utility poles started by Vietnam-vet Jim Power in the 1980s, when this was the main drag for NYC's vibrant, artistic counterculture in the pre-gentrification days.

❷ German Library & Clinic

On Second Ave find the ornate terra-cotta facades of a public library and a former medical clinic (now offices) at Nos 135 and 137; built in 1884, they served the sizable German immigrant population that lived here back when the neighborhood was nicknamed 'Kleindeutschland' (Little Germany).

❸ St Mark's Church in-the-Bowery

In 1660 Dutch colonial governor Peter Stuyvesant built his family chapel on the site of this **church** (www.stmarksbowery.org), making this NYC's oldest religious site still in use. He's buried in the crypt.

❹ Yiddish Theater Memorial

Set into the pavement at the southeast corner of E 10th St and Second Ave (formerly a Jewish deli, now a Chase Bank) are the names of actors and playwrights from the many Jewish theaters that thrived here pre-WWII, including crossover stars Molly Picon and Fyvush Finkel.

❺ Russian & Turkish Baths

Locals have been *shvitzing* in the saunas and steam rooms at these homey public **baths** (www.russianturkishbaths.com) since 1892. Join the crowds for a sensible soak.

❻ Charlie Parker's House

Head to Ave B between 9th and 10th Sts. No 151, a brownstone from 1849, was the home of legendary jazz saxophonist Charlie Parker in the 1950s.

❼ Museum of Reclaimed Urban Space

Visit this former **tenement building** (www.morusnyc.org) reclaimed by squatters in the 1980s to learn about grassroots urban activists fighting against corporate power in the East Village and beyond.

❽ Tompkins Square Park

This bustling **green space** (www.nycgovparks.org) has offered respite to all of the neighborhood's various demographics over the years: German, Polish and other European immigrants of the 1800s and early 1900s; Alphabet City's postwar Puerto Rican populace; the revolutionaries, musicians and artists of the mid-20th century and today's medley of young professionals, middle-class families and punk-rock kids who call this park home.

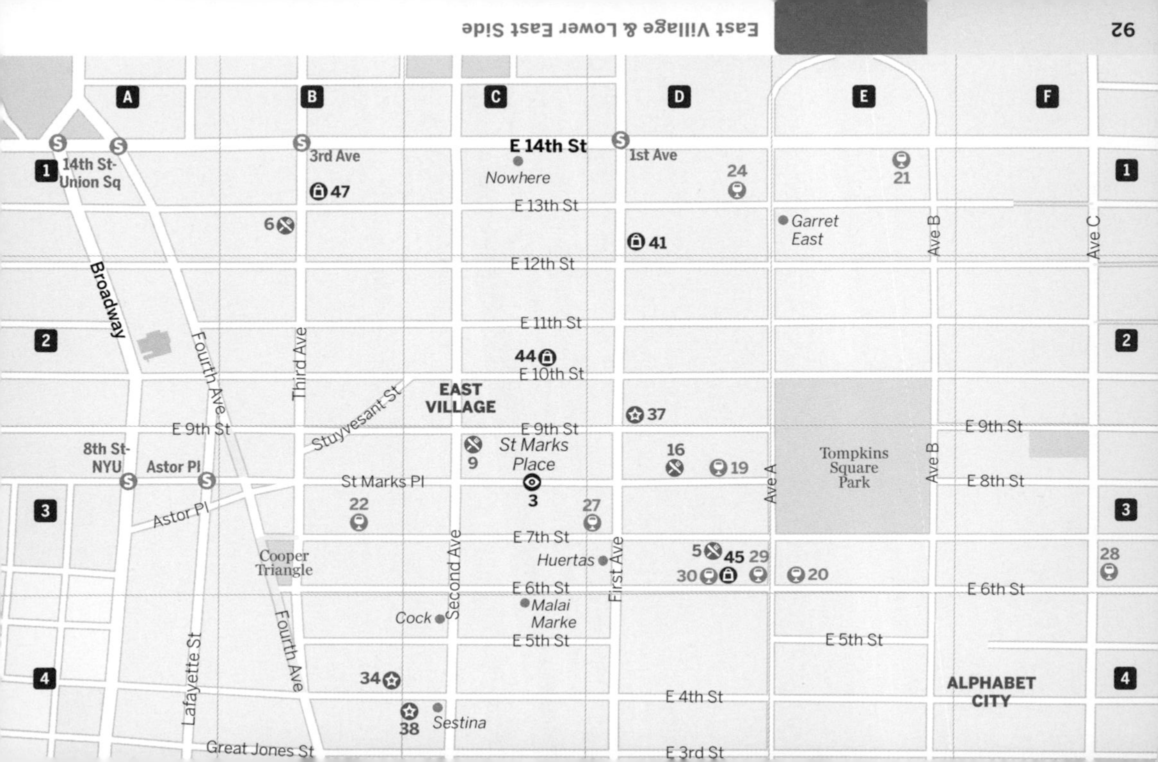
A
B
C
D
E
F
1
2
3
4
14th St-Union Sq
3rd Ave
E 14th St
1st Ave
Nowhere
47
24
21
E 13th St
6
41
Garret East
Ave B
Ave C
Broadway
E 12th St
E 11th St
Fourth Ave
Third Ave
44
E 10th St
EAST VILLAGE
37
Stuyvesant St
E 9th St
8th St-NYU
Astor Pl
9
St Marks Place
16
19
Ave A
Tompkins Square Park
E 8th St
St Marks Pl
3
22
27
Astor Pl
E 7th St
Cooper Triangle
Huertas
5
45
29
28
30
20
Second Ave
First Ave
E 6th St
Malai Marke
Cock
E 5th St
Lafayette St
34
ALPHABET CITY
38
Sestina
E 4th St
Great Jones St
E 3rd St

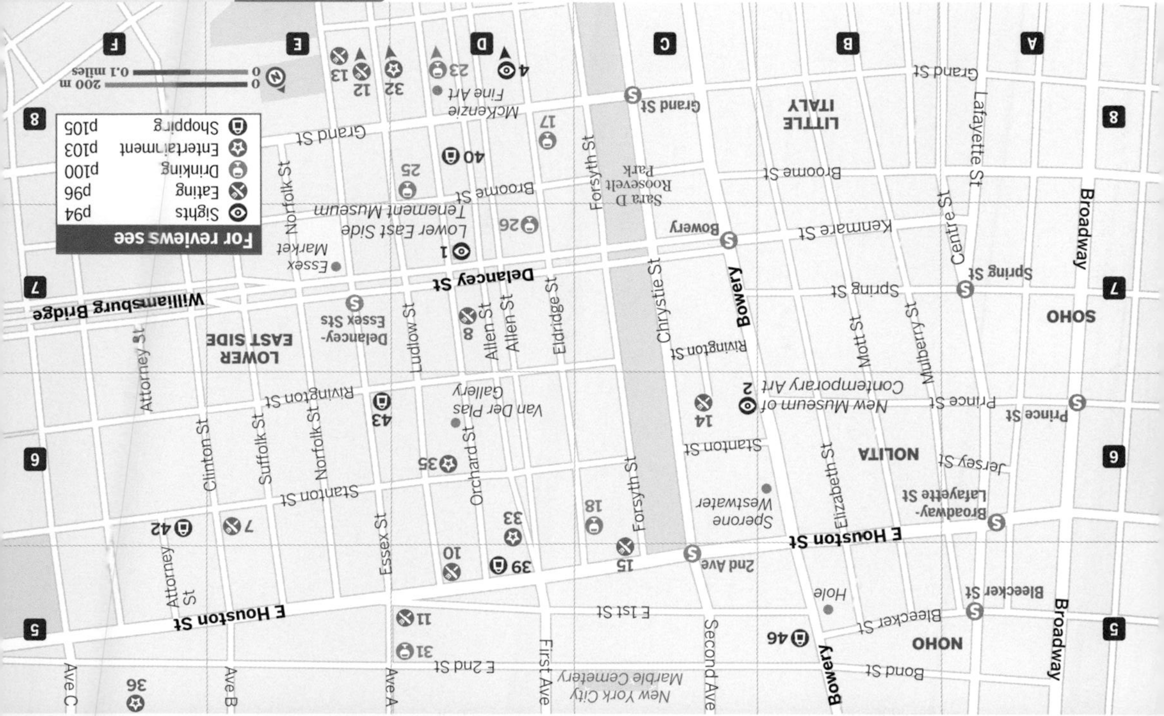

For reviews see

Sights	p94
Eating	p96
Drinking	p100
Entertainment	p103
Shopping	p105

0 — 200 m
0 — 0.1 miles

A B C D E F
5 6 7 8

NOHO
SOHO
NOLITA
LITTLE ITALY
LOWER EAST SIDE

Ave C
Ave B
Ave A
First Ave
Second Ave
E 2nd St
E 1st St
E Houston St
Attorney St
Clinton St
Suffolk St
Norfolk St
Essex St
Ludlow St
Orchard St
Allen St
Eldridge St
Forsyth St
Chrystie St
Bowery
Elizabeth St
Mott St
Mulberry St
Centre St
Lafayette St
Broadway
Bond St
Bleecker St
Jersey St
Prince St
Spring St
Kenmare St
Broome St
Grand St
Stanton St
Rivington St
Delancey St
Williamsburg Bridge

Bleecker St
Broadway-Lafayette St
2nd Ave
Prince St
Spring St
Bowery
Grand St
Delancey-Essex Sts

New York City Marble Cemetery
Hole
Sperone Westwater
New Museum of Contemporary Art
Van Der Plas Gallery
Essex Market
Lower East Side Tenement Museum
McKenzie Fine Art
Sara D Roosevelt Park

1 2 4 7 8 10 11 12 13 14 15 17 18 23 25 26 31 32 33 35 36 39 40 42 43 46

Alphabet City Community Gardens

After a stretch of arboreal abstinence in the East Village, the community gardens of Alphabet City are a welcome sight. The network of gardens, started in the 1970s, was carved out of abandoned lots to provide low-income residents in the mainly Hispanic neighborhood (nicknamed 'Loisada,' for the local pronunciation of Lower East Side) with communal backyards.

Trees and flowers were planted, sandboxes built, found-art sculptures erected and domino games played – all within green spaces wedged between buildings or even claiming entire blocks. The **6th & B Garden** (www.6bgarden.org) is a well-organized space that hosts free music events and workshops, while three dramatic weeping willows and a koi pond grace the twin plots of **La Plaza Cultural** (www.laplazacultural.com).

And while some green spots started getting destroyed in the early 2000s – replaced by new developments and faced with much protest – plenty have held their ground.

You can visit on weekends from April through October, when most gardens tend to be open to the public; many gardeners are activists within the community and are a good source of information about local politics. A map of all the area's gardens can be found on the website for **Loisada United Neighborhood Gardens** (www.lungsnyc.org).

Sights

Lower East Side Tenement Museum MUSEUM

1 MAP P92, D7

This museum allows visitors to briefly inhabit the Lower East Side's heartbreaking, hardscrabble but unexpectedly inspiring heritage. Two remarkably preserved (and minimally restored) 19th-century tenements are the focus of various tours, including the impossibly cramped home and garment shop of the Levine family from Poland, and two immigrant dwellings from the Great Depressions of 1873 and 1929. Visits to the tenement building are available only as part of scheduled guided tours, with many departures each day. (www.tenement.org)

New Museum of Contemporary Art MUSEUM

2 MAP P92, C6

The New Museum of Contemporary Art is a sight to behold: a seven-story stack of ethereal, off-kilter white boxes (designed by Tokyo-based architects

Kazuyo Sejima and Ryue Nishizawa of SANAA and New York firm Gensler) rearing above its medium-rise neighborhood. It was a long-awaited breath of fresh air along what was a completely gritty Bowery strip when it arrived back in 2007. Since the museum's opening, many glossy new constructions have joined it, quickly transforming this once down-and-out avenue. (www.newmuseum.org)

St Marks Place

STREET

3 MAP P92, C3

A hallowed stomping ground for bohemian boundary-breakers (including anarchist Emma Goldman, jazz fiend Thelonius Monk, beatnik Allen Ginsberg and punk queen Debbie Harry) walking this graffitied strip of 8th St is like stepping into the shoes of NYC's edgiest icons. While gentrification has softened its bite, there's still gritty flavor to savor along the three-block stretch. Smoke shops, dumpling spots, tattoo parlors and drinking dens like speakeasy PDT (p100) attract new generations of rabble-rousers raring to make their mark.

Museum at Eldridge Street

MUSEUM

4 MAP P92, D8

This landmark synagogue, built in 1887, was a center of Jewish life before suffering a decline in the congregation in the late 1920s. After WWII, the main sanctuary was closed off and services relocated to the basement.

Lower East Side Tenement Museum

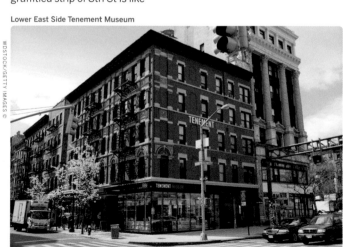

Lower East Side Art Galleries

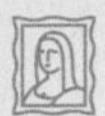

Chelsea may be the heavy hitter in New York's gallery scene, but the Lower East Side still has dozens of quality showplaces. One of the early pioneers, the **Sperone Westwater gallery** (Map P92, B6; www.speronewestwater.com; 257 Bowery, btwn E Houston & Stanton Sts, Lower East Side), which opened in 1975, represents art-world darlings like William Wegman and Richard Long. The gallery's futuristic building is an artwork itself, designed by the famed Norman Foster, who made a splash in NYC with his designs for the Hearst Tower and 425 Park Ave. Near the New Museum of Contemporary Art (p94) is the 4000-sq-ft **Hole** (Map P92, B5; www.theholenyc.com; 312 Bowery, at Bleecker St, East Village) – known for both its art and its rowdy openings, which bring together downtown art-circuit scenesters and the occasional famous face.

Walk up Orchard St from Hester to Stanton, and there's a gallery on nearly every block, starting with sleek **McKenzie Fine Art** (Map P92, D8; http://mckenziefineart.com; 55 Orchard St, btwn Hester & Grand Sts, Lower East Side) and ending with the colorful collections at **Van Der Plas** (Map P92, D6; www.vanderplasgallery.com; 156 Orchard St, btwn Rivington & Stanton Sts, Lower East Side). Grand and Delancey between Forsyth and Allen Sts are equally art-filled, and a fine afternoon could be spent roaming the area with a coffee in hand, peeking in places that catch your eye.

The badly deteriorated synagogue was restored following a 20-year-long, $20m restoration that was completed in 2007, and it now shines with its original splendor – it's a real stunner.

It's now the only remaining marker of Jewish migration to the Lower East Side that is open to the public.

Admission includes a 45-minute self-guided tour, or an hour-long tour with a docent (check the website for availability). (www.eldridgestreet.org)

Eating

Cadence

VEGAN **$$**

5 MAP P92, D3

Chef Shenarri Freeman's native Virginia roots shine in this restaurant's entirely vegan menu doused with Southern soul. Plates are made for sharing, but you might want to hog the collard-green-wrapped succotash, tart potato salad and the savory-sweet pancake made with black-eyed-pea-and-garlic batter. The rose banquette, floral wallpaper and forest-green bar make the entire experience a veritable garden party. (www.overthrowhospitality.com/venues/cadence)

Yellow Rose

TEX-MEX $$

6 MAP P92, B1

Flour tortillas give Tex-Mex taquerias their north-of-the-border flair, and the toasty wheat creations in this far-north-of-Texas outpost make a winning case for Lone Star style.

The bean-and-cheese taco is tried-and-true, the *carne guisada* is chili-gravy greatness, and vegans can rejoice over dairy-free queso.

With swinging saloon doors and Willie Nelson on the stereo, it doesn't get more Texas than this. (www.yellowrosenyc.com)

Ivan Ramen

RAMEN $$

7 MAP P92, E6

After creating two thriving ramen spots in Tokyo, Long Islander Ivan Orkin brought his talents back home.

Few can agree about NYC's best ramen, but this intimate shop, where solo ramen heads sit at the bar watching their bowls take shape, is on every short list. The seafood *tsukumen* (dipping-style) ramen with lobster and shrimp broth is unbeatable. (www.ivanramen.com)

Russ & Daughters Cafe

JEWISH $$

8 MAP P92, D7

Feast on shiny boiled bagels and perhaps the best lox (smoked salmon) in the city at this classic-diner extension of the storied Jewish delicatessen Russ & Daughters (p105), just up Orchard St.

Aside from thick, smoky fish, there are potato latkes, borscht, eggs plenty of ways, and even chopped liver, if you must. (www.russanddaughterscafe.com)

Veselka

UKRAINIAN $$

9 MAP P92, C3

This beloved vestige of the area's Ukrainian past has been serving up handmade pierogi (cheese, potato or meat dumplings), borscht and goulash since 1954. The cluttered spread of tables was once a 24/7 go-to for loungers and carb-loaders, and though the restaurant keeps more civilized hours these days, it's still a heart-warming haunt for the East Village's colorful band of characters. (www.veselka.com)

Katz's Delicatessen

DELI $$

10 MAP P92, D5

Though visitors won't find many remnants of the classic, old-world Jewish Lower East Side dining scene, there are a few stellar holdouts – among them Katz's Delicatessen, where Meg Ryan faked her famous orgasm in the 1989 movie *When Harry Met Sally.*

Essex Market

In 2019, after nearly 80 years in a cramped building across from its current Delancey St location, the wide-ranging specialty food-and-dining hall **Essex Market** (Map P92, E7; www.essexmarket.nyc) unveiled its expansive new digs. Browse fresh seafood, meats and artisanal cheeses before taking lunch upstairs to sunny, open-atrium seating. Vendors offer Scandinavian smoked fish, traditional Dominican food, gourmet ice cream, platters of Indian and much more.

If you love classic deli grub like pastrami and salami on rye, it just might have the same effect on you. (www.katzsdelicatessen.com)

Punjabi Grocery & Deli

PUNJABI $

11 MAP P92, D5

If you spot yellow taxis parked out front, you're in the right place. Former cabbie Kulwinder Singh opened this no-frills food counter in 1993 as a taxi-driver haven for home-cooked Punjabi food, and the bodega-style establishment quickly became a stalwart for affordable veggie fare. Order plates heaped with favorites like *chana masala* (chickpea curry) and well-spiced *samosa chaat*; wash it down with a steaming cup of chai.

Dimes

CAFE $$

12 MAP P92, E8

The LES gets a taste of SoCal at this restaurant with healthy, good-value dishes. Join the design-minded group at Crayola-colored tables for spicy breakfast sandwiches, acai bowls, creative salads (with sunchokes, anchovies, goat cheese), and heartier dishes for dinner (bavette steak, seed-crusted salmon and pulled pork with pineapple are a few). (www.dimesnyc.com)

Partybus Bakeshop

BAKERY $

13 MAP P92, E8

The scent of sourdough is a sweet surprise when stepping into this pretty-in-pink pastry shop. Grab a seat and stay awhile – you'll need time to savor the decadent cinnamon bun and almond-chocolate croissant (buy a loaf of fresh-baked bread for later). While nibbling, search the flower-filled wallpaper for the bakery's eponymous partybus and a few famous neighborhood sites. (www.partybusbakeshop.com)

Freemans

AMERICAN $$$

14 MAP P92, C6

Tucked at the end of Freeman Alley, this charming place draws a hip crowd who gather around the wooden tables to sip cocktails and snack on dishes like roast chicken or grilled brook trout. Potted plants and taxidermied antlers lend a rustic-cabin vibe.

Banzarbar, a 20-seat drink den hidden on the 2nd floor, is an excellent spot for intimate imbibing. (www.freemansrestaurant.com)

Yonah Schimmel Knish Bakery
JEWISH $

15 MAP P92, C5

Step back in time at this bakery-cafe that's been selling old-fashioned Jewish knishes – a pocket of baked dough filled with mashed potatoes, buckwheat, cabbage, spinach, blueberries and sweet cheese – since 1910.

Other classic dishes (potato pancakes, apple strudel) are available, as are egg cream and lime rickey sodas. It doesn't get more authentic than this. (www.knishery.com)

Cafe Mogador
MOROCCAN $$

16 MAP P92, D3

Mogador is a long-running East Village classic, serving fluffy piles of couscous, chargrilled lamb and *merguez* (a spicy lamb or beef sausage) with basmati rice and Arabic salad, as well as satisfying platters of hummus with chickpeas, tomato and parsley.

The standouts are the tagines – fragrantly spiced, claypot-simmered chicken or lamb dishes in four different sauces. (www.cafemogador.com)

Vegan Valhalla

New York's vegan scene is approachable, innovative and exciting. In the East Village alone, there's vegan soul food, Mexican, Italian and more. Here are some of my neighborhood favorites, including plant-based and vegan-friendly spots:

Garret East (Map P92, E1; www.thegarreteast.com) It's a speakeasy that isn't completely vegan, but I like its vegan taco and funky decor.

Sestina (Map P92, C4; www.matthewkenneycuisine.com/sestina) Vegan Italian – come for the seasonal ravioli.

Malai Marke (Map P92, C4) Flavorful Indian with a solid lunch special and plenty of veggie options; it's never too busy.

Huertas (Map P92, D3; www.huertasnyc.com) Basque-style tapas – order the blistered *shishito* peppers.

Cadence (p96) Bring a friend and try multiple dishes. Definitely order the lasagna.

Recommended by Shenarri Freeman, *executive chef of the plant-based restaurant Cadence*

Drinking

Flower Shop

BAR

17 MAP P92, D8

Take the stairs under the humming same-named restaurant to discover a basement bar with such meticulously retro furnishings you'll feel you've stumbled into a mash-up of your dad's pool room and your grandparents' 'best' room. The randomly assembled photos and posters often raise a smile, while flowery banquettes and good cocktails encourage lingering. (www.theflowershopnyc.com)

Bar Goto

COCKTAIL BAR

18 MAP P92, C6

Maverick mixologist Kenta Goto has cocktail connoisseurs spellbound at his eponymous, intimate bar. Expect meticulous, elegant drinks that draw on Goto's Japanese heritage (the Far East Side – with sake, tequila, shiso, lemon, elderflowers and yuzu bitters – is inspired), paired with authentic Japanese comfort bites, such as *okonomiyaki* (savory cabbage pancakes). (www.bargoto.com)

PDT

BAR

19 MAP P92, D3

PDT (Please Don't Tell) scores high on novelty. Pick up the receiver in the phone booth at the hot-dog shop Crif Dogs (www.crifdogs.com); once you're given the OK (reservations are recommended to avoid being turned away), the wall swings open and you step into an intimate, low-lit bar with the odd animal head on the wall and first-rate cocktails. (www.pdtnyc.com)

Club Cumming

LGBTIQ+

20 MAP P92, E3

Anything goes and all are welcome at this slender slip of a nightclub owned by actor and LGBTIQ+ icon Alan Cumming. Every night brings a bevy of debauched delights: nerdy B'way open-mikes, naughty-bawdy burlesque, sweaty dance fêtes, figure-drawing sessions, and the occasional surprise appearance by Cumming's glitzy gaggle of celeb pals. Don't worry about fitting in – by last call, everyone's family. (www.clubcummingnyc.com)

Otto's Shrunken Head

BAR

21 MAP P92, E1

Sling yourself into one of the curved vinyl booths at this rockabilly tiki bar with a Mai Tai or Zombie served up in a classic skull mug (yours to keep for an extra $7). The back room hosts nightly live music, comedy and the like, while DJs spin up front; there's never a cover. (www.ottosshrunkenhead.com)

Proletariat

CRAFT BEER

22 MAP P92, B3

Don't be fooled by the menacing wolf logo – no one's eating meat inside this dimly lit beer den, which serves 100% vegan fare with its list of exceptional suds. Craft-beer cognoscenti sidle up to the bar for 'rare, new and unusual' brews, while hungry hounds down plates of plant-based pub grub in an adjoining room covered in traditional American tattoo art. (www.proletariatny.com)

Lobby Lounge

COCKTAIL BAR

23 MAP P92, D8

If you like your lilies gilded, the Nine Orchard hotel's street-level cocktail lounge (drinks $17 to $22) provides the requisite opulence. Housed in a beaux-arts bank from 1912, every corner stuns with Vanderbilt-era grandeur. Sink into the plush Aperol-pink banquette to sip martinis and enjoy the best view; glass tables reflect the vaulted ceilings above, rich with original ornamentation. (www.nineorchard.com)

Phoenix

GAY & LESBIAN

24 MAP P92, D1

Literally risen from the ashes of its predecessor, The Bar (which burned down), the Phoenix is less 'divey' than it once was, but it's just as friendly. It also has a happy hour from 3pm to 8pm, a pool table, karaoke and trivia nights. (www.phoenixbarnyc.com)

Ten Bells

WINE BAR

25 MAP P92, D8

This charmingly tucked-away natural-wine-and-tapas bar has a grotto-like design, with flickering candles, dark tin ceilings, brick walls and a U-shaped bar that's an ideal setting for a conversation with a new friend. (www.tenbellsnyc.com)

PDT

Alternative LGBTIQ+

NYC's LGBTIQ+ community isn't relegated to one gayborhood – it's a vast archipelago stretching from hot-and-heavy Hell's Kitchen's to Brooklyn's bohemian Bushwick. In the geographic center sits the East Village, where punk attitude provides an antidote to HK's pretty-boy posturing. **Nowhere** (Map p92, C1; www.nowherebarnyc.com), **Phoenix** (p101) and **Club Cumming** (p100) are great places to meet friendly faces, while the **Cock** (Map p92, C4) caters to a friskier male crowd. Drinks are typically cheaper than those you'll find on Manhattan's west side.

Attaboy COCKTAIL BAR

26 MAP P92, D7

Another no-door-sign, speakeasy-vibe bar, but Attaboy is a notch above, serving knockout artisanal cocktails concocted by expert bartenders. Drinks aren't cheap, and you'll likely have to wait for a seat, but the atmosphere and alcohol are worth it. (www.attaboy.us)

Abraço CAFE

27 MAP P92, D3

Abraço is an East Village refuge in an open, ground-level space that serves up perfectly prepared espressos and lattes alongside housemade sweets. Find a table and sip your nicely balanced cappuccino while inhaling a slice of its dangerously addictive olive-oil cake. (www.abraconyc.com)

Accidental Bar BAR

28 MAP P92, F3

'I want more people to drink more sake more irresponsibly,' declares a sign at this relaxed hang dedicated to alcoholic fermented rice. The quote is from owner Austin Power, a sake sommelier whose passion for the Japanese juice inspires indulgence. Join him by sipping a variety of styles with descriptions like 'creamed corn at a summer BBQ' and 'drinking gin with a delightful Swamp Witch.' (www.accidentalbar.com)

Amor y Amargo BAR

29 MAP P92, D3

'Love and Bitters' is like a crafty cocktail chemistry lab, showcasing its namesake selection of amaro. Walk through the apothecary-style entrance filled with tinctures for sale, and enter the tasting room where knowledgeable barkeeps offer their advice on flavors. (www.amoryamargony.com)

Death & Co COCKTAIL BAR

30 MAP P92, D3

Despite the morbid name, the flagship location of this national-award-winning cocktail bar is full of life.

Relax in the dim, stylish interior and let the skilled bartenders shake, rattle and roll some of the best cocktails in town (classics and new creations from $19). It's usually packed – if there's no room, staff take your number and call once there is. (www.deathand company.com)

Berlin

CLUB

31 MAP P92, D5

This brick-vaulted cavern beneath Avenue A does its best to hide – access is through an unmarked door around the corner on the side of the bar that seems to occupy Berlin's address, then steep stairs lead down into a dim, riotous indie lair.

Once you're in, relax and enjoy a night of rock, funk, disco, house and other party tunes in close proximity with your fellow revelers. (www.berlinundera.com)

Entertainment

Metrograph

CINEMA

32 MAP P92, D8

Serious cinephiles should consider devoting a few hours to this indie movie mecca. Two screens, equipped with state-of-the-art digital projectors and an old 35mm reel-to-reel, play a mix of premieres and rare archival videos, and an on-site Commissary drips with classic Hollywood style. Drop by prefilm for the European-influenced dinner menu (mains $27 to $31), or stop by the bar for a postmovie digestif. (www.metrograph.com)

Amor Y Amargo

Rockwood Music Hall

LIVE MUSIC

33 MAP P92, D6

Opened by indie rocker Ken Rockwood, this breadbox-sized concert space has three stages and a rapid-fire flow of bands and singer-songwriters. If cash is tight, try stage 1, which has free shows with a maximum of one hour per band (die-hards can see five or more performances a night). Music kicks off at 3pm on weekends and 6pm on weeknights. (www.rockwoodmusichall.com)

New York Theatre Workshop

THEATER

34 MAP P92, B4

New York Theatre Workshop is like Broadway's scrappier (and secretly cooler) little sister. Going strong since 1979, this innovative production house is the place to see contemporary plays with purpose.

It was the originator of big Broadway hits like *Rent* and *Urinetown* – plus it's where the musicals *Once* and *Hadestown* had their off-Broadway premieres – and each season offers a constant supply of high-quality drama. (www.nytw.org)

Arlene's Grocery

LIVE MUSIC

35 MAP P92, D6

This Lower East Side institution (found in a former bodega) has been hosting a wide swath of nightly live music – but especially local rock, punk and alternative bands – since 1995. Everyone from Arcade Fire to the Strokes to Lady Gaga has played here.

Upstairs is a separate bar where you can keep the night going after the show. (www.arlenesgrocery.net)

Nuyorican Poets Café

LIVE PERFORMANCE

36 MAP P92, F5

Going strong since 1973, the legendary Nuyorican is home to poetry slams, hip-hop performances, plays, films, dance and music. It's living East Village history, but also a vibrant, still-relevant non-profit arts organization. Check the website for events and buy tickets online for the more-popular weekend shows. Or try out your lyrical skills at Monday's open-mike night (8pm; $15). (www.nuyorican.org)

Performance Space New York

THEATER

37 MAP P92, D2

Founded in 1980 as Performance Space 122, this cutting-edge theater once housed in an abandoned public school now boasts state-of-the-art performance spaces, artist studios, a new lobby and a roof deck.

The bones of the former schoolhouse remain, as does its experimental-theater bona fides: Eric Bogosian, Meredith Monk, Justin Vivian Bond and Elevator Repair Service have all performed here. (https://performancespacenewyork.org)

La MaMa ETC

THEATER

38 MAP P92, C4

A long-standing home for onstage experimentation (the ETC stands for Experimental Theater Club), La MaMa is now a three-theater complex with a cafe, an art gallery and a separate studio building that features inventive dramas, sketch comedy and readings of all kinds. Founded in 1961, it's a home for artists of all identities, races, ages and cultures.

All artists in the theatre's programme each season receive a developmental residency, including rehearsal and performance space. There are $10 tickets for each show, available (until they run out) by booking online. (www.lamama.org)

Shopping

Russ & Daughters

FOOD

39 MAP P92, D5

Since 1914 this much-loved deli has served up Eastern European Jewish delicacies, such as caviar, herring, sturgeon and, of course, lox. Proudly owned by four generations of the Russ family, it's a great place to load up for a picnic or stock your fridge with breakfast goodies. Foodies, history buffs and interior designers will love it. (www.russanddaughters.com)

LAAMS

CLOTHING, ART

40 MAP P92, D8

Upon entering this street-culture clubhouse, a laidback posse will likely greet you with a preamble

Concord America plays at Arlene's Grocery

JOHN MARSHALL MANTEL/ZUMA WIRE/ALAMY LIVE NEWS ©

about its three floors of streetwear, records, femme-forward vintage collection and walls filled with urban art. It's worth touring the entire operation – treasures await on every floor, and taking sartorial cues from this crew will grant you major style cred on Orchard St. (www.laams.nyc)

No Relation Vintage

VINTAGE

41 MAP P92, D1

Among the many vintage shops of the East Village, No Relation is a winner for its wide-ranging collections that run the gamut from designer denim and leather jackets to vintage flannels, funky sneakers, plaid shirts, irreverent branded T-shirts, varsity jackets, clutches and more. Sharpen your elbows: hipster crowds flock here on weekends. (www.ltrainvintagenyc.com)

Only NY

CLOTHING

42 MAP P92, F6

Forget the 'I Love NY' shirts – this street-smart independent fashion label sells cool-kid city merch dripping with local swagger.

Vintage-style tees repping Rockaway Beach, bagel-loving totes that say 'Everything's & More,' and clothing dedicated to hot spots like Lincoln Center and the Museum of Natural History: these '90s-style duds will make you look like a native New Yorker. (https://onlyny.com)

A-1 Records

Economy Candy FOOD

43 MAP P92, E6

Bringing sweetness since 1937, this candy shop is stocked with floor-to-ceiling goods in package and bulk, and is home to some beautiful antique gum machines. You'll find everything from childhood favorites like jelly beans, lollipops, gum balls, Cadbury imports, gummy worms and rock candy, to more grown-up delicacies such as halvah, green tea bonbons, hand-dipped chocolates, dried ginger and papaya. (www.economycandy.com)

Archie's Press STATIONERY

44 MAP P92, C2

Archie Archambault's paper-thin print shop features a splendid collection of letterpress art (mainly posters and cards), including his distinctive pieces: city maps from around the world simplified into a series of circles. The shop does double duty as a printing studio, using a Vandercook SP-15 Letterpress from 1960.

New artists regularly exhibit their work, which ranges from cute kitsch to museum-worthy wonder. (https://archiespress.com)

A-1 Records MUSIC

45 MAP P92, D3

One of the last of the many record stores that once graced the East Village, A-1 has been around since 1996. The cramped aisles, filled with a large selection of jazz, funk and soul, draw vinyl fans and DJs from far and wide. (www.instagram.com/a1recordshop)

John Varvatos FASHION & ACCESSORIES

46 MAP P92, B5

Occupying the former location of legendary punk club CBGB, this John Varvatos store goes to great lengths to acknowledge the site's rock-and-roll heritage, with records, high-end audio equipment and even electric guitars for sale alongside JV's denim, leather boots, belts and graphic tees.

Don't expect to see Patti Smith – sales associates dressed in Varvatos seem far removed from the Bowery's gritty past. (www.johnvarvatos.com)

Kiehl's COSMETICS

47 MAP P92, B1

Making and selling skincare products since it opened in NYC as an apothecary in 1851, this Kiehl's flagship store has doubled its shop size and expanded into an international chain, but its personal touch remains – as do the coveted, generous sample sizes.

No

Explore

West Village, Chelsea & the Meatpacking District

The West Village's charming streets and well-preserved town houses offer intimate spaces for dining, drinking and wandering; hugging the river is the Meatpacking District, a see-and-be-seen spot for shopping and nightlife. North is Chelsea, home to art galleries and a vibrant gay community.

The Short List

- ***High Line (p110)*** *Packing a picnic lunch from Chelsea Market for a pastoral moment above the city grid.*
- ***Chelsea Galleries (p112)*** *Checking out the city's brightest art stars at top galleries.*
- ***Washington Square Park (p116)*** *People-watching at this beloved Greenwich Village gathering spot.*
- ***Rubin Museum of Art (p118)*** *Exploring fascinating exhibitions from the Himalayas and beyond.*
- ***Stonewall National Monument (p118)*** *Seeing where the LGBTIQ+ equal rights movement began.*

Getting There & Around

S Sixth Ave, Seventh Ave and Eighth Ave have convenient subway stations, but options narrow further west. Take the A/C/E or 1/2/3 lines to 14th St and walk from there, or to W 4th St-Washington Sq for the heart of the Village.

Neighborhood Map on p114

Washington Square Park (p116) DANOR_A/GETTY IMAGES ©

Top Experience

Wander Along the High Line

Snaking from the Meatpacking District to Hudson Yards at 30ft above street level, this 1.5-mile urban park is a fabulous example of industrial reuse. Once a freight line linking slaughterhouses to the Hudson River, it fell into disuse by the 1980s, only to be resurrected as a green, art-strewn ribbon running between galleries, hotels and chic modern high-rises blossoming below.

MAP P114, C4

www.thehighline.org

Gansevoort St, Meatpacking District

M14 crosstown along 14th St, M23 along 23rd St, S A/C/E, L to 8th Ave-14th St; 1, C/E to 23rd St; 7 to 34th St-Hudson Yards

From Rails to Real Estate

In the early 1900s the area around the Meatpacking District and Chelsea was Manhattan's largest industrial zone. With street-level freight lines causing disruption and fatalities (Tenth Ave was nicknamed 'Death Ave'), an elevated freight track was built. The 'West Side Elevated Line' ran its first train in 1933, but when it fell into disuse, demolition was mooted. In 1999 a plan was hatched to convert the rusting, weed-strewn metal viaduct into public green space. Phase one of this beloved urban-renewal project opened with much ado in 2009; it's been one of NYC's star attractions ever since.

Visiting the High Line

The first completed section starts at Gansevoort St and runs north along Tenth Ave. Glimpse public artworks, spot Little Island (p116), recline on giant chaise longues and rest on wooden bleachers facing huge glass panes framing the traffic below. Food carts will fuel your journey with coffee, *currywurst (a German sausage dish)*, empanadas and gelato.

Over the next several years, the second and third sections opened. Look out for the bulbous bay-windowed **Lantern House** (www.lantern-house.com) – designed by Heatherwick Studio, the team behind the Vessel at Hudson Yards – and architect Zaha Hadid's futuristic glass-and-metal apartment complex at **520 W 28th St** (www.520w28.com).

Finally, the trail curves around Hudson Yards (p163) to reveal supertall skyscrapers shining eastward, and the Hudson River rolling westward. Here the path widens, with rusting, weed-filled railroad tracks alongside the walkway to evoke the overgrown industrial wilderness that pre-existed the park's creation. Access the park via stairways at Gansevoort, 14th, 16th, 17th, 20th, 23rd, 26th, 28th, 30th and 34th Sts, or via elevators at Gansevoort, 14th, 23rd and 30th Sts.

★ Top Tips

- Crowds can cause major congestion along the High Line, particularly during summer's weekend afternoons. Start early at 30th or 34th St to avoid the swarms, then wander south toward Gansevoort St to explore the Whitney Museum (p116) and the West Village.
- Download the Bloomberg Connects app for an in-depth look at art and gardens along the trail; you'll also find schedules for free docent-led tours.

✕ Take a Break

- A wonderland of food vendors awaits behind the brick walls of Chelsea Market (p117), near the 14th St exit of the High Line.
- For Spanish-style treats, peruse the tapas kiosks at Mercado Little Spain (p166), located at the 30th St exit next to Hudson Yards.

Walking Tour

Ogle Art at Chelsea's Galleries

Zigzagging through west Chelsea is like visiting a contemporary-art museum. The neighborhood is home to the densest concentration of galleries in NYC, and while purchasing pieces costs big bucks, perusing the showrooms is free. Most lie in the 20s, between Tenth and Eleventh Aves, and open from Tuesday to Saturday until 6pm. Join the city's well-heeled aesthetes by hunting the streets for a visual feast.

Walk Facts

Start de Vera; S 23rd St

End David Zwirner; S 14th St

Length 1.3 miles; three hours

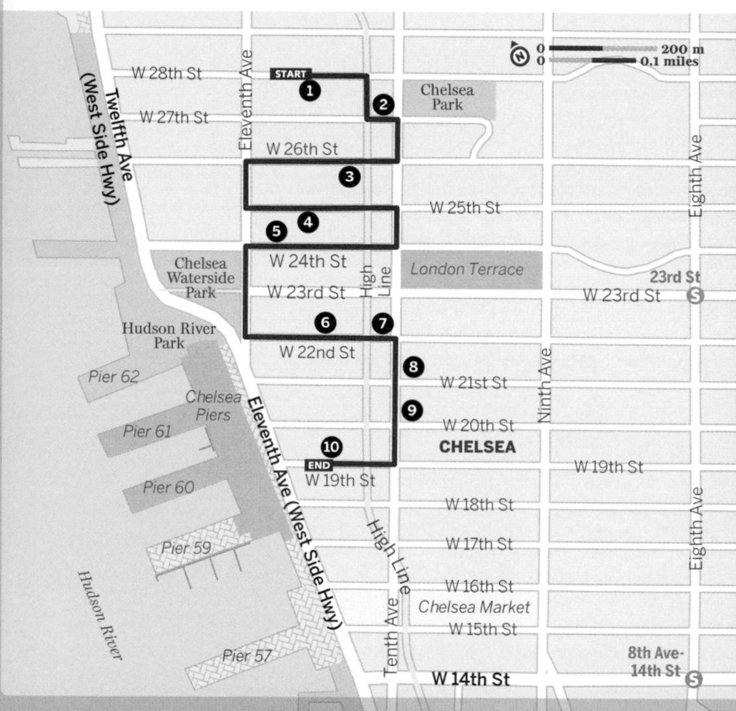

❶ de Vera

Venetian glass, baroque pearls, marble busts and portraits spanning classic to contemporary: Federico de Vera's collection (www.deveraobjects.com) of curious objects might seem more at home in the Met than on 28th St.

❷ High Line Nine

Walk through this block-long hallway (https://highlinenine.org) linking 28th and 27th Sts underneath the High Line – it's a classy strip mall for contemporary galleries, where budding collectors can spot the next big thing.

❸ Paula Cooper Gallery

Paula Cooper started SoHo's gallery explosion in 1968, then moved to Chelsea (www.paulacoopergallery.com) in the 1990s before it became cool. Her mission never falters: expose the world to conceptual and minimal art.

❹ Pace Gallery

Eight floors and 75,000 sq ft can fit quite a lot of work, and this international gallery (www.pacegallery.com) fills it with leading artists of the day. Don't miss the smaller 8000-sq-ft space at 510 W 25th St.

❺ Gagosian

Global chain Gagosian (www.gagosian.com) rotates through exhibits of greats like Jeff Koons, Andy Warhol and Nam June Paik. It's basically a mini MoMA – except everything is for sale.

❻ Dia Chelsea

The massive pieces in this cavernous 20,000-sq-ft space (https://diaart.org) would dwarf most of Manhattan's jewel-box galleries. Marvel at their size before perusing the art bookshop – it's pretty as a picture.

❼ Tía Pol

Refuel and relax with tapas and wine at this intimate Spanish restaurant (www.tiapol.com).

❽ 192 Books

Search the well-curated shelves of this darling bookshop (www.192books.com) for artist monographs, children's books and fantastic new fiction.

❾ Intelligentsia

Walk beyond the High Line Hotel's green hedges and Gothic facade for a jolt of espresso from this hidden coffee counter (www.thehighlinehotel.com), tucked past the lobby entrance.

❿ David Zwirner

Prince of the art world's Blue Chip empire, German curator David Zwirner (www.davidzwirner.com) stages shows featuring celebrated artists from Dan Flavin to Yayoi Kusama.

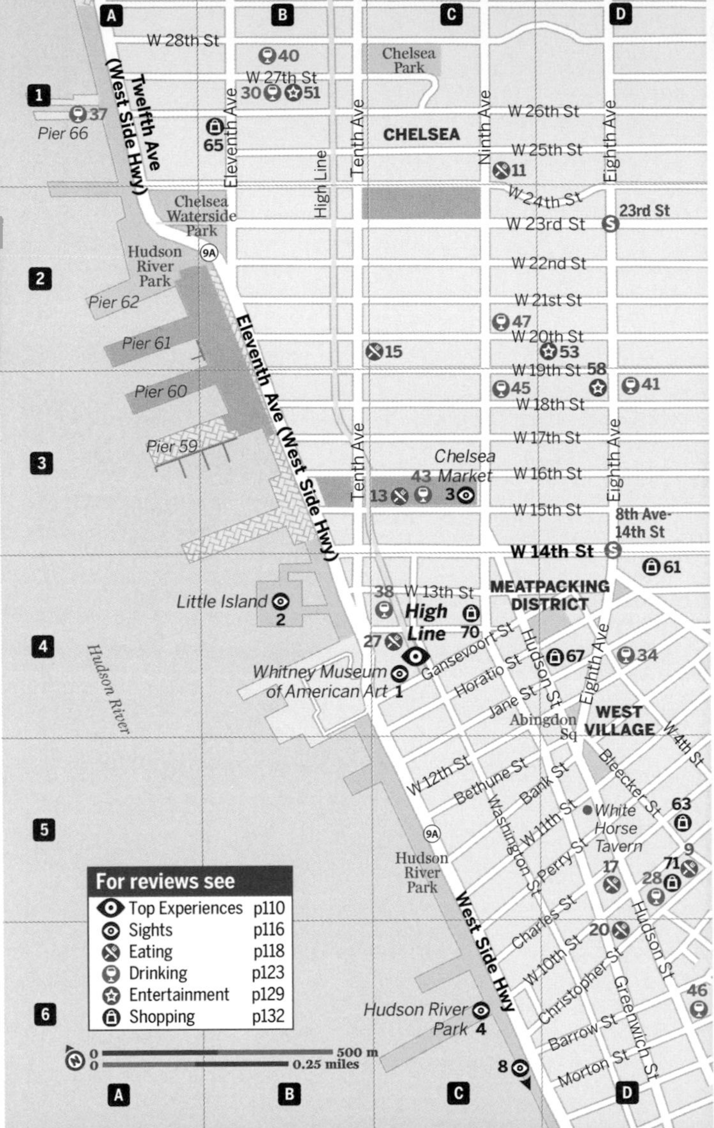
A
B
C
D
1
2
3
4
5
6
W 28th St
40
W 27th St
30
51
Chelsea Park
W 26th St
37
Pier 66
Twelfth Ave (West Side Hwy)
65
Eleventh Ave
High Line
Tenth Ave
CHELSEA
Ninth Ave
W 25th St
Eighth Ave
11
W 24th St
Chelsea Waterside Park
W 23rd St
23rd St
Hudson River Park
9A
W 22nd St
Pier 62
W 21st St
47
Pier 61
W 20th St
15
53
W 19th St
58
Pier 60
45
41
W 18th St
Eleventh Ave (West Side Hwy)
W 17th St
Pier 59
Chelsea Market
43
W 16th St
13
3
W 15th St
8th Ave-14th St
W 14th St
61
MEATPACKING DISTRICT
38
W 13th St
Little Island
2
High Line
70
27
Gansevoort St
Hudson St
67
Eighth Ave
34
Hudson River
Whitney Museum of American Art
1
Horatio St
Jane St
Abingdon Sq
WEST VILLAGE
W 4th St
W 12th St
Bethune St
Bank St
Bleecker St
Washington St
W 11th St
White Horse Tavern
63
Hudson River Park
Perry St
9
71
17
28
Charles St
20
Hudson St
West Side Hwy
W 10th St
Christopher St
Greenwich St
46
Hudson River Park
4
Barrow St
Morton St
8
For reviews see
Top Experiences p110
Sights p116
Eating p118
Drinking p123
Entertainment p129
Shopping p132
0 500 m
0 0.25 miles

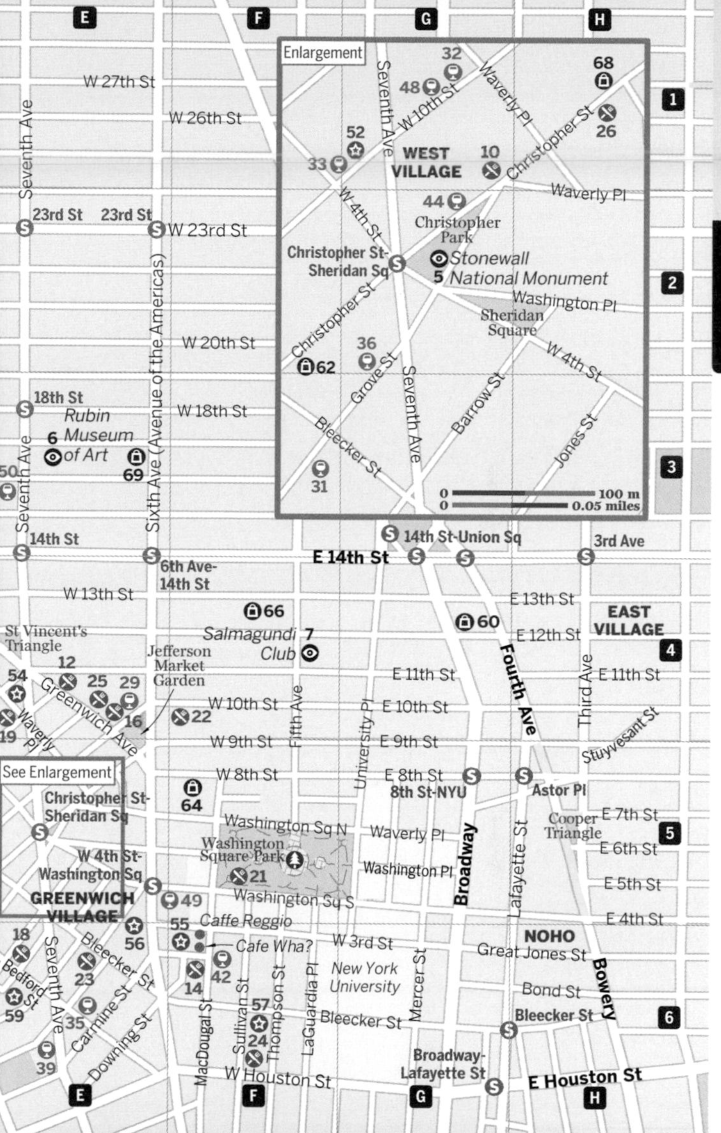

Enlargement
WEST VILLAGE
Christopher Park
Stonewall National Monument
Sheridan Square
Christopher St-Sheridan Sq
Seventh Ave
W 10th St
Waverly Pl
Christopher St
W 4th St
Washington Pl
Grove St
Barrow St
Jones St
Bleecker St
100 m
0.05 miles
W 27th St
W 26th St
23rd St
W 23rd St
W 20th St
18th St
W 18th St
Rubin Museum of Art
Sixth Ave (Avenue of the Americas)
14th St
6th Ave-14th St
14th St-Union Sq
E 14th St
3rd Ave
W 13th St
E 13th St
E 12th St
EAST VILLAGE
St Vincent's Triangle
Jefferson Market Garden
Salmagundi Club
Greenwich Ave
Fourth Ave
Third Ave
E 11th St
E 10th St
W 10th St
W 9th St
E 9th St
Fifth Ave
University Pl
Stuyvesant St
W 8th St
E 8th St
8th St-NYU
Astor Pl
See Enlargement
W 4th St-Washington Sq
GREENWICH VILLAGE
Washington Sq N
Washington Square Park
Washington Sq S
Waverly Pl
Washington Pl
Cooper Triangle
E 7th St
E 6th St
E 5th St
E 4th St
Broadway
Lafayette St
Caffe Reggio
Cafe Wha?
W 3rd St
New York University
NOHO
Great Jones St
Bond St
Bowery
Bleecker St
Bedford St
Carmine St
Downing St
MacDougal St
Sullivan St
Thompson St
LaGuardia Pl
Mercer St
Broadway-Lafayette St
W Houston St
E Houston St

Wander Washington Square Park

Once a potter's field and square for public executions, **Washington Square Park** (Map p114, F5; www.nycgovparks.org) is now a bohemian green space and the unofficial town square of Greenwich Village, hosting lounging NYU students, tuba-playing street performers, socializing canines, fearless squirrels, speed-chess pros and barefoot children who splash about in the fountain on warm days.

Locals have resisted changes to the shape and uses of the park, and its layout has remained largely the same since the 1800s. Check out the Washington Square Park Conservancy (www.washingtonsquareparkconservancy.org) for news and events.

The iconic Stanford White Arch (colloquially known as the Washington Square Arch) dominates the park with its 73ft of gleaming white Tuckahoe marble.

Originally designed in wood to celebrate the centennial of George Washington's inauguration in 1889, it proved so popular that it was replaced with a stone version six years later.

Sights

Whitney Museum of American Art

MUSEUM

1 MAP P114, C4

Anchoring the southern reaches of the High Line (p110), this modern marvel's glass-and-cement shell – designed by Renzo Piano and opened in 2015 – provides 63,000 sq ft of space for the museum's unparalleled collection of American art. Wander light-filled galleries to see pieces by greats like Edward Hopper, Jasper Johns, Georgia O'Keeffe and Mark Rothko, and escape the crowds on three outdoor terraces for a smattering of sculptures and skyline views. Unlike many museums, special emphasis is given to works by living artists. (www.whitney.org)

Little Island

PARK

2 MAP P114, B4

This 2.4-acre park floating above the Hudson appeared like a surrealist dream when unveiled in 2021: 132 concrete pods shoot from the water like tulips, crowned by undulating green hills, outdoor performance spaces and lookouts peering from pretty flower beds to Manhattan's skyscraper forest. Snake along footpaths to enjoy gentle breezes and expansive views or check the seasonal event schedule to see live theater, music and dance with the rippling river as a backdrop. (https://littleisland.org)

Chelsea Market

MARKET

3 MAP P114, C3

In a shining example of redevelopment and preservation, the Chelsea Market has transformed a former Nabisco factory into a shopping concourse catering to foodies and fashion hounds. Over three dozen vendors ply their temptations, including Mokbar (ramen with Korean accents), Pia (vegan Mexican and natural wine), Fat Witch Bakery (brownies and other decadent hits) and Day Drinks (on-tap espressos, teas and botanicals). Once you've had your fill, make sure to check out Artists and Fleas – a small market where local artists sell their wares. (www.chelseamarket.com)

Hudson River Park

PARK

4 MAP P114, C6

The High Line may be all the rage these days, but one block away from the famous elevated park stretches a 5-mile stream of recreational space that has transformed the city over the past decade.

Covering 550 acres (400 of which are on the water) and running from Battery Park at Manhattan's southern tip to 59th St in Midtown, Hudson River Park is Manhattan's wondrous waterfront backyard. The long riverside path is a great spot for cycling, running and strolling. (www.hudsonriverpark.org)

Chelsea Market

KRISTI BLOKHIN/SHUTTERSTOCK ©

Stonewall National Monument NATIONAL PARK

5 MAP P114, G2

In 2016, a 7.7-acre area in the West Village, including tiny triangular Christopher Park, became the first US national monument dedicated to LGBTIQ+ history. The monument protects the site of the 1969 Stonewall Uprising (p130), when patrons at the Stonewall Inn fought against police brutality, sparking the modern LGBTIQ+ rights movement. Today, NYC's LGBTIQ+ community comes here to celebrate, mourn, party and protest. The city boasts many gayborhoods, but this is its beating heart. (www.nps.gov/ston)

Rubin Museum of Art GALLERY

6 MAP P114, E3

The Rubin is the first museum in the Western world dedicated to the art of the Himalayas and surrounding areas. Its impressive collection spans 1500 years to the present day, and includes Chinese embroidered textiles, Nepalese gilt-copper bodhisattvas, Pakistani stone sculptures and intricate Bhutanese paintings, as well as ritual objects and dance masks from various Tibetan regions. Fascinating rotating exhibitions have included The Tibetan Buddhist Shrine Room – an immersive installation incorporating sights, sounds and scents found in a traditional household shrine. (https://rubinmuseum.org)

Salmagundi Club GALLERY

7 MAP P114, F4

One of the oldest art clubs in the US (founded in 1871), this free-to-visit space focused on representational American art is far removed from Chelsea's flashy gallery scene. Set in a stunning 19th-century brownstone below Union Sq, the trip is worth it if only to linger in the parlor, which is decked in period decor and historic paintings. (www.salmagundi.org)

New York Trapeze School HEALTH & FITNESS

8 MAP P114, C6

Fulfill your circus dreams on the flying trapeze in this open-air tent by the Hudson River, open from May through October and located atop Pier 40. The school also has an indoor facility in South Williamsburg, Brooklyn, that's open year-round. No prior experience necessary; call or check the website for daily class times. (www.newyork.trapezeschool.com)

Eating

I Sodi ITALIAN $$$

9 MAP P114, D5

Booking a reservation at this romantic Italian osteria is like winning the lottery: challenging to get, potentially life-changing. Each bite is a tastebud trip to Tuscany, and the simple decor ensures the food is the focus. Follow the traditional three-course menu, starting with antipasti (sliced meats, cheeses, salads), moving to *primi* (the house-made lasagna is high-class comfort food) and rounding it out with a meat-focused secondi. (www.isodinyc.com)

Jeffrey's Grocery AMERICAN $$$

10 MAP P114, G1

This lively eating and drinking spot started making waves in the West Village over a decade ago. Seafood is the focus: well-executed dishes include a spicy ceviche, mussels with chili soffritto and lobster spaghetti in tarragon butter, but the real star is the raw bar. Wash down oysters and king crab legs with the Tides (vodka, contratto, pineapple and lime). (www.jeffreysgrocery.com)

Shukette MIDDLE EASTERN $$

11 MAP P114, C1

It takes a strong constitution not to fill up on piles of fluffy pita, grilled *laffa* flatbread, and Moroccan *frena* bread – but it's worth saving room for the entrees and dips that make this Middle Eastern spot sizzle. Bring a group, order tons of plates, and try everything: dollops of *labne* (strained yoghurt), tahini and baba ghanoush (eggplant dip), then perhaps crispy eggplant and Arctic char meatballs. No dish disappoints. (www.shukettenyc.com)

Semma INDIAN $$$

12 MAP P114, E4

Experience summer in South India by ordering the spicy chutneys and sauces on Semma's menu. The lingering heat of each dish is bound to make you sweat. (Spice-averse eaters should order the gunpowder dosa instead.) Kaleidoscopic murals of jungle plants and Hindi gods add to the Indian authenticity, but the artful presentation plants this restaurant firmly in New York's upscale dining scene. (www.semma.nyc)

West Side Art Crawl

Join fashionable art hounds at the latest gallery shows (p112) in Chelsea. Thursday nights from 6pm to 9pm are most common for openings, and if planned correctly, it's possible to roam from one party to the next while enjoying free wine and eavesdropping on sharp-tongued critics. Find listings on artforum.com/artguide/place/new-york.

During the day, the Meatpacking District wows with the Whitney Museum of American Art (p116) and the High Line (p110) – chock-full of sculptures, murals and paintings beloved by locals and tourists alike.

Los Tacos No 1 MEXICAN $

13 MAP P114, C3

It's worth waiting in line for these authentic Mexican tacos served at a counter inside Chelsea Market (p117). Get a fresh corn tortilla filled with your choice of meat or *nopal* (grilled cactus), and ask for *con todo* to get all the fixings: cilantro, onion, salsa and guacamole. Successful expansions to Tribeca, NoHo, Grand Central and Times Sq prove this chain means business. (www.lostacos1.com)

Minetta Tavern

BISTRO **$$$**

14 MAP P114, F6

Initially opened in 1937, this tavern was once frequented by literary bohemians like Ernest Hemingway and EE Cummings. A 2009 renovation nods to the historic setting with snug red-leather banquettes, dark-paneled walls and glowing yellow bistro lamps – but the pricey menu winks at the West Village's modern-day elite. The Black Label Burger is a smoky sensation; follow it with a Manhattan for a boozy-cherry dessert. (www.minettatavernny.com)

Cookshop

AMERICAN **$$**

15 MAP P114, C2

A brilliant brunching pit stop before (or after) tackling the verdant High Line (p110) across the street, Cookshop is a lively place that knows its niche and nails it. Excellent service, eye-opening cocktails (good morning, Cookshop Mary!), a perfectly baked bread basket, outdoor seating for warm days and inventive egg dishes make this a Chelsea favorite. (www.cookshopny.com)

Rosemary's

ITALIAN **$$$**

16 MAP P114, E4

One of the West Village's liveliest restaurants, Rosemary's serves high-end Italian fare that lives up to the hype. In a farmhouse-like setting, diners tuck into generous portions of house-made pastas, rich salads, and cheese and cured-meat boards.

Some of the produce is grown in-house – or rather *over* the house – with a rooftop garden producing everything from crisp dandelion greens to plump zucchinis. (www.rosemarysnyc.com)

RedFarm

ASIAN FUSION **$$$**

17 MAP P114, D5

Dim sum diners cram into this small, buzzing space to experience Chinese cooking as a delectable art form. 'Pac Man' shrimp dumplings deliver on the name, pastrami egg rolls get served with deli mustard and the three-colored veggie dumplings look like sci-fi sea creatures. Don't worry about filling up on small stuff – starters and dumplings make for a fine feast. (www.redfarmnyc.com)

Sushi Nakazawa

SUSHI **$$$**

18 MAP P114, E6

The price is high, but the quality is phenomenal at this tiny sushi spot that opened to much acclaim in 2013. There are no cooked dishes and little in the way of individual choice. Instead the meal is a 20-course fixed-price affair created by chef Daisuke Nakazawa, who served under Jiro Ono, probably the world's finest sushi chef. (www.sushinakazawa.com)

Taïm

ISRAELI $

19 MAP P114, E4

This chain's original outpost whips up some of the city's best falafel in tiny quarters.

Order it green (traditional style) or harissa (with Tunisian spices) – whichever you choose, you'll get it stuffed into pita with tahini, salad and pickles, on a platter with sides such as Moroccan carrots and marinated beets, or over Israeli salad.

Take it to go and chow down on a bench at St Vincent's Triangle. (www.taimfalafel.com)

JeJu Noodle Bar

NOODLES $$$

20 MAP P114, D6

Don't be fooled by the 'Nighthawks' awning out front. You won't find any Edward Hopper paintings here – you'll find Michelin-starred Korean ramen (called *ramyun*). Sit counterside to watch chefs prepare dishes like *toro ssam bap* (fatty tuna, toasted seaweed, *tobiko* rice and scrambled egg) – a perfect starter before slurping down *gochu ramyun* with pork belly and noodles in a spicy red broth. (www.jejunoodlebar.com)

NY Dosas

SOUTH INDIAN $

21 MAP P114, F5

It's easy to spend an entire afternoon in Washington Square Park, and during that time, you'll likely

RedFarm

ROBERT K CHIN/ALAMY STOCK PHOTO ©

Dining Out

With a bit of research and cash in your pocket, you can eat like royalty at every meal in these neighborhoods. The West Village is known for classy, cozy and intimate spots, with much of the good grub lining Greenwich Ave, Hudson St and Bleecker St. The adjacent Meatpacking District's dining scene is generally more ostentatious, trend-driven and pricey.

Chelsea strikes a balance between the two, with a brash assortment of eateries between Seventh and Ninth Aves, and a few tasty stragglers further west on Tenth Ave.

need food. If you're lucky, hunger will strike midday when Sri Lanka–born Thiru Kumar sells his South Indian–style dosas, samosas and roti from a tiny pushcart near the park's dog run. The all-vegan, gluten-free fare is delicious, cheap and ideal for outdoor snacking. (http://nydosas.com)

Alta

TAPAS **$$**

22 MAP P114, F4

This gorgeous 19th-century town house highlights the neighborhood's character, with exposed brick, wood beams, massive mirrors and romantic fireplaces. A small-plates Mediterranean menu inspires overordering with the likes of lamb tagine, fried goat cheese, mushroom flatbread and seared sea scallops; reading the encyclopedic wine list is enough to get a buzz. Keep your eyes peeled for the garden-level entrance. www.altarestaurant.com)

Faicco's Italian Specialties

DELI **$$**

23 MAP P114, E6

Family-run since 1900, this classic Italian deli earned early fame thanks to its house-made pork sausages; today, it's hyped for sandwiches so big they could feed an entire wolf pack.

Step up to the counter, take a number and wait until you're called. Standing in line with the lunch crowd affords time to decide on a hero: perhaps meatball, mozzarella, chicken or fried eggplant. (https://faiccosnyc.com)

Banter

AUSTRALIAN **$**

24 MAP P114, F6

Fed up with greasy NY diner food? Opt for this cheery Australian cafe's colorful veggie bowls, loaded avocado toast or homemade granola with fresh berries and yogurt. Pair it with a flat white or Aperol spritz.

This casual brunch-lunch hang is ideal for coffee, cocktails and hours of conversation. As for its two outposts located a mile apart? That's what Aussies call 'ace.' (www.banternyc.com)

Mah Ze Dahr

BAKERY $

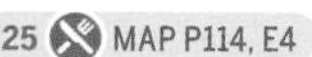
25 MAP P114, E4

Tangy, creamy cheesecakes and rich chocolate brownies are on offer at this bakery opened by former financial advisor Umber Ahmad, who was discovered when she baked for one of her clients, celebrity chef Tom Colicchio. When you try one of the sugared brioche doughnuts filled with silky vanilla cream you'll understand why Colicchio suggested the change of career. (www.mahzedahrbakery.com)

Délice and Sarrasin

VEGAN $$

26 MAP P114, H1

Tahini 'foie gras,' oyster mushroom 'escargot,' and a 'boeuf' bourguignon made with pea protein: navigating French menus can be a vegan nightmare, but inside this petite exposed-brick bistro, each dish is a veggie dream. Dine on savory galettes, sweet crepes, crème brûlée, and even 'steak' tartare – all those meat-and-dairy no-no's are finally *oui-oui*'s. (http://delicesarrasin.com

Hector's Café & Diner

CAFE $

27 MAP P114, C4

Time stands still at this old-school diner hunkered below the High Line – the last humble (and reasonably priced) eatery in the Meatpacking District. Join wise guys, construction crews and the odd tourist over heaping plates of pancakes, omelets, hot pastrami sandwiches and cheeseburgers.

Drinking

Employees Only

BAR

28 MAP P114, D5

This divine speakeasy-style cocktail bar, tucked behind a discreet green awning on Hudson St, is a world-beater. Ace mixologists shake up crazy libations like the Ginger Smash, and the wood-rich art deco space makes everyone feel glamorous. The kitchen plays its part, too, producing decadent hits like bacon-wrapped lamb chops and eggplant ravioli to help soak up the booze. (www.employeesonlynyc.com)

Happiest Hour

COCKTAIL BAR

29 MAP P114, E4

A supercool, tiki-licious cocktail bar splashed with palm prints, '60s pop and playful mixed drinks that provide a chic take on the fruity beach cocktail. If the setting summons fantasies of West Coast living, order the Happiest Burger – a beef double-decker akin to the double-double at California's In-N-Out (there's a veggie option, too). After one bite, you're toeing the Pacific. (www.happiesthournyc.com)

Gallow Green

BAR

30 MAP P114, B1

Run by the innovative team behind the immersive show *Sleep No More*, Gallow Green is a rooftop sanctuary for food and drinks, festooned with vines, potted plants and fairy lights. It's a great hang whether you're seeing the show or not, with live music for weekend brunch and Sunset Sundays. The space becomes a cozy chalet in winter.

Reservations recommended. (www.mckittrickhotel.com/gallow-green)

Buvette

WINE BAR

31 MAP P114, F3

Bubbling with the animated conversation of locals, courting couples and theater types, this devotedly Francophile cafe-bar-restaurant makes a great rest stop while wandering around the West Village. Sip an espresso, order a glass of wine or settle in for a full meal. Brunch dishes such as croque monsieurs are replaced by tartines and small plates at dinner. (www.ilovebuvette.com)

Julius'

GAY

32 MAP P114, G1

One of NYC's longest-running gay joints, this cozy dive is refreshingly unpretentious. The clientele is an intergenerational mix of LGBTIQ+ old-guard and scruffy upstarts, and the mostly fried food, cooked opposite the bar, is also without pretense.

Search the walls for a black-and-white photo from 1966, when members of the Mattachine Society came here to stage a 'Sip-In,' protesting a discriminatory law against serving homosexuals. (www.juliusbarny.com)

St Jardim

CAFE WINE BAR

33 MAP P114, F1

Perched on a lively West Village side street with oversized windows and outdoor tables, this all-day cafe and natural wine bar is perfect for people watching.

Coffee beans from Brooklyn-based Sey (p231) ensure smooth brews, and the mostly French vino list appeals to picky oenophiles. Pair them with morning bites (breakfast sandwiches, omelets and more) or dinner's Mediterranean-inspired plates. (www.stjardimnyc.com)

Cubbyhole

LESBIAN

34 MAP P114, D4

This snug West Village dive started serving the LGBTIQ+ community and their allies in 1994. While the crowd's mostly women, it welcomes anyone looking for a drink in good company beneath a ceiling festooned with lanterns, toys and other ephemera. It's got a great jukebox, friendly bartenders and regulars who prefer to hang and chat rather than hook up and leave. (www.cubbyholebar.com)

Bandits

BAR

35 MAP P114, E6

Squeeze into a pea-green booth, find Farrah Fawcett on the wood-paneled portrait gallery and down enough 'dressed-up' beers to confidently fondle the shag wall leading to the bathroom. The disco ball and classic rock might feed the need to show off smooth moves, but hold off – the vibe here is less 'dance club' and more '1970s diner,' tasty bar bites included. (www.banditsnyc.com)

Marie's Crisis

BAR

36 MAP P114, G2

Aging Broadway queens, bright-eyed chorus kids, giggly tourists and other musical theater fans assemble around this bar's lovingly beat-up piano to take turns belting out campy show tunes, often joined by the entire crowd – and the occasional celebrity. It's old-school fun, no matter how jaded you might be upon entering. It's also historic: Thomas Paine (author of *The American Crisis*) died here in 1809. (www.mariescrisiscafe.com)

Frying Pan

BAR

37 MAP P114, A1

Salvaged from the bottom of the sea (or at least the Chesapeake Bay), the lightship *Frying Pan* and the two-tiered dockside bar where it's moored are fine go-to spots for a summer sundowner. On balmy days the rustic open-air space brings in rowdy crowds, who laze on deck chairs and down ice-cold beers while enjoying Hudson River breezes. (www.pier66maritime.com)

Top of the Standard

BAR

38  MAP P114, C4

Afternoon tea morphs into evening cocktails at this golden perch atop the oh-so-ritzy Standard hotel. Live jazz and glittering views add to the picture of sophistication; if

Julius'

Greenwich Village Bohemia

It's hard to imagine today, but this entire neighborhood once brimmed with bohemian revelry. In the mid-20th century, author James Baldwin and beatnik Jack Kerouac got rowdy at the **White Horse Tavern** (Map p114, D5; www.whitehorsetavern1880.com); Bob Dylan and Jimi Hendrix crooned at **Cafe Wha?** (Map p114, F6). Haunts where writers like F Scott Fitzgerald found inspiration have mostly shuttered, making way for high-end boutiques and million-dollar residences. But if you tuck into works by these Village bohemians – perhaps at **Caffe Reggio** (Map p114, F6; www.caffereggio.com), open since 1927 – it's possible to conjure their spirits.

you want to join in, reserve a table in advance and show up wearing smart-casual attire. Le Bain, a connected penthouse discotheque, attracts stylish crowds with legendary DJs and a giant Jacuzzi. (www.standardhotels.com)

Little Branch — COCKTAIL BAR

39 MAP P114, E6

If it weren't for lines later in the evening, you'd never guess a charming bar hides beyond the plain metal door set in a brick wall on a triangular corner.

Walking downstairs to the basement den feels like a Prohibition throwback: patrons clink glasses and sip artfully prepared cocktails; live jazz occasionally accompanies the percussion of mixologists at work. (www.instagram.com/lbbarnyc)

Eagle NYC — GAY

40 MAP P114, B1

Leather fetishists and those who love them gather at this three-level sleaze palace for dancing, drinking and cruising, all done with abandon.

Theme nights throughout the week encourage appropriate attire (if you forget yours, there's an on-site fetish shop), but jeans and a tee are often acceptable. Come for summer's Sunday beer blasts, when bears and daddies down brews on the roof deck. (www.eagle-ny.com)

Jungle Bird — BAR

41 MAP P114, D3

Classy cocktails with tropical touches splish-splash around this vibrant two-floor lounge. Downstairs is ideal for intimate groups or dates, with rich green walls, brown-leather banquettes and brass peacock kegs pumping the bar's eponymous drink (created in the 1970s for the Kuala Lumpur Hilton).

Upstairs feels friskier: slosh onto plush-pink seats to nibble Southeast Asian bites and imbibe. (https://junglebirdnyc.com)

124 Old Rabbit Club

BAR

42 MAP P114, F6

You'll wanna pat yourself on the back when you find this well-concealed craft-beer haunt (hint: look for the tiny word 'Rabbit' over the door). Once you're inside the cavern-like space, grab a seat at the dimly lit bar and reward yourself with a rare imported brew or something more local (Brooklyn-based Grimm ales are generally great). (www.rabbitclubnyc.com)

Tippler

COCKTAIL BAR

43 MAP P114, C3

Paying material homage to its once-industrial setting, this spacious brick-and-wood cellar bar beneath Chelsea Market serves up properly blended cocktails and a decent selection of craft beer. The decor makes use of materials from vintage sources – including an old NYC water tower and the nearby High Line – to create a warm and relaxing space. (www.thetippler.com)

Stonewall Inn

GAY & LESBIAN

44 MAP P114, G2

Site of the 1969 Stonewall Uprising and birthplace of the modern movement seeking equal rights for gay people, Stonewall is a National Historic Monument and place of pilgrimage. Despite its international fame, it's a laid-back dive that welcomes the entire rainbow mafia (and their allies) to nightly events like drag shows and cabarets. Order something stiff and salute the legends who came before you. (www.thestonewallinnnyc.com)

Cafe Wha?

Bathtub Gin

COCKTAIL BAR

45 MAP P114, C3

Amid NYC's obsession with speak-easy-styled hangouts, Bathtub Gin manages to poke its head above the crowd with its supersecret front door hidden on the wall of the Stone Street Coffee Shop (look for the 'Stone Street Standard' sign). Once inside, chill seating, soft background beats and an actual clawfoot tub make this a chic place to enjoy bespoke cocktails with friends. (www.bathtubginnyc.com)

Henrietta Hudson

LESBIAN

46 MAP P114, D6

In 2021 this long-running lesbian club renovated its interior and transformed from 'Bar & Girl' to 'Queer Human Bar.' The crowd still favors the Sapphic set, who cram in on weekends for late-night dancing and 'gender fluids' with cheeky names like 'margarita-tas.' Come earlier in the week to shoot pool and chat over pub grub. Happy hour is 6pm to 8pm daily. (www.henriettahudson.com)

Milk & Hops

CRAFT BEER

47 MAP P114, C2

Craft connoisseurs come to this beer bar and bottle shop to sample the 10 rotating taps and scour its cold case, sporting 300 styles of brews. The laid-back atmosphere encourages lingering: nab a banquette, order some comfort food (deviled eggs, grilled cheese, bratwurst etc) and order a flight from the list scribbled on the white-tiled wall behind the bar. (www.milknhops.com)

Té Company

TEAHOUSE

48 MAP P114, G1

If you prefer oolongs to oat lattes, you've come to the right place: these loose full-leaf teas, sourced from Taiwanese farmers, are served with sweets so pretty they belong in a Wes Anderson film (pineapple linzers, mooncakes and bars). Sit inside and try a three-tea flight or take one to go for an afternoon stroll. (https://tecompanytea.com)

Vol de Nuit

PUB

49 MAP P114, F5

Even all the NYU students can't ruin this: a cozy Belgian beer bar with Delirium Tremens on tap and a few dozen bottle options, including Duvel and Lindemans Framboise (raspberry beer!). You can order *moules* (mussels) and *frites* (fries) to share at the front patio seats, the lounge, the communal wood tables or under the bar's dangling red lights. (www.voldenuitbar.com)

Yanni's Coffee

CAFE

50 MAP P114, E3

After 17 years as a sports marketing executive, Ioannis Blentzas (better known as Yanni) decided to open his dream business: selling brews and baked goods. Going strong since 2018, this Chelsea favorite lures in crowds with the nutty nose of drip coffee – made with beans from Sey (p231) – and the buttery scent of fresh-baked cookies (dangerously delicious). (www.facebook.com/yanniscoffee)

Entertainment

Sleep No More

THEATER

51 MAP P114, B1

Choose your own adventure at this immersive noir retelling of *Macbeth*, set inside a series of Chelsea warehouses meticulously redesigned to look like the 1930s-era 'McKittrick Hotel' (a nod to Hitchcock's *Vertigo*).

For a postperformance debrief, linger at the Manderley, a jazz bar referencing Hitchcock's film adaptation of Daphne du Maurier's *Rebecca*. Be prepared: you must wear a mask, à la *Eyes Wide Shut*. (www.sleepnomorenyc.com)

Smalls

JAZZ

52 MAP P114, G1

Living up to its name, this cramped but appealing basement jazz den offers a grab-bag collection of acts who sweat out riffs, trills and improvised solos mere feet from the front row.

Founded in 1994 by 'a former Navy submariner, registered nurse, philosopher & jazz violinist,' Smalls opened a second venue, Mezzrow (www.mezzrow.com), down the street in 2014. Reserve seats in advance. (www.smallslive.com)

Bathtub Gin

A Brief History of LGBTIQ+ New York

The West Village is out and damn proud. This is where the Stonewall rebellion erupted, the modern movement seeking equal rights for gay people blossomed and America's first Pride march hit the streets. For LGBTIQ+ folks, it's a ROY-G-BIV mecca.

Before Stonewall

During the 1850s and '60s, men like Walt Whitman found kindred queer spirits at Pfaffs – a beer cellar at 647 Broadway – and by the early 20th century, a number of gay-owned businesses lined MacDougal St in Greenwich Village. Among them was Eve's Hangout at number 129, run by lesbian Polish-Jewish émigré Eve Adams, who made it famous for poetry readings. But a new conservatism replaced the era's relative freethinking in the following decades: tougher policing aimed to eradicate queer visibility, forcing the scene underground in the 1940s and '50s.

The Stonewall Revolution

In the early hours of June 28, 1969, officers began a routine raid at the Stonewall Inn (p127) – a Greenwich Village gay bar – and patrons did the unthinkable: they revolted. Fed up with harassment, they bombarded the officers with coins, bottles, bricks and chants of 'gay power' and 'we shall overcome.' Their collective anger and solidarity was a turning point, igniting passionate debate about discrimination and beginning the modern LGBTIQ+ fight for equal rights – not just in New York but around the world.

Marriage & the New Millennium

The fight for equality took two steps forward in 2011. A federal law banning LGBTIQ+ military personnel from serving openly – the 'Don't Ask, Don't Tell' policy – was repealed after years of intense lobbying. Persistence led to an even greater victory that year – the right to marry. The New York State Assembly passed the Marriage Equality Act, which was signed into law on the eve of NYC Pride. State victory became national on June 26, 2015, when the US Supreme Court ruled that same-sex marriage is a legal right across the country, striking down the remaining marriage bans in 13 US states.

But the fight for equality isn't over. Attacks on the community, often targeting transgender individuals and people of color, continue around the US – all the more reason to celebrate and honor this unique LGBTIQ+ haven.

Atlantic Theater Company

THEATER

53 MAP P114, D2

Founded by David Mamet and William H Macy in 1985, the Atlantic is a pivotal anchor for the off-Broadway community, hosting many Tony Award and Drama Desk winners since its inception. The Linda Gross Theater, housed in a Gothic Revival church, presents high-profile shows like Broadway transfer *Kimberly Akimbo*; Stage 2 presents smaller black-box productions. (www.atlantictheater.org)

Village Vanguard

JAZZ

54 MAP P114, E4

Possibly NYC's most prestigious jazz club, the Vanguard has hosted every major star of the past 50 years. Starting in 1935 as a venue for beat poetry and folk music, it occasionally returns to its roots, but mostly it's big, bold jazz. The **Vanguard Jazz Orchestra** has been a Monday-night mainstay since 1966. (www.villagevanguard.com)

Comedy Cellar

COMEDY

55  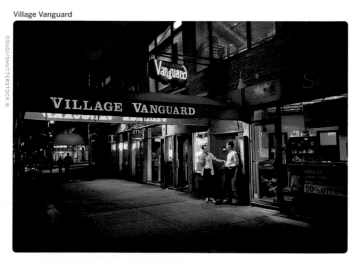 MAP P114, F6

This legendary, intimate comedy club beneath the Olive Tree cafe features a cast of talented regulars, including up-and-coming tv writers and personalities, plus occasional high-profile drop-ins by folks like Wanda Sykes, Jerry Seinfeld and Amy Schumer. Its success has spawned offspring in Las Vegas and at the Village Underground, around the corner at 130 W 3rd St. (www.comedycellar.com)

Village Vanguard

IFC Center CINEMA

56 MAP P114, E6

This art-house cinema in NYU land has a solidly curated lineup of new indies, cult classics and foreign films. Catch shorts, documentaries, mini festivals, '80s revivals, director-focused series, weekend classics and frequent special series, such as cult favorites *(The Shining, Taxi Driver, Alien)* at midnight. (www.ifccenter.com)

(Le) Poisson Rouge LIVE MUSIC

57 MAP P114, F6

This high-concept art space hosts a wide-ranging lineup of live performances, with musical acts that cover classical, folk, opera and more – Charlie XCX, Os Mutantes and Anna Netrebko are just a few past headliners. Children of the '90s should consider popping in on Friday nights, when the Fresh Kids of Bel-Air rock out like it's MTV's *Total Request Live.* (www.lpr.com)

Joyce Theater DANCE

58 MAP P114, D3

A favorite among dance enthusiasts thanks to its excellent sight lines and offbeat offerings, this is an intimate venue, seating 472 in a renovated cinema. Its focus is on traditional modern companies, such as Martha Graham, Garth Fagan and Parsons Dance, as well as global stars like Dance Brazil, Ballet Hispanico and Malpaso Dance Company. (www.joyce.org)

Cherry Lane Theatre THEATER

59 MAP P114, E6

A little backstreet theater of distinctive charm, Cherry Lane has a long and distinguished history. Started by poet Edna St Vincent Millay in 1924, it has given a voice to numerous playwrights and actors over the years, showcasing the early work of such dramaturgical heavyweights as Harold Pinter and Edward Albee. Readings, plays and one-person comedy shows rotate frequently. (www.cherrylanetheatre.org)

Shopping

Strand Book Store BOOKS

60 MAP P114, G4

Beloved and legendary, the iconic Strand embodies downtown NYC's intellectual bona fides – a bibliophile's Oz, where generations of book lovers carrying the store's trademark tote bags happily lose themselves for hours. In operation since 1927, the Strand sells new, used and rare titles, spreading an incredible 18 miles of books (over 2.5 million of them) among three-and-a-half labyrinthine floors. (www.strandbooks.com)

Screaming Mimis VINTAGE

61 MAP P114, D4

If you dig vintage, designer and rare threads, or flamboyant costumes, you may just scream, too. This funtastic shop carries an excellent selection of yesteryear pieces, organized by decade, from the '40s to Y2K. From prim beaded cardigans to macrame minidresses, Dior bikinis, white leather go-go boots, sequined band jackets and accessories up the wazoo, the stock is in great condition. (www.screamingmimis.com)

Cueva

CLOTHING

62 MAP P114, F2

A streetside sandwich board showcases the eclectic set of designers represented by this seasonally curated menswear collection, circling the globe from America to Sweden and on to Japan. Search the racks for shirts, slacks, shoes and caps. There's not a particular style but a cohesive quality: well-made, sartorially original and bound to turn heads. (https://cuevashop.com)

Zuri

CLOTHING

63 MAP P114, D5

On a shop-heavy stretch of Bleecker St, Zuri stands out from the crowd with its riotously colorful racks of one-style-fits-all dresses. Derived from the Swahili word for 'good,' Zuri lives up to its name: all clothes are ethically sourced from Kenya, and the customer service is both welcoming and warm. Don't need a dress? Check out the woven baskets, belts and bags. (www.shopzuri.com)

Goods for the Study

STATIONERY

64 MAP P114, F5

Hard-core journalers and sketchpad fanatics go gaga for the assortment of paper and writing

Cherry Lane Theatre

West Village Wandering

Most of the West Village isn't served by subway lines, and the L train goes only as far as Eighth Ave, so if you want to access the westernmost areas of Chelsea and the West Village by public transport, try the M14 or the M8 bus. But it's a shame to get around the West Village by vehicle – this postcard-perfect neighborhood is ideal for strolling. It's absolutely acceptable to arm yourself with a map (or smartphone) to navigate the charming-but-challenging blocks. When Manhattan's street grid was established in 1811, the already-bustling West Village was left alone, cementing the meandering trails established by waterways, indigenous folks, animals, early Dutch colonizers and property lines. In short, it gets confusing; even locals have trouble finding their way here.

utensils on display at this den for desk goodies. Leather-bound traveler's notebooks, aluminum fountain pens, supertrendy pencil pouches and quirky 'thank you' cards – all laid out like pieces of art. If there's such a thing as home-office heaven, this is it. (www.goodsforthestudy.com)

Printed Matter, Inc — BOOKS

65 MAP P114, B1

Printed Matter is a wondrous little shop dedicated to limited-edition artist monographs and strange little zines. Here you will find nothing carried by mainstream bookstores; instead, trim shelves hide call-to-arms manifestos, critical essays about comic books, flip books that reveal Jesus' face through barcodes and how-to guides written by prisoners. (www.printedmatter.org)

Beacon's Closet — VINTAGE

66 MAP P114, F4

At Beacon's, which has three other locations in Brooklyn, you'll find a good selection of gently used clothes beloved by vintage hunters and penny-pinching fashion hounds. Thrift shops are thin on the ground in this area, which makes this even more of a draw. Come midweek or be prepared to brave the crowds. (www.beaconscloset.com)

Myers of Keswick — FOOD

67 MAP P114, D4

If the Union Jacks don't tip you off, the foreign brands will: Parsons pickled cockles, Percy Pig gummy candies, and enough British bangers to feed His Majesty's Armed Forces. This West Village grocer started hocking hard-to-get UK imports to New York Anglophiles in 1985, and it still serves the savory pies that made it famous – try the chicken and leek or curried lamb. (https://myersofkeswick.com)

Greenwich Letterpress

GIFTS & SOUVENIRS

68 MAP P114, H1

Founded by two sisters, this cute card shop specializes in wedding announcements and other specially made letterpress endeavors, so skip the stock postcards of the Empire State Building and send your loved ones a bespoke greeting card from this stalwart stationer. (www.greenwichletterpress.com)

Pippin Vintage Jewelry

JEWELRY

69 MAP P114, E3

The bangles, baubles, brooches and beads you'll find inside this sparkling jewelry shop look like a million bucks, but they're mainly under $100.

Curious about heritage? Check the tag for a year – vintage, costume and fine jewels range from 19th century to present day. Extra points if you spot the 'I heart NY' mural on the parking lot wall next door. (https://pippinvintage.com)

RH New York

DESIGN

70 MAP P114, C4

Interior-design junkies beware: once you step inside this 90,000-sq-ft gallery spread across six floors, you might never leave. Luckily, there's no need to go hungry while drooling over sumptuous modern living spaces, outdoor set-ups and sections for babies and teens: a glass elevator in the central atrium swoops ravenous guests to a swanky rooftop restaurant with sweeping vistas. (https://rh.com/newyork)

McNulty's Tea & Coffee Co, Inc

FOOD & DRINKS

71 MAP P114, D5

If the worn wooden floorboards, fragrant sacks of coffee beans and large glass tea jars seem steeped in another era, it's because they are. This charmingly gritty shop started selling gourmet teas and coffees in 1895. Overwhelmed by exotic aromas? Ask the team behind the counter for help – they're experts. (www.mcnultys.com)

Explore

Union Square, Flatiron District & Gramercy

Between creative downtown and businessy Midtown, these few blocks combine the spirit of both, converging at the transit hub that is Union Sq. Broadway leads north to pretty Madison Square Park, a popular food destination. East, Gramercy Park is a subdued, beautiful residential area.

The Short List

- ***Flatiron Building (p140)*** *Appreciating the angles on this architectural icon.*
- ***Union Square (p139)*** *People-watching on a park bench, in what's essentially the town square for the bottom half of Manhattan.*
- ***Union Square Greenmarket (p139)*** *Admiring the season's best veg and sampling artisanal treats.*
- ***Raines Law Room (p144)*** *Sipping flawless cocktails in upholstered-leather luxury from another era.*
- ***Eataly (p142)*** *Savoring a culinary trip through Italy at this gigantic food hall and grocery store.*

Getting There & Around

S At Union Sq, the 4/5/6 lines come from the Upper East Side, the L from Williamsburg and the N/Q/R lines from Queens and Brooklyn. Take the Q for an express link to Herald Sq and Times Sq.

The M14A and M14D speed cross-town along bus-only 14th St; the M23 runs on 23rd St.

Neighborhood Map on p138

The Flatiron Building (p140) ALEXANDER SPATARI/GETTY ©

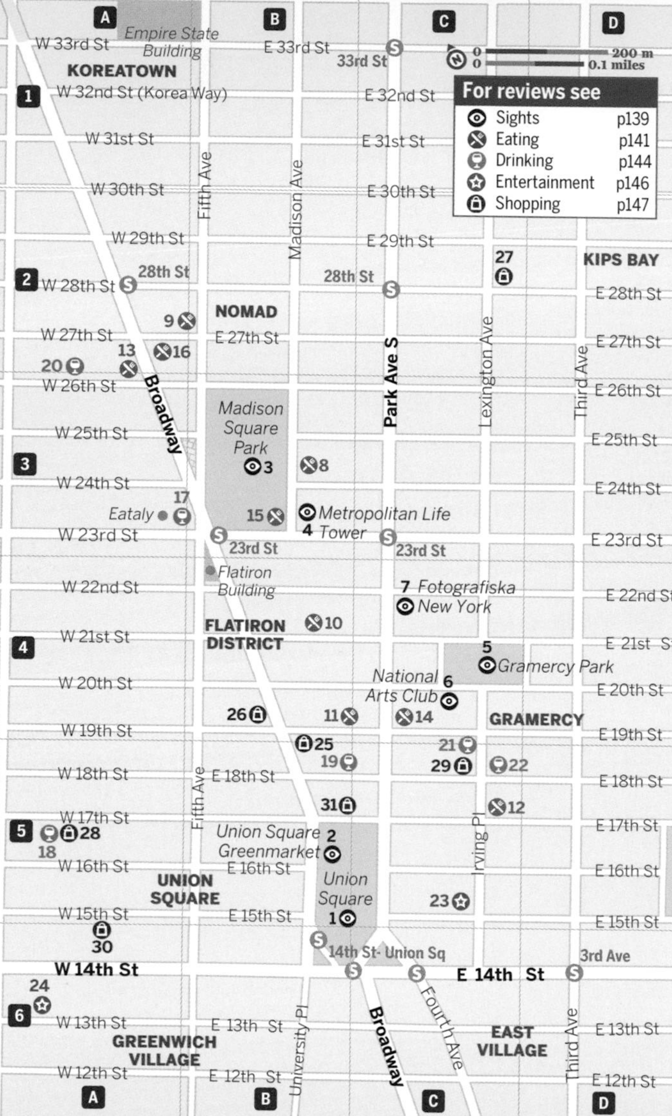

For reviews see
Sights p139
Eating p141
Drinking p144
Entertainment p146
Shopping p147
200 m
0.1 miles
Empire State Building
KOREATOWN
NOMAD
KIPS BAY
Madison Square Park
Eataly
Metropolitan Life Tower
Flatiron Building
Fotografiska New York
FLATIRON DISTRICT
Gramercy Park
National Arts Club
GRAMERCY
Union Square Greenmarket
Union Square
UNION SQUARE
GREENWICH VILLAGE
EAST VILLAGE
33rd St
28th St
23rd St
14th St- Union Sq
3rd Ave
Broadway
Fifth Ave
Madison Ave
Park Ave S
Lexington Ave
Third Ave
Irving Pl
University Pl
Fourth Ave
W 33rd St
E 33rd St
W 32nd St (Korea Way)
E 32nd St
W 31st St
E 31st St
W 30th St
E 30th St
W 29th St
E 29th St
W 28th St
E 28th St
W 27th St
E 27th St
W 26th St
E 26th St
W 25th St
E 25th St
W 24th St
E 24th St
W 23rd St
E 23rd St
W 22nd St
E 22nd St
W 21st St
E 21st St
W 20th St
E 20th St
W 19th St
E 19th St
W 18th St
E 18th St
W 17th St
E 17th St
W 16th St
E 16th St
W 15th St
E 15th St
W 14th St
E 14th St
W 13th St
E 13th St
W 12th St
E 12th St

Sights

Union Square

SQUARE

1 MAP P138, B5

Union Sq is like the Noah's Ark of New York, rescuing at least two of every kind from the curling seas of concrete. In fact, you'd be hard pressed to find a more eclectic cross-section of locals gathered in one public place: suited business-folk gulping fresh air during their lunch breaks, blissed-out loiterers tapping beats on their tablas, skateboarders flipping tricks on the southeastern stairs, old-timers poring over chess boards, and throngs of protesting masses chanting fervently for various causes. (www.unionsquarenyc.org)

Union Square Greenmarket

MARKET

2 MAP P138, B5

On the north half of Union Sq, the city's best farmers market draws famous chefs and mere civilians, united in their love of seasonal bounty from farms around the city. Even if you won't be cooking, it's worth a visit for some of the artisanal goodies, such as breads, cheeses and cider. It's on every Monday, Wednesday, Friday and Saturday. (www.grownyc.org/unionsquaregreenmarket)

Madison Square Park

PARK

3 MAP P138, B3

This park defined the northern reaches of Manhattan until the island's population exploded after

Madison Square Park

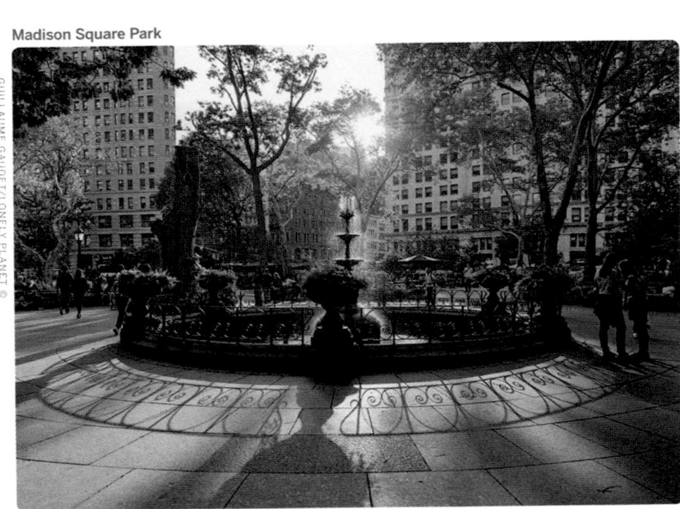

The Flatiron Building

Elegant as a ship sailing uptown, the 20-story triangular **Flatiron Building** (Map p138, B4) grows more beautiful the longer you stare at its ornate limestone-and-terracotta facade.

Its construction in 1902 coincided with the rise of picture postcards, so that images of the world's tallest tower (until 1909, anyway) quickly circled the globe, and many painters and photographers have immortalized it. (See Alfred Stieglitz's moody image in the Met, for example.) Actress Katharine Hepburn once quipped that *she'd* like to be admired as much as the grand old building.

For decades the Flatiron was associated with the publishing industry. An original tenant was Frank Munsey, who published such pulp-fiction magazines as *Argosy* and *The All-Story*, and in 1959, St Martin's Press moved in.

By 2004 its parent company, Macmillan, took over the whole building, and employees in the prow offices had some of the most coveted desks in the city. But Macmillan moved out in 2019: for now, the building is a hollow icon of old New York.

the Civil War. These days it's a welcome oasis, with a popular children's playground, a dog run and the original Shake Shack (p144) burger joint. It's also one of the city's most cultured parks, with specially commissioned art installations and (in warmer months) activities ranging from literary discussions to live-music gigs. (www.madisonsquarepark.org)

Metropolitan Life Tower

HISTORIC BUILDING

4 MAP P138, B3

This 700ft-tall clock tower soaring above Madison Square Park's southeastern corner was completed in 1909. If it looks familiar, it's because it was modeled after Venice's world-famous *campanile* (bell tower) in Piazza San Marco. Ironically, this New World version is now older than its muse: the original Venetian tower collapsed in 1902, with its replacement not completed until 1912.

Gramercy Park

PARK

5 MAP P138, C4

You may not be able to go in (only local residents have the key), but you can peer through the fence and imagine the romantic scenes that have transpired here – or the tough-guy ones, as James Cagney used to live at 34 Gramercy Park E. It's the core of this English-style neighborhood, built by Samuel Ruggles in 1831 after he drained the area's swamp.

National Arts Club ARTS CENTER

Founded in 1898 to promote public interest in the arts, the National Arts Club holds art exhibitions, with free admission to the public on weekdays; check the website for a schedule, including evening events and drawing classes. Calvert Vaux – cocreator of Central Park – designed the building itself, with a picture-lined front parlor adorned with a beautiful, vaulted stained-glass panel. The mansion was once home to Samuel J Tilden, a former New York governor and the failed 1876 presidential candidate. (www.nationalartsclub.org)

Fotografiska New York MUSEUM

7 MAP P138, C4

An outpost of a popular Stockholm arts club, this giant building celebrates photography in its most vivid and arresting forms: fashion glam from David LaChapelle, say, and the stark photojournalism of James Nachtwey. Visitors are encouraged to treat it like a social space: take wine from the cafe up to the galleries (especially at evening events), or have a chat in the velvet armchairs on the top floor. (www.fotografiska.com/nyc)

Eating

Eleven Madison Park AMERICAN $$$

8 MAP P138, B3

Consistently excellent (Michelin agrees: three stars) and dedicated to sustainability, chef Daniel Humm raised the stakes after the COVID lockdown, when he reopened with a fully plant-based menu. Whether you're vegetar-

Counting the Minutes

Union Sq features statues of George Washington (one of the first public pieces of art in New York City) and peacemaker Mahatma Gandhi, but what usually draws the eye is *Metronome*, a giant mixed-media installation on a 10-story building along the south side of the square.

Installed in 1999, it functioned as a cryptic art piece (Why did occasional puffs of steam waft from the hole in the rippling ceramic? And what's with the giant rock?), but more practically as an elaborate digital clock that savvy New Yorkers simply used to check the time. In 2020, in a collaboration between the original artists and two artist-activists, the clock was reprogrammed as a so-called Climate Clock. Now the digital display counts down the seconds we have left to reverse the toll of climate change, before the temperature rises another 1.5°C.

Graze through Eataly

A sprawling temple to Italian gastronomy, **Eataly** (Map p138, A3; www.eataly.com) is both a functional grocery store and a grazer's delight of a food hall, with counters and sit-down restaurants set among the food aisles – and a bar-restaurant, Serra (p144), on the roof. Whether you want gelato, pizza, pasta or snacks for a picnic in Madison Square Park, it's all here. There's another big branch downtown at the World Trade Center.

ian or not – perhaps especially if you're not – come for a mind-expanding meal ($365, eight to 10 tasting courses). A shorter bar tasting menu ($195) is also an option. Prepaid reservations required. (www.elevenmadisonpark.com)

Ilili

LEBANESE **$$**

9 MAP P138, A2

Pomegranate seeds glitter like jewels at this elegant restaurant, where Lebanese cuisine gets its dressed-up due. This is a great place for a special meal if a group is split between vegetarians and meat-eaters, with a dazzling selection of veg dishes (mmm, cauliflower and tahini), as well as home-style recipes such as grape leaves with shredded lamb (or a vegan alternative). (www.ililirestaurants.com)

Cosme

MEXICAN **$$$**

10 MAP P138, B4

Mexico City culinary royalty Enrique Olvera has been reeducating stereotype-burdened New Yorkers since 2014, showing them the ways of Oaxacan chili pastes, heirloom beans, a glistening pool of mole that's a universe of flavor and cult-status duck carnitas. The setting is very 'fine dining' (ie, sedate); book ahead or try for a walk-in seat at the livelier bar. (www.cosmenyc.com)

Craft

AMERICAN **$$$**

11 MAP P138, B4

Chef Tom Colicchio flies the flag for small, family-owned farms and food producers, transforming their bounty into pure, polished dishes. Whether flawlessly charred braised octopus, juicy roasted quail or pumpkin *mezzaluna* pasta with sage, brown butter and Parmesan, expect every ingredient to sing with flavor. Next-door Vallata is Colicchio's more homespun, purely Italian restaurant – and where tables are more available. (www.craftrestaurant.com)

Casa Mono

TAPAS **$$$**

12 MAP P138, C5

Casa Mono features a long bar where you can sit and watch your Michelin-starred tapas being prepared, or dine at tables for more discreet conversation. Either way, get set for flavor-packed bites like creamy eggs with sea urchin, walnuts, lime and anchovy oil. No reservation? Pop in to adjoining Bar Jamón. (www.casamononyc.com)

Tortazo

MEXICAN

13 MAP P138, A2

Chicago chef Rick Bayless brings his brand of fast-casual super-fresh Mexican food to this pleasant stretch of Broadway, which is increasingly known for great places to eat.

Tortas (sandwiches) are packed with flavorful meats and salsas, and there are big bowls and salads, as well as kid-friendly quesadillas (and margaritas for grown-ups). (www.tortazo.com)

Union Square Cafe

ITALIAN $$

14 MAP P138, C4

Opened in 1985, this was restaurateur Danny Meyer's first effort, and it's still a wild success. The vibe is grown-up (among publishing execs, it's a business-lunch mainstay) but very comfortable, with creative-but-satisfying seasonal Italian dishes and the signature Meyer warm service that can be found at all of his dozen or so restaurants around the city. Considered by many to be the birthplace of a generation of New York City's most renowned chefs and restaurateurs. (www.unionsquarecafe.com)

Eataly

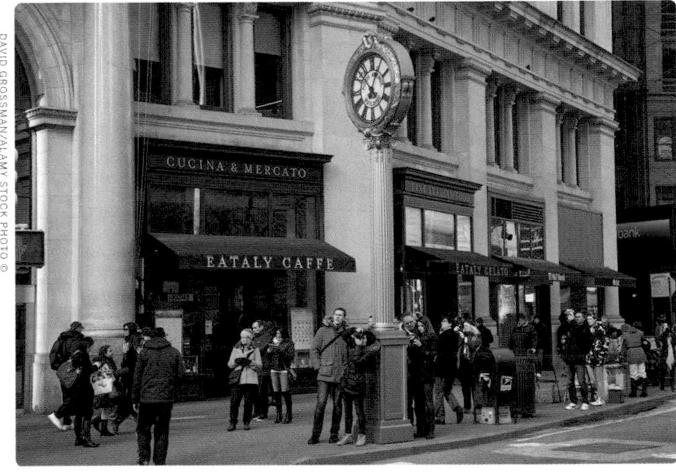

NoMad Piazza

With the introduction of COVID-friendly outdoor dining and city experiments in car-free streets, the stretch of Broadway between 25th St and 31st St (dubbed NoMad, short for North of Madison Square Park) has blossomed into a social destination. In what will hopefully be a permanent pattern, the six blocks have been closed to cars during the summer and filled with cafe tables for the many new restaurants around here.

Shake Shack

BURGERS **$**

15 MAP P138, B3

The flagship of Danny Meyer's fast-food chain (arguably where the whole premium-burger trend started) this park snack stand uses high-quality meat and local produce. Vegetarians can have a crisp portobello burger, and for dessert, there's frozen custard. The line can look long, but it usually moves fast, and the park is a great spot for people-watching. (www.shakeshack.com)

Smith

AMERICAN **$$**

16 MAP P138, A2

For reliable, crowd-pleasing food with a bit of flair, head for this bustling brasserie and sociable bar, on a prime corner on Broadway. Think: hot potato chips with blue-cheese fondue, spicy fried chicken and a veggie Korean bibimbap. The original is in the East Village, and there are other outposts in Midtown East and on the Upper West Side (www.thesmithrestaurant.com)

Drinking

Serra

ROOFTOP BAR

17 MAP P138, A3

The crown jewel of Italian food emporium Eataly (p142) is this covered rooftop garden where the decorative theme is refreshed seasonally: a Mediterranean beach escape one month, an alpine country retreat the next. Relax with a cold beer, or dig in to pasta and seafood.

Look for the elevator on the 23rd St side of the store - you'll find it near the checkout stands. (www.eataly.com)

Raines Law Room

COCKTAIL BAR

18 MAP P138, A5

Velvet drapes and overstuffed leather lounge chairs, the perfect amount of exposed brick, and expertly crafted cocktails using hard-to-find spirits – these folks are as serious as a mortgage payment when it comes to amplified atmosphere.

There's no sign; look for the '48' on the awning above the stairs down, and ring the bell to gain entry. (www.raineslawroom.com)

Old Town Bar & Restaurant

BAR

19 MAP P138, B5

It still looks like 1892 in here, with the mahogany bar, original tile floors, tin ceilings and even a surprisingly impressive old urinal. Although it's often used for TV and film shoots, most of the time it's not too busy.

It also does a decent, unfancy burger (from $12.50). (www.oldtownbar.com)

Flatiron Room

COCKTAIL BAR

20 MAP P138, A2

'Bar' doesn't do this place justice: it's more of a sedate, elegant living room with an expert focus on fine and rare whiskeys. The scene is set with vintage wallpaper and a glittering chandelier, plus nightly live music, pitched to a level that allows for conversation. Fine cocktails pair nicely with high-end snacks, such as charcuterie plates. Reservations highly recommended. (www.theflatironroom.com)

Irving Farm

CAFE

21 MAP P138, C5

Yes, hand-picked beans are lovingly roasted and then brewed expertly and served along with light snacks and pressed sandwiches. But really this bustling downstairs cafe (the original of a local mini-chain) is a nice excuse to hang out alongside all the neighborhood regulars, on an exceptionally pretty street – with a view straight uptown to the Chrysler Building, no less. (www.irvingfarm.com)

Madison Square Park

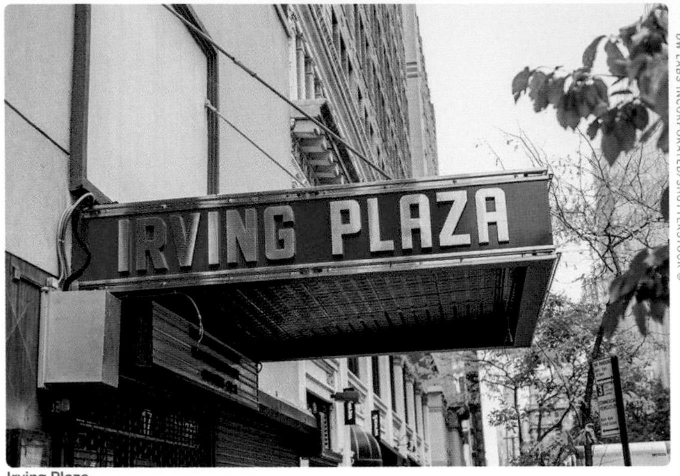

Irving Plaza

Pete's Tavern

BAR

22 MAP P138, C5

With its original 19th-century mirrors, pressed-tin ceiling and rosewood bar, this dark, atmospheric watering hole has all the earmarks of a New York classic – and indeed, it's been slinging beers since 1864. Choose from 17 draft beers, joined by everyone from posttheater couples to the odd celebrity (see photos by the restrooms). (www.petestavern.com)

Entertainment

Irving Plaza

LIVE MUSIC

23 MAP P138, C5

Rocking since 1978, Irving Plaza has seen them all: the Ramones, Bob Dylan, U2, Pearl Jam, you name it. These days it's a great in-between stage for quirkier rock and pop acts, both young up-and-comers and reuniting old-timers. It has a cozy floor around the stage, and good views from the mezzanine. (www.irvingplaza.com)

Stone

LIVE MUSIC

24 MAP P138, A6

Created by renowned downtown jazz-cat legend John Zorn, the Stone is about the music and nothing but the music, in all its experimental and avant-garde glory.

Concerts are held at the New School Glass Box Theater, and admission is a flat $20 at the door (but register ahead). (www.thestonenyc.com)

Shopping

ABC Carpet & Home

HOMEWARES

25 MAP P138, B5

Manhattan's biggest, most eclectic furniture store, ABC is an inspiration for designers and a fantasyland for apartment dwellers. The ground floor stocks easy-to-pack knickknacks, boho textiles and jewelry; wander upstairs (seven floors in all!) for statement furniture, lighting, bedding and antique carpets. During the holidays the shop is a terrific place to buy home and tree decorations. (www.abchome.com)

Fishs Eddy

HOMEWARES

26 MAP P138, B4

This family-owned shop, open since 1986, carries a near-overwhelming stock of old vintage plates and other dishes, along with its own excellent new designs, often with major New Yorker attitude (the shop is a favorite of homemaker comedian Amy Sedaris). At last pass, hand-drawn pigeons were popular, alongside its iconic city-skyline table settings. (http://fishseddy.myshopify.com)

Kalustyan's

SPICES

27 MAP P138, C2

A stalwart of the so-called Curry Hill district, a strip of mostly Indian shops and restaurants on Lexington, this epic shop (two

Fishs Eddy

storefronts, multiple floors) grants virtually every foodie wish, from asafetida to za'atar. It must be seen to be believed. (www.kalustyans.com)

Books of Wonder

BOOKS

28 MAP P138, A5

Devoted to children's and young-adult titles, this wonderful bookstore is a great place to take little ones on a rainy day, especially when an author is giving a reading or a storyteller is on hand. There's an impressive range of NYC-themed picture books, plus a section dedicated to rare and vintage children's books and limited-edition artwork. (www.booksofwonder.com)

Bedford Cheese Shop

FOOD

29 MAP P138, C5

Brooklyn's most celebrated cheesemonger brings the artisanal outer-borough foodie vibe to Manhattanites, in the form of some 200 expertly curated marvels of dairy culture. Make a picnic with artisanal charcuterie and other deli treats (many also proudly Made in Brooklyn), or eat in with a tasting board or a sandwich ($14). (www.bedfordcheeseshop.com)

Rent the Runway

CLOTHING

30 MAP P138, A6

This popular fashion-rental service maintains a flagship store stocked with looks by high-end designers (Narciso Rodriguez, Badgley Mischka, Nicole Miller and many

Barnes & Noble

Where to Shop

A relatively small area, the blocks around Union Square nonetheless harbor some retail gems. Along **14th Street** (more west than east) is an eclectic stretch of shops, everything from guitars and furniture to sportswear, wigs and tattoos. For midrange to more upscale chains like Zara, Banana Republic, Club Monaco, J Crew, Anthropologie and Intermix, head north up **Fifth Avenue**.

more). For health reasons, it's currently closed to browsing, but you can shop on the app and arrange pickup here or delivery to a hotel. Perfect for light packers who still want to make a splash.

Rental fees differ by look. If you already use one of Rent the Runway's subscription services, you can use them at the store. (www.renttherunway.com)

Barnes & Noble

BOOKS

31 MAP P138, B5

Once bemoaned as an invader, B&N has hung on through the years to now be viewed with some affection. Its four floors are filled with books, plus magazines, toys and games, gifts and accessories and even a vinyl-LP section. (It also happens to be a good place to use the bathroom, on the same floor as the Starbucks cafe.)

Check the schedule for free readings by top authors. (www.barnesandnoble.com)

RADIO CITY
MUSIC HALL
RADIO
TONIGHT HARRY STYLES
RADIO CITY
Harry Styles

Explore Midtown

The field of office towers south of Central Park is where New Yorkers get the job done. It's bustling by day and windswept at night – except in ever-glowing Times Square and Broadway theaters. To the west, gay-friendly Hell's Kitchen has more character but gives way to slick Hudson Yards.

The Short List

- ***Times Square (p152)*** *Basking in the glow of several million lightbulbs and an impressive sea of humanity.*
- ***Museum of Modern Art (p156)*** *Hanging out with Picasso, Warhol and Rothko at this vast, world-class museum.*
- ***Bryant Park (p164)*** *Lunching alfresco, watching a movie under the stars or just relaxing in this Midtown oasis.*
- ***Jazz at Lincoln Center (p171)*** *Gazing at the spectacular view while listening to world-class musicians hit their groove.*
- ***Broadway – or Off-Broadway (p170)*** *Adding a little sparkle to life with a hot-ticket musical or the next Tony-award-winning drama.*

Getting There & Around

S Times Sq-42nd St, Grand Central-42nd St and 34th St-Herald Sq are Midtown's main hubs. A/C/E and 1/2/3 lines run north–south through Midtown West; 4/5/6 through Midtown East. The central B/D/F/M lines follow Sixth Ave, while N/Q/R/W follow Broadway. The 7, E and M lines offer some crosstown service.

Neighborhood Map on p158

Radio City Music Hall (p172)

Top Experience

Light up the Night in Times Square

Love it or loathe it, Times Square – in the low 40s, where Broadway crosses Seventh Ave – is undeniably the city's heart, and even the most hardened urbanites can be mesmerized by the glittering lights, giant billboards and raw urban energy, round the clock. It's nearly as busy in the wee hours as it is in the afternoon.

MAP P158, D4

www.timessquarenyc.org

Broadway, at Seventh Ave

S N/Q/R/W, S, 1/2/3, 7 to Times Sq-42nd St

Everyone's Invited

Times Square proves that New York truly is the city that never sleeps. Massive billboards stretch half a skyscraper tall, and LED and neon signs glow bright as day. A jumble of humanity from every corner of the globe is joined by costumed characters that range from cute Elmo to noble Statue of Liberty to, well, the Naked Cowboy. When you're tired of circulating, enjoy the people-watching from a perch on the bright red stairs at the north end.

Times Square Transformed

This is the New York of collective fantasies, the place where Al Jolson 'makes it' in the 1927 film *The Jazz Singer* and Alicia Keys and Jay-Z sing 'These lights will inspire you' – not to mention the world's most famous place to ring in the new year.

For several decades, though, when the city struggled through an economic trough, Times Square fueled different fantasies, as it accommodated porn cinemas and strip clubs. In 1981 *Rolling Stone* magazine dubbed West 42nd St 'the sleaziest block in America.' That all changed in the mid-1990s, when a business-improvement district (BID) lured in 'respectable' retail chains such as a Virgin megastore, and targeted policing chased out the three-card-monte hucksters. By the new millennium, Times Square had gone from X-rated to G-rated (there was even a giant Toys 'R' Us). In 2009 Broadway was closed to cars, enhancing the plaza-like feel. Now the dazzling lights – required on every business, per BID zoning rules, in fact – draw almost 50 million visitors annually.

★ Top Tips

- Pass through by day, to get oriented, but the real scene is at night, to soak up the lights.
- If you take photos of, or with, any of the costumed characters, or take videos of dancers, give a few dollars as a tip.
- Need help? Stop by the police station on the south side.

Take a Break

Only a few steps from the chaos is the no-frills Cuban lunch counter Margon (p166), open till 5pm. Later, or for more room to sit, head north to family-friendly, cheesecake-lovely **Junior's Restaurant & Bakery** (www.juniorscheesecake.com; 1626 Broadway, at W 49th St). Just need a drink? Jimmy's Corner (p169) is your spot.

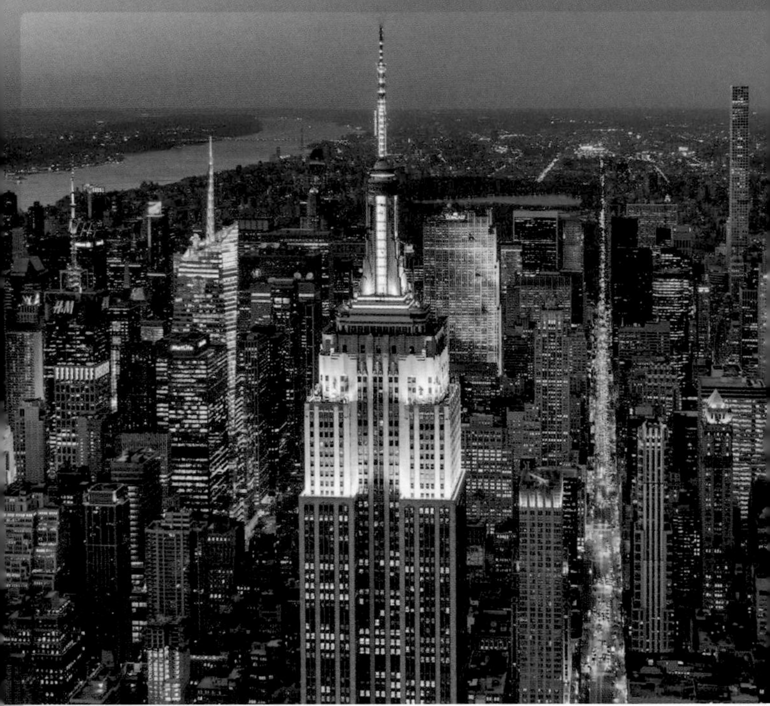

Top Experience

Scale the Heights of the Empire State Building

The Chrysler Building may be prettier, and One World Trade Center taller, but the queen of the New York skyline remains the Empire State Building – especially since a 2020 renovation shined up its spire. As Deborah Kerr told Cary Grant in An Affair to Remember, *the deco skyscraper is 'the nearest thing to heaven we have in New York.'*

MAP P158, E5

www.esbnyc.com

20 W 34th St

86th-fl observation deck adult/child $38/32

8am-2am, last elevators up 1:15am

A Bird's-Eye View

The ESB has two observation decks: the main one on the 86th floor (tickets from $44), which is outdoors, and a tiny round room with floor-to-ceiling windows on the 102nd floor, at the tippy-top of the mast. (Given the 102nd floor costs at least an additional $33, it's fair to say the 86th alone is plenty satisfying.) On the way up, the elevators let you out on the 80th floor for some exhibits and views, and you can make like Ann Darrow (the unfortunate woman caught in King Kong's grip) in a photo-op replica of the gorilla's giant paw. On the 86th floor, train the binoculars on the nearby Chrysler Building, to admire its splendid deco details.

Building the Legend

Built in a frenzied 410 days, this limestone tower – 102 stories and 1250ft tall – opened on May 1, 1931, to claim the title of world's tallest building. The rival Chrysler Building had previously set the record less than a year earlier, with a last-minute spire, hoisted in secret. Not to be outdone, the ESB's developers went back to the drawing board and added another 250ft in the form of a skinny round 'mast,' allegedly for mooring airships – a plan abandoned as soon as the building's status was secured.

Exhibits on the 2nd floor detail the impressive construction feat with surprisingly good immersive video and other neat tricks. Also take time to watch some of the affectionate video recollections of longtime ESB employees, and look out for gorgeous art deco details, even as you exit.

★ Top Tips

- Timed tickets are required, but are usually available the same day. Buy online (for a $2 fee) or on-site.
- Sunset has great views, but tickets come with a surcharge. Visit late (after 10pm) for city lights and fewer crowds.
- Allow an hour or more for a visit, including the good exhibits on the 2nd floor and the 80th floor.
- Download the ESB tour app to hear an audio tour as you go (there's free wi-fi).

Take a Break

Grab tacos at the local branch of Mexican mini-chain **Tacombi** (www.tacombi.com), in the building on the W 33rd St side. Or head for nearby Koreatown's abundant eating options, including peaceful HanGawi (p165).

Top Experience

Discover the Museum of Modern Art

Name a notable artist from the late 19th century on – Van Gogh, Picasso, Cassatt, Mondrian, Pollock, Bourgeois – and MoMA probably has some of their best work among its collection of some 200,000 pieces. For art buffs, it's paradise. For the uninitiated, it's a crash course, with enough variety that everyone will find something that resonates.

MoMA

www.moma.org

11 W 53rd St

adult/child $25/free, 5:30-9pm Fri free

10am-5:30pm Sat-Thu, to 9pm Fri & 1st Thu

More Art on View

In 2019 MoMA expanded next door, adding a much-needed 40,000 sq ft of gallery space over six floors. The collection is no longer arranged by medium, but rather chronologically, then by theme, so that a single room might contain masterworks in painting, sculpture, photography, film and design, all with similar subject or concept. Work your way down: floor 5 is 1880s–1940s; floor 4, 1940s–1970s; and floor 2, 1970s–present. Floor 3 features temporary exhibits, and the 4th-floor Kravis Studio is a dedicated space for performance art.

Highlights of the Collection

Following the redesign, works are now rotated through the galleries at least once a year, which means a fresh experience even for repeat visitors. On the downside, for first-timers, it also means that not all the most most famous works are on permanent display. You can, however, count on seeing Van Gogh's dreamy *Starry Night*, for instance, as well as Picasso's *Demoiselles d'Avignon* and Henri Rousseau's *Sleeping Gypsy*. There will certainly be some Andy Warhol prints (such as *Soup Cans*), as well as works by Henri Matisse and Edward Hopper.

Abby Aldrich Rockefeller Sculpture Garden

On the north side of the main building, this space was laid out in 1953 by designer Philip Johnson as 'a sort of outdoor room.' On warm, sunny days, you can sit in pleasant shadows cast by the works of greats such as Matisse, Giacometti, Calder and Picasso. Best of all, it's free to enter (no need for museum admission).

★ Top Tips

- The museum is open daily, with later hours on Saturdays.
- Timed tickets are required, and same-day tickets are usually available, if not for ideal time slots. In general, Mondays and Tuesdays are less crowded than Friday nights and weekends.
- Each spring, the New Directors/New Films series, in partnership with Lincoln Center, is reliably good.

Take a Break

The museum has two dining spaces inside. On the 2nd floor, casual Cafe 2 serves coffee and fresh Italian-inspired food with counter service and shared tables.

For table service, opt for Terrace Café on the 6th floor, with its outdoor space overlooking 53rd St.

A B C D

1 2 3 4 5 6

UPPER WEST SIDE
HELL'S KITCHEN
THEATER DISTRICT
GARMENT DISTRICT
HERALD SQUARE

W 59th St
W 58th St
W 57th St
W 56th St
W 55th St
W 54th St
W 53rd St
W 52nd St
W 51st St
W 50th St
W 49th St
W 48th St
W 47th St
W 46th St
W 45th St
W 44th St
W 43rd St
W 42nd St
W 41st St
W 40th St
W 39th St
W 38th St
W 37th St
W 36th St
W 35th St
W 34th St
W 33rd St
W 32nd St
W 31st St
W 30th St
W 29th St
W 28th St

Twelfth Ave (West Side Hwy)
Eleventh Ave
Tenth Ave
Ninth Ave
Columbus Ave
Eighth Ave
Broadway
Seventh Ave
6½ Ave
Sixth Ave (Avenue of the Americas)
Dyer St
Central Park South
57th St

Hudson River Park
Dewitt Clinton Park
9A
Columbus Circle
Central Park
Hearst Tower
Worldwide Plaza
TKTS Booth
Times Square
Bank of America Tower
Signature Theatre
Port Authority Bus Terminal
Lincoln Tunnel
NYC Information Center
Macy's
Edge
Hudson Yards
High Line
Moynihan Train Hall
Penn Station

57th St-7th Ave
7th Ave
50th St
49th St
47th-50th Sts-Rockefeller Center
42nd St-Port Authority
42nd St-Times Sq
42nd St-Bryant Park
34th St-Penn Station
34th St-Hudson Yards
34th St-Herald Sq

32 33 18 34 31 15 30 14 44 40 26 24 21 25 22 20 27 37 13 39 28 38 45 46 11 10 35 41 19

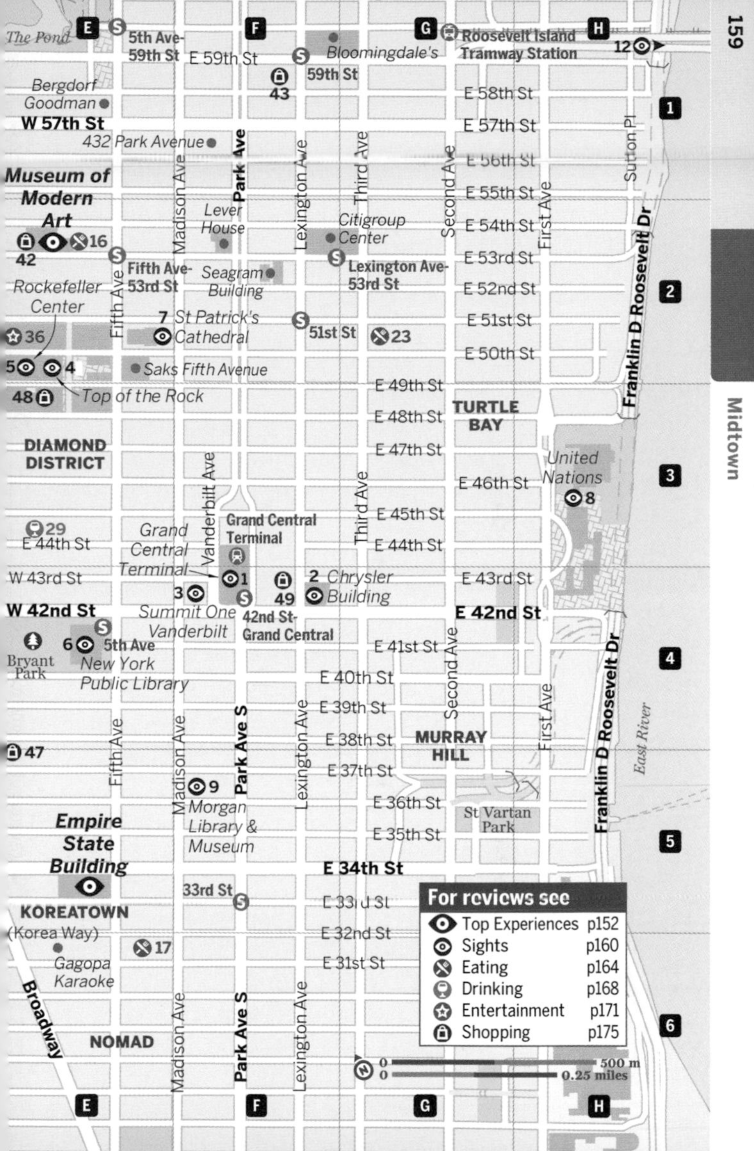
E
F
G
H
The Pond
5th Ave-59th St
E 59th St
Bloomingdale's
59th St
Roosevelt Island Tramway Station
12
43
Bergdorf Goodman
W 57th St
E 58th St
E 57th St
432 Park Avenue
E 56th St
E 55th St
E 54th St
E 53rd St
E 52nd St
E 51st St
E 50th St
E 49th St
E 48th St
E 47th St
E 46th St
E 45th St
E 44th St
E 43rd St
E 42nd St
E 41st St
E 40th St
E 39th St
E 38th St
E 37th St
E 36th St
E 35th St
E 34th St
E 33rd St
E 32nd St
E 31st St
Sutton Pl
Madison Ave
Park Ave
Lexington Ave
Third Ave
Second Ave
First Ave
Museum of Modern Art
16
42
Lever House
Citigroup Center
Fifth Ave-53rd St
Seagram Building
Lexington Ave-53rd St
Rockefeller Center
Fifth Ave
7 St Patrick's Cathedral
51st St
23
36
5
4
Saks Fifth Avenue
48
Top of the Rock
Franklin D Roosevelt Dr
TURTLE BAY
DIAMOND DISTRICT
Vanderbilt Ave
United Nations
8
29
Grand Central Terminal
E 44th St
W 43rd St
1
2 Chrysler Building
3
49
W 42nd St
Summit One Vanderbilt
42nd St-Grand Central
6
5th Ave
Bryant Park
New York Public Library
Park Ave S
47
MURRAY HILL
East River
9
Morgan Library & Museum
St Vartan Park
Empire State Building
33rd St
KOREATOWN
(Korea Way)
17
Gagopa Karaoke
Broadway
NOMAD
1
2
3
4
5
6
0 500 m
0 0.25 miles
For reviews see
Top Experiences p152
Sights p160
Eating p164
Drinking p168
Entertainment p171
Shopping p175

Sights

Grand Central Terminal

HISTORIC BUILDING

1 MAP P158, F4

Completed in 1913, this enormous station hall is one of New York's beaux-arts treasures. Commuters churn through the glorious marble-trimmed concourse, around a glowing opal-glass clock, beneath the vaulted ceiling. It depicts (inaccurately) the constellations, and what's visible today is a 1944 copy, on asbestos board, to cover water damage in the original fresco, designed by French painter Paul César Helleu. A 1990s renovation added twinkling lights (per Helleu's plan) and cleaned the ceiling. Follow Cancer's claws (northwest corner) to a tiny black rectangle: an unretouched patch of soot. (www.grandcentralterminal.com)

Chrysler Building

HISTORIC BUILDING

2 MAP P158, F4

The 77-floor Chrysler Building, opened in 1930 as the headquarters of the auto empire, is New York's purest art deco architecture, guarded by stylized eagles of chromium nickel and topped by a beautiful seven-tiered spire reminiscent of the rising sun. The best view is from the corner of Third Ave and 44th St. The lobby, closed to visitors for COVID-19 safety, is one of Gotham's most beautiful; it's worth checking if it has reopened.

Summit One Vanderbilt

VIEWPOINT

3 MAP P158, F4

Hall of mirrors, but make it skyscraper: the 91st and 92nd floors of this new skyscraper are tricked out with infinity mirrors and other shiny Instagram bait, including a small glass-floor terrace; the 93rd floor is a cafe-bar and outdoor terrace.

Gimmicks aside, the view is great: you're eye level with the best details of the nearby Chrysler and Empire State Buildings. Timed tickets only; online surcharge is $3. Floor mirrors make skirts inadvisable; sunglasses are recommended for the daytime glare. (www.summitov.com)

Rockefeller Center

HISTORIC BUILDING

4 MAP P158, E2

This 22-acre, 'city within a city' debuted at the height of the Great Depression, and its gorgeous art deco towers were designated a National Landmark in 1987. Visit for the Top of the Rock observation deck, the towering Christmas tree and ice-skating and, when they resume, **NBC Studio Tours** (www.thetouratnbcstudios.com) – or just to admire the great exterior bas-reliefs and the murals in the building lobbies. Underground is a warren of shops and tunnels connecting to the subway and neighboring buildings. (www.rockefellercenter.com)

Midtown Skyscrapers

The Empire State and Chrysler Buildings get all the love, but Midtown is also defined by some newer towers. Six landmarks:

Lever House (1950–52; 306ft) Stark international style, and the first NYC tower built without setbacks. (Map p158, F2)

Seagram Building (1956–58; 514ft) Mies van der Rohe and Philip Johnson's modernist classic, trimmed in bronze and often imitated. (Map p158, F2)

Citigroup Center (1974–77; 915ft) Its triangular roof adds variety to the skyline. (Map p158, F2)

Hearst Tower (2003–06; 597ft) Built atop the 1928 original Hearst HQ, this tower is marked by a distinctive diagonal grid structure. (Map p158, C1)

Bank of America Tower (2004–09; 1200ft) Across from Bryant Park, with a multifaceted glass top and lit-up spire. (Map p158, D4; www.durst.org)

432 Park Avenue (2011–15; 1396ft) One of the new 'supertalls'; architect Rafael Viñoly said he was inspired by a trash can. (Map p158, F1; www.432parkavenue.com)

Top of the Rock VIEWPOINT

5 MAP P158, E2

Designed in homage to ocean liners and opened in 1933, this 70th-floor observation deck sits atop the tallest tower at Rockefeller Center.

While it's not as iconic as the Empire State Building (p154), the Top of the Rock does have several selling points: it's less crowded, it's a bit cheaper, it has wider observation decks (both outdoor and indoor) – and of course it offers a view of the ESB itself. (www.topoftherocknyc.com)

New York Public Library HISTORIC BUILDING

6 MAP P158, E4

Guarded by two marble lions (south: 'Patience'; north: 'Fortitude'), this was the largest marble structure in the US when it opened in 1911. To this day, it is a lavish public temple, particularly in the gorgeous **Rose Main Reading Room**, with its soaring coffered ceiling and serene rows of gleaming work tables. To admire the whole structure, head across Fifth Ave to the 7th-floor terrace of the Stavros Niarchos Foundation branch library. (www.nypl.org)

Midtown Breaks

6½ Ave You can walk through passageways from 51st to 57th St. A nice break from crowds, with plenty of shade and seating for a quick rest.

Dainobu (www.dainobunyc.com; 36 W 56th St) Japanese grocery with ready-made lunches, good for Central Park. Always fresh and delicious.

MoMA movies (www.moma.org/calendar/film) The best ticket in town! With museum admission, you can see every film showing that day (or use ticket cost toward museum entry within a month). With membership, you can see hundreds a year.

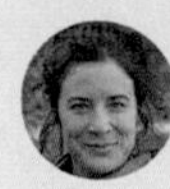

Recommended by Katie Trainor, *film collections manager at the Museum of Modern Art*

St Patrick's Cathedral CATHEDRAL

7 MAP P158, E2

Gracing an entire city block since 1875, this huge Gothic Revival church replaced a smaller one in Soho as the seat of the Archbishop of New York. With elaborate stained glass, enormous organs and grand bronze doors, it's a prestige spot for a wedding. In its crypt are buried all the state's archbishops, as well as one layman, the freed slave Pierre Toussaint, a champion of the poor who was declared Venerable in 1996. Audio tours are $25. (www.saintpatrickscathedral.org)

United Nations HISTORIC BUILDING

8 MAP P158, H3

Peek into the hallowed headquarters of the UN on an hour-long guided tour (prebooking required; check in at the visitors office at 801 First Ave). It's gratifying to see the very meeting halls so often captured in news photos, and to glimpse the interpreters' booths and other odd corners. The whole place has the mid-century flair you'd expect in a complex designed by Le Corbusier and Oscar Niemeyer. Bonus: an extremely eclectic art collection, donated by member states. (http://visit.un.org)

Morgan Library & Museum MUSEUM

9 MAP P158, F5

Bibliophiles especially will appreciate this sumptuous cultural center, built around steel magnate JP Morgan's mansion. The star attraction is Morgan's vaulted, three-story library, with a 16th-century Dutch tapestry, a zodiac-theme ceiling and no fewer than three Gutenberg Bibles. To make the steep entry price worthwhile, check to see if the other rotating exhibits (in new modern wings of the building) are of interest – but along with the Frick (p189), this is one of the city's less-visited gems. (www.themorgan.org)

Hudson Yards

AREA

10 MAP P158, B6

A slice of Dubai on the Hudson, this luxury megadevelopment opened in 2019 and will expand west. It may not have much character, but it's at the north end of the High Line (p110), so most visitors will pass through.

There's a seven-story mall with good food at Mercado Little Spain (p166), a promising arts center (p174) and the observation deck, Edge.

The adjacent development, Manhattan West, between Ninth and Tenth Aves, has a very large food hall, Citizens (www.ctzns.com). (www.hudsonyardsnewyork.com)

Edge

VIEWPOINT

11 MAP P158, B5

Probably the least interesting of NYC's observation decks, Edge compensates for its poor location (no major landmarks nearby) with adrenaline boosters such as slanted glass fencing that encourages you to lean out, and a small glass floor, to peer down at taxis 100 floors below. On the plus side, it's seldom crowded.

For real thrills, don a helmet and harness and climb outside ($185, minus deck entry price). (www.edgenyc.com)

Rockefeller Center (p160)

S4SVISUALS/SHUTTERSTOCK ©

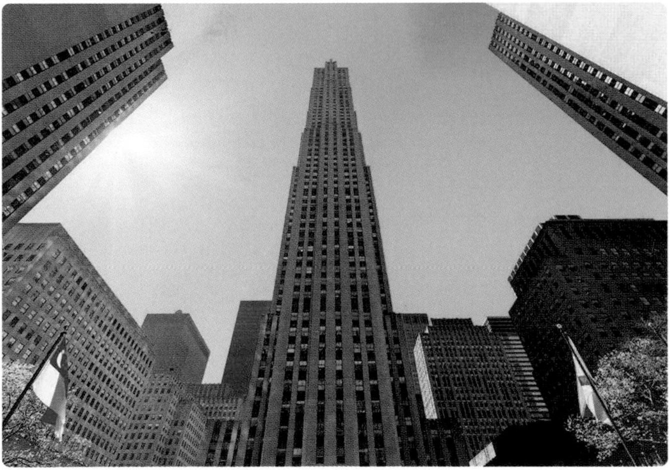

Bryant Park

Like Times Square, **Bryant Park** (Map p158, E4; www.bryantpark.org) is a mid-1990s transformation tale, as a public-private partnership remade scary 'Needle Park' into a thoroughly inviting oasis. Coffee kiosks, alfresco chess games, summer film screenings and winter ice skating are the norm at this half-block behind the main library; check the schedule for daily activities, from yoga classes to bird-spotting. It also has NYC's best public restrooms, as luxurious as the finest hotels, and free to all goers.

Roosevelt Island AREA

12 MAP P158, H1

In the East River, this skinny island is an odd planned neighborhood, mostly built in the 1970s, that feels more like a northern European suburb. At the southern tip is architect Louis Kahn's striking **Four Freedoms Park** (www.fdrfourfreedomspark.org), planted with beautiful cherry trees. At the north end, **Manhattan Park Pool Club** (www.manhattanpark.com) is a good swimming getaway. A short **aerial tram** (www.rioc.ny.gov/tramtransportation.htm) – yeah, the one Spider-Man hopped on – connects to Midtown; it's worth a trip in itself for the stunning view. (www.rihs.us)

Eating

Grand Central Oyster Bar & Restaurant SEAFOOD $$$

An absolute classic and a blessed time warp, set under a vaulted tiled ceiling, with efficient union waiters serving simple, great seafood. Prime seats at the Grand central Oyster (see 1 Map p158, F4) are at the counter to your far right: watch the signature rich lobster stew made to order, in pots heated by the NYC steam system. Savvy commuters slurp oysters from a window behind. (www.oysterbarny.com)

Pio Pio PERUVIAN $$

13 MAP P158, B3

A mini-chain started in Queens, Pio Pio dresses up a bit at this Hell's Kitchen branch, with a long bar (the frothy pisco sours are like drinking a booze-soaked cloud) and a longer ceviche menu. Still, the star is absolutely flawless roast chicken, served with plenty of tangy, green *ají* sauce. (www.piopio.shop)

Totto Ramen JAPANESE $

14 MAP P158, B2

The name Totto is synonymous with great (and great value) Japanese food in Midtown. This place, along with another branch in Midtown East, specializes in extraordinarily rich and soothing noodles, ladened with chicken fat. If your taste runs to grilled chicken, check out Yakitori Totto (W 55th St); for buckwheat noodles, visit Totto Soba (E 43rd St). (www.tottoramen.com)

Le Bernardin

SEAFOOD $$$

15 MAP P158, D2

If you love seafood and have the budget, triple-Michelin-starred Le Bernardin is your fine-dining holy grail.

For decades, French-born chef Eric Ripert has been steering this restaurant on a course of deceptively simple seafood (one menu category is 'barely touched') that can border on transcendent. The three-course prix-fixe menu (lunch/dinner $120/195) has ample choice. Book a month ahead. (www.le-bernardin.com)

Modern

FRENCH $$$

16 MAP P158, E2

MoMA's formal restaurant shines with two Michelin stars. In a light-filled spaced with giant windows overlooking the sculpture garden, British-born chef Thomas Allan does rich, confident seasonal food that gleams like fine art. The dining room is a set tasting menu (lunch/dinner $150/250); the (unfortunately dim) Bar Room is à la carte (mains $40) and takes walk-ins. (www.themodernnyc.com)

HanGawi

KOREAN $$

17 MAP P158, E6

Leave your shoes at the entrance and slip into a soothing space of meditative music, low seating and clean, complex and entirely

Roosevelt Island Tram

Putting the K in Koreatown

K-beauty, K-pop, really K-everything-you-can-imagine can be found on W 32nd St between Fifth Ave and the intersection of Sixth Ave and Broadway, and a bit on nearby blocks. The cafes, restaurants, salons, spas and shops are dense on the ground and often occupy 2nd and 3rd floors too. Bars are plentiful – or try **Gagopa** (Map p158, E6; www.gagopakaraoke.com) for private karaoke – and the block stays lively late into the night.

meat-free dishes. Favorites include stuffed shiitake mushrooms, spicy kimchi-mushroom pancakes and a seductively smooth tofu claypot in ginger sauce. Weekend lunch has a four-course prix-fixe deal for $35. Book ahead for dinner. (www.hangawirestaurant.com)

Burger Joint

BURGERS $

18 MAP P158, D1

Walk into the swanky lobby of the Thompson Central Park hotel and turn left just before the red velvet drapes. By the tiny neon burger sign is the door to a disorientingly different world: graffiti-strewn walls, retro booths and simple, high-quality beef 'n' patty brilliance. The same great burgers can be had at Penn Station, though without the magic-trick setting. (www.burgerjointny.com)

Mercado Little Spain

FOOD HALL $$

19 MAP P158, B6

Celebrity chef José Andrés has given the food court a welcome makeover: the lower level of the Hudson Yards mall is filled with kiosks and sit-down restaurants serving specialties from all the regions of Spain, from simple cured-ham sandwiches and churros to more elaborate paella and other seafood, all washed down with Spanish wines. (www.littlespain.com)

Margon

CUBAN $

20 MAP P158, D3

A timeless treasure just a few steps from glitzy Times Square, this narrow Cuban lunch spot (open till 5pm) is packed with loyal regulars. Up front, grab a quick *cubano* sandwich (roast pork, salami, pickles, *mojo* sauce and mayo; $10), or join the line in the back for hearty hot stews, with rice and beans ($12). Limited seating. (www.instagram.com/margonrestaurantnyc)

Barbetta

ITALIAN $$$

21 MAP P158, C3

This block of 46th St, known as Restaurant Row, is typically for quick pretheater meals, and Barbetta does offer a set menu before 7:30pm. But it's worth lingering in this gorgeous time warp (it's run by the same family that established it in 1906), for the impeccable service, a lush garden and the Piedmontese specialties such as gnocchi and risotto. (www.barbettarestaurant.com)

All'antico Vinaio

SANDWICHES $

22 MAP P158, C3

A branch of a renowned Florence institution, this tiny tiled place serves high-quality sandwiches ($14-18): signature big squares of *schiacciata* (like focaccia but thinner), with all-Italian ingredients, such as silky mortadella, pistachio paste and creamy buffalo-milk cheese. It also does a nice pretheater combo of charcuterie plates and wine – though you might have to eat standing up. (www.allanticovinaio.com)

Ess-a-Bagel

DELI $

23 MAP P158, G2

Perfectly toothsome bagels have made this kosher deli an institution; expect a queue. Pick your bagel (plain, poppy seed, etc), specify toasted or untoasted, and select, from a sprawling display, cream cheese or other spreads. Classic: scallion cream cheese with lox, capers, tomato and red onion ($15.50.) If the weather's fine, turn into 51st St and lunch in pretty Greenacre Park. (www.ess-a-bagel.com)

Amy's Bread

BAKERY $

24 MAP P158, C3

Amy's has been in Hell's Kitchen since 1992 and has outposts at several museums and libraries.

Mercado Little Spain

BIBIKOW WALTER/HEMIS.FR ©

Amy's Bread (p167)

Pop in to the creaky old store, painted a cheerful turquoise blue, for chewy baguettes, sandwiches or sweet treats like almond brioche toast or a rich lemon olive-oil cake. (www.amysbread.com)

Drinking

Campbell — COCKTAIL BAR

In the 1920s, this was financier John W Campbell's office. It fell into varied misuses before being restored to its original grandeur, complete with a stunning hand-painted ceiling. Come to Campbell (see 1 Map p158, F4) for cocktails and you'll feel like you're waiting for Rockefeller or Carnegie to join you. Book ahead Thursday to Sunday; Saturday has live jazz.

It's a little tricky to find: outside on Vanderbilt (a pedestrian plaza), look for the red awning; inside, take the stairs to the right. From inside Grand Central Terminal, walk up the west marble stairs and outside to Vanderbilt. (www.thecampbellnyc.com)

Bar Centrale — BAR

25 MAP P158, C3

Set in an old brownstone, this unmarked bar is a favorite of Broadway actors, often seen here postcurtain unwinding to sultry jazz. It's an intimate spot with a no-standing policy, so consider calling ahead (reservations are taken up to a week in advance). It's just up the stairs to the left of Joe Allen's. (www.barcentrale.nyc)

Q

CLUB

26 MAP P158, C3

Opened in 2021, this multilevel space rapidly became known as one of the best gay clubs for a sweaty night out dancing. Events vary, but the standard parties are Pop Rave on Fridays and QAF on Saturdays. Buy tickets ahead (sliding scale; pick the price bracket you're comfortable with) to guarantee admission. (www.theqnyc.com)

Rudy's Bar & Grill

BAR

27 MAP P158, B3

The big pants-less pig outside should have told you: this is Hell's Kitchen's best dive bar, with cheap pitchers of draft beer, vinyl booths patched with duct tape, a great variety of patrons and (budget-travel alert!) free hot dogs. The soundtrack is classic rock, with muted Knicks games on TV. (www.rudysbarnyc.com)

Jimmy's Corner

BAR

28  MAP P158, D3

Longtime owner Jimmy Glenn, a former boxing trainer, was lost to COVID in 2020, but his legacy lives on at his welcoming, unpretentious dive, a narrow space lined with boxing memorabilia. The excellent, Stax-heavy jukebox is kept low enough for talking.

Lantern's Keep

COCKTAIL BAR

29  MAP P158, E3

This dark, intimate salon, set off the lobby of the Iroquois Hotel,

Jimmy's Corner

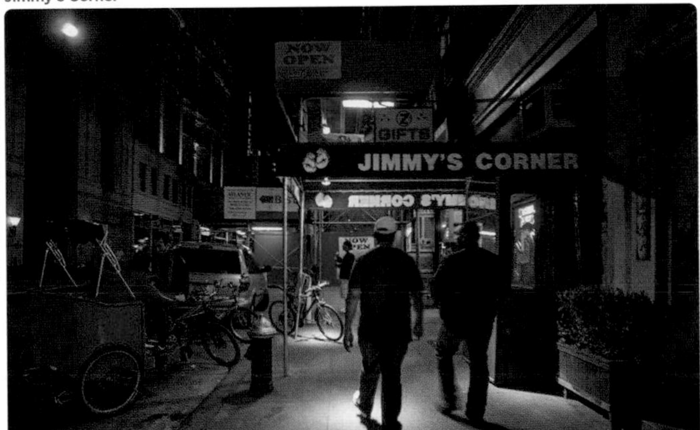

NYC Theater: Broadway & Beyond

'Broadway' as a concept got its start in the early 20th century, when theaters around Times Square opened with popular plays and suggestive comedies that in the 1920s evolved into full musical narratives like Oscar Hammerstein's *Show Boat*. In 1943, Broadway had its first runaway hit – *Oklahoma!* – which remained on stage for a record 2212 performances.

Today, Broadway is an official designation, established with IATSE, the performers' union, for theater size (500-plus seats) and minimum wages. Many of the 41 Broadway theaters are still well-maintained vintage jewels, producing both musicals and non-musicals.

'Off-Broadway' refers not to location but to smaller size and lower minimum salary – which translates to lower ticket prices, plus a good chance of seeing a hit in the making. The Public Theater (p84) has a decades-long record of great debuts, from *Hair* to *Hamilton*, but also check out Playwrights Horizons (p173), Second Stage (p173) at the Tony Kiser Theater, Signature Theatre (Map p158, B4; www.signaturetheatre.org), tiny Soho Rep (p63) and Ars Nova (www.arsnovanyc.com).

As for 'Off-Off-Broadway,' it's an unofficial term, more a state of mind, used for small, mostly downtown theaters dedicated to experimental and avant-garde material.

specializes in classic drinks, some straight from the late 19th century and others inspired by the era. Chat with the passionate, bow-tied bartenders for a recommendation, and reserve if you can. (www.iroquoisny.com)

As Is

CRAFT BEER

30 MAP P158, B2

Done with dark dives? Sip a beer by the big windows at this airy, coffee-bar-ish corner spot. There are 20 beers on tap, plus cocktails, natural wine and interesting sodas. Hearty bar snacks (nachos, fancy sardines) stand up to the hops. And if, after a few drinks, you hanker for a dive again, honky-tonk Waylon (www.thewaylon.com) is right next door. (www.asisnyc.com)

Industry

GAY

31 MAP P158, C2

This slick, 4000-sq-ft watering hole is one of Hell's Kitchen's biggest scenes, with handsome lounge areas, a pool table and a stage for top-notch drag divas. Head in between 6pm and 9pm for the two-for-one drinks special or squeeze in later to party with the eye-candy party hordes. (www.industry-bar.com)

Entertainment

Jazz at Lincoln Center
JAZZ

32 MAP P158, C1

Perched atop the Time Warner Center, Jazz at Lincoln Center comprises three state-of-the-art venues: midsized Rose Theater; panoramic, glass-backed Appel Room; and chummy Dizzy's Club. It's the last of these that you're most likely to visit, given its nightly shows (cover charge $5 to $45). The talent here is often exceptional, as is the dazzling Central Park view. (www.jazz.org)

Carnegie Hall
LIVE MUSIC

33 MAP P158, D1

This legendary concert hall (how do you get here? Practice, practice, practice!) may not be the world's biggest nor its grandest, but it's definitely one of the most acoustically blessed. Classical, jazz and folk greats feature in the main Isaac Stern Auditorium. Smaller Zankel Hall hosts edgier, eclectic names, and intimate Weill Recital Hall is for chamber music.

Guided tours ($20) shed light on the venue's storied history. If you're attending a concert, allow time to visit the Rose Museum, which opens a bit before showtime and documents the venue's illustrious history. (www.carnegiehall.org)

The Ambassador on Broadway

TV Show Tapings

Being the 'live studio audience' is fun and free, but requires some planning (and, currently, proof of vaccination against COVID). Most don't allow kids under 16. Some of the best known are:

Saturday Night Live (www.bit.ly/SNLtickets) The trickiest ticket to get: try for standby tickets by emailing snltickets@nbcuni.com at 10am Thursday, for the Saturday show. Or email in August to try your luck with the lottery for the whole season.

Last Week Tonight with John Oliver (www.lastweektickets.com) Tickets are available online up to a month in advance of taping dates (Saturdays at 6:30pm).

Late Night with Seth Meyers and **The Late Show with Stephen Colbert** (www.1iota.com) As they're taped multiple times a week, the late-night talk shows are easier tickets to get. They're usually released three or four weeks in advance; for *Colbert*, keep tabs on the Twitter feed (@colbertlateshow).

New York City Center

LIVE PERFORMANCE

34 MAP P158, D1

In 1943 a converted Masonic temple (hence the neo-Moorish fantasia) became 'The People's Theater,' a pioneer in the practice of hosting all manner of performance on a single stage. In particular look for the excellent Alvin Ailey American Dance Theater, which does an annual performance here; it also does short-run Broadway revivals. Tickets are usually quite reasonable. (www.nycitycenter.org)

Madison Square Garden

LIVE PERFORMANCE

35 MAP P158, C5

NYC's best-known arena – set above Penn Station – hosts major pop stars, as well as New York Knicks (www.nba.com/knicks) basketball and New York Rangers (www.nhl.com/rangers) hockey.

One-off boxing matches and annual events like the Annual Westminster Kennel Club Dog Show (www.westminsterkennelclub.org) happen here too. There is also a smaller upstairs theater, often used for comedy shows. (www.msg.com)

Radio City Music Hall

CONCERT VENUE

36 MAP P158, E2

In the early 1930s, vaudeville producer Samuel Lionel 'Roxy' Rothafel pulled out all the stops on this art deco palace and an over-the-top extravaganza featuring the dance troupe the Roxyettes – later streamlined to the Rockettes, and still the core of the campy-glitzy annual Christmas Spectacular.

For concerts, it's a sumptuous setting, but the size of the place (and the comfy seats) can make for a sedate night. That said, arena-fillers like Dolly Parton play here in relative intimacy. (www.radiocity.com)

Birdland

JAZZ

37 MAP P158, C3

Bebop legend Charlie Parker (aka 'Bird') lent his name, and the club still has major jazz cachet. These days, the intimate space features big names; a smaller basement theatre hosts newer artists. Every Friday at 5:30pm, the house big band does an electrifying set, often drawing excellent dancers. Ticket prices are reasonable, but there's a $20 drink minimum. www.birdlandjazz.com)

Playwrights Horizons

THEATER

38 MAP P158, B4

An excellent place to catch what could be the next big thing, this "writers' theater," established in 1971, is dedicated to fostering contemporary American works.

Notable playwrights here include recent Pulitzer Prize winners Michael R Jackson (*A Strange Loop*) and Annie Baker (*The Flick*), as well as theater legends like Kenneth Lonergan, AR Gurney and Christopher Durang. (www.playwrightshorizons.org)

Second Stage

THEATER

39 MAP P158, C3

Since 1979, this theater company has been building a reputation for well-crafted American theater, with both debut works and shows by better-known playwrights. Recent hits have included *Dear Evan Hansen* and a revival of *Take Me Out*.

Its main theater is the Off-Broadway Tony Kiser; the larger Hayes is nearby (W 44th St); and uptown is pocket-sized McGinn Cazale. (www.2st.com)

Broadway on a Budget

If you want to see several shows, consider joining the TDF (www.tdf.org), which offers discount tickets, though rarely to the hottest shows. For one-off, same-day deals, line up at TDF's **TKTS Booth** (Map p158, D3; www.tdf.org/tkts) in Times Square, under the big red stairs. Some block-busters – such as Hamilton (www.hamiltonmusical.com) and Book of Mormon (www.bookofmormonbroadway.com) – run online ticket lotteries for same-day cheap seats. Many theaters offer standing-room spots or last-minute sales; if you have your eye on a specific show, check the theater's website or enquire directly at the box office.

Carolines on Broadway COMEDY

40 MAP P158, D2

You may recognize this big (300 seat), bright, mainstream classic from comedy specials filmed on location here. Carolines first opened as a small cabaret club in 1982. Owner Caroline Hirsch, a lifelong comedy fan, soon began booking comedians in her room. It's been a huge success and is a top spot to catch US comedy big guns and sitcom stars. Tickets range from $25 to $45. (www.carolines.com)

Shed ARTS CENTER

41 MAP P158, A6

While much of Hudson Yards is blandly luxurious, this giant performance space adds an artsy edge by commissioning original works in dance and music and hosting theatrical productions.

The Shed brings together established and emerging artists to create new work in fields ranging from pop to classical music, painting to digital media, theater to literature to dance. It also has a smaller performance area, galleries, a bookshop and a bar-lounge. Pop stars such as Björk and Sia have played here. (www.theshed.org)

Shopping

MoMA Museum & Design Stores GIFTS & SOUVENIRS

42 MAP P158, E2

The enormous gift shop at the Museum of Modern Art (p156)

Macy's (p176)

stocks gorgeous books (criticism, architecture, kids' picture books) as well as art posters and one-of-a-kind knickknacks.

For furniture, homewares, jewelry, bags and artsy gifts, head across the street to the **MoMA Design Store**, which also has a branch in SoHo. (www.momastore.org)

Argosy BOOKS

43 MAP P158, F1

Since 1925 this landmark has filled its six stories (accessible via a tiny staffed elevator) with fine antiquarian items such as books, art monographs and more. Travelers will love the 2nd floor, which is devoted to maps; there's also historical, literary and show-biz memorabilia, from personal letters and signed books to autographed publicity stills. Prices range from costly to clearance. (www.argosybooks.com)

FAO Schwarz TOYS

Claiming to be America's oldest toy store, FAO Schwarz started in Baltimore in 1862, but has been synonymous with NYC since 1870.

Its only been located in Rockefeller Plaza since 2018, (see 4 Map p158, E2) but it has the giant floor piano that Tom Hanks made famous in the movie *Big*, and the uniformed human nutcrackers at the door, so all is well. (www.faoschwarz.com)

Fine & Dandy FASHION & ACCESSORIES

44 MAP P158, B2

This pocket-square-sized haberdashery specializes in retro fashion accessories for dapper folk: proper bow ties, ascots, embroidered suspenders and cuff links, plus an array of hats, from straw boaters to newsboy caps. Yes, it even sell spats.

You've likely never seen so much tweed, tartan, paisley and argyle in one spot before. (www.fineanddandyshop.com)

New York Transit Museum Store GIFTS & SOUVENIRS

On the east side of Grand Central Terminal (see 1 Map p158, F4), next to the stationmaster's office, this nifty shop is filled with transit-themed swag: T-shirts for your favorite subway line, pencil cases, toy trains and much more. Like the star-studded Grand Central ceiling pattern? Buy it here, in chiffon-scarf form.

There's also a mini-gallery with rotating transit exhibits; if you like what you see, head to the main **New York Transit Museum** (www.nytransitmuseum.or) in downtown Brooklyn. (www.nytransitmuseumstore.com)

Drama Book Shop BOOKS

45 MAP P158, C4

If you want a script, any script, this legendary theater-industry shop (open since 1917) likely has

Department Stores

New York's great retail palaces are a good reminder of the pleasures of hands-on browsing, and perfect if you're traveling with a group: there's something for everyone, from lipsticks to tea towels. At most places, out-of-town shoppers are granted an immediate 10% discount (ask at the store's info desks), and don't feel shy about asking sales reps if any additional discounts are available.

Macy's (Map p158, D5; www.macys.com) The most mass-market. It's also the oldest: check out the wooden escalators on the upper floors on the west side.

Saks Fifth Avenue (Map p158, E2; www.saksfifthavenue.com) Absolutely enormous (10 floors!), and its Christmas windows and lightshow are legendary.

Bloomingdale's (Map p158, F1; www.bloomingdales.com) Occupies a beautiful black art deco building. Its 'brown bags' are iconic.

Bergdorf Goodman (Map p158, E1; www.bergdorfgoodman.com) Hits the high end, with especially sharp fashion (and supercreative Christmas windows). Menswear is across the avenue.

it, along with a huge selection of industry books and magazines.

This location is new since 2021 (thanks to the intervention of megafan Lin-Manuel Miranda), and has a pleasant coffee bar and a busy event schedule; check the website for details. (www.dramabookshop.com)

B&H

ELECTRONICS

46 MAP P158, C5

What Blimie & Herman started as a camera store in 1973 is now a multistory temple to electronic gadgetry that's worth a visit for the experience alone.

Check out the elaborate overhead conveyor-belt stock system, chat with expert staff, and you might leave with a new drone or set of binoculars. Note that it's closed Saturdays. (www.bhphotovideo.com)

M&J Trimming

ARTS & CRAFTS

47 MAP P158, E5

Since 1936, this Garment District mainstay has been inspiring designers with a dazzling array of buttons, beads, sequins, ribbons, rhinestones, feathers and plenty more – worth a browse whether you want to zhuzh up an existing outfit or dream about a new one. (www.mjtrim.com)

Christie's

ART

48 MAP P158, E3

This celebrated auction house (established in London in 1766) is a great place to see surprising treasures for free. Before every auction, most items are on view in the exhibition halls, and the collections are a grab bag: Chinese ceramics, perhaps, or 1980s hip-hop memorabilia. To attend an auction, you must preregister. (www.christies.com)

Grand Central Market

MARKET

49 MAP P158, F4

This 240ft corridor on the east side of the terminal features NYC grocery stalwarts like Zabar's, Li-Lac Chocolates and Murray's Cheese, along with prime fresh produce, meat and fish. It's convenient for gifty treats or quick more-like-home nosh, such as antipasti or a slab of lasagna. (www.grandcentralterminal.com/market)

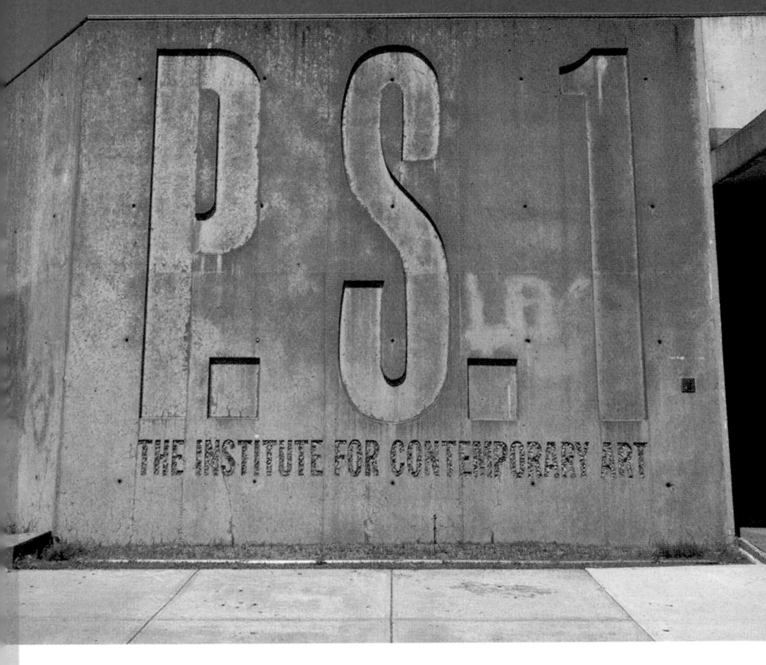

Top Experience

Experiment with Art at MoMA PS1

The smaller, hipper sibling of Manhattan's Museum of Modern Art, MoMA PS1 showcases global, experimental contemporary work. Installations make creative use of the space – a big old redbrick school building – and summer DJ parties in the courtyard can be a major scene. Whatever's on, it's a good excuse to hop the East River to Queens.

www.momaps1.org

22-25 Jackson Ave, Long Island City

adult/child $10/free

noon-6pm Thu-Mon

Experimental Classics

In 1976 artist Alanna Heiss took possession of an abandoned school building in Queens. The inaugural exhibit, *Rooms,* invited artists like Richard Serra, James Turrell and Keith Sonnier to create site-specific works. Some survive, along with later permanent 'interventions,' making a building-wide scavenger hunt. Right in the lobby is a Pipilotti Rist tiny video set in a floorboard hole; then check the basement, the stairwells (Richard Artschwager's painted oval *blps* are from 1976), and a hole in the wall on the 3rd floor (Alan Saret, also from 1976). Also ask about James Turrell's *Meeting,* one of his signature Skyspaces, which is open periodically around dusk.

The MoMA Era

Since PS1 affiliated with MoMA in 2001, the space has shown off that institution's contemporary acquisitions. Shows rotate every few months, with a global approach to curation that features, for example, Egyptian puppeteers and German video artists. At the same time, some landmark shows have a more local slant: every few years, the Greater New York survey show, say, and a more recent focus on socially engaged art that reflects city social issues.

Special Events

Programming may still be impacted by the pandemic, so check for two key series during your visit. In summer Warm Up is a Saturday-afternoon DJ party that started way back in 2001, each year in a new custom-built architectural creation in the museum courtyard. Check the website ticket prices. It finishes at 9pm. November to April, Sunday Sessions is a varied series of lectures, screenings, live music, performance art and more.

★ Top Tips

- Admission prices are a suggestion only; pay less if you like.
- The bookstore (www.artbook.com) here is less crowded than MoMA's, and it stocks many of the same exhibition catalogs and coffee-table tomes, as well as edgier media.

Take a Break

Greek chef Mina Stone offers wholesome comfort food in the museum's restaurant, **Mina's** (www.minas.nyc). It's closed Mondays, though; in that case go for quiche or a flaky pastry at Cannelle Patisserie (www.cannellepatisserie.com), or a Michelin-starred Mexican dinner at Casa Enrique (www.casaenriquelic.com).

★ Getting There

S E or M to Court Sq-23 St, or 7 to Court Sq.

East River line to Hunters Point, or Astoria line to Long Island City.

Walking Tour

Eat Everything in Astoria

Directly across the East River from Manhattan's Upper East Side, Astoria is quintessential Queens: diverse, energetic and creative even in drab surrounds (no Brooklyn-style brownstone grandeur here, only midrise brick and vinyl siding). In many cases, that creativity comes out in food, so bring an appetite.

Getting There

NYC Ferry to Astoria. From the dock, it's a five-minute walk south to Socrates Sculpture Park.

S N/W to Broadway, then 15-minute walk west to Socrates. Leaving MoMI, take M/R from Steinway St.

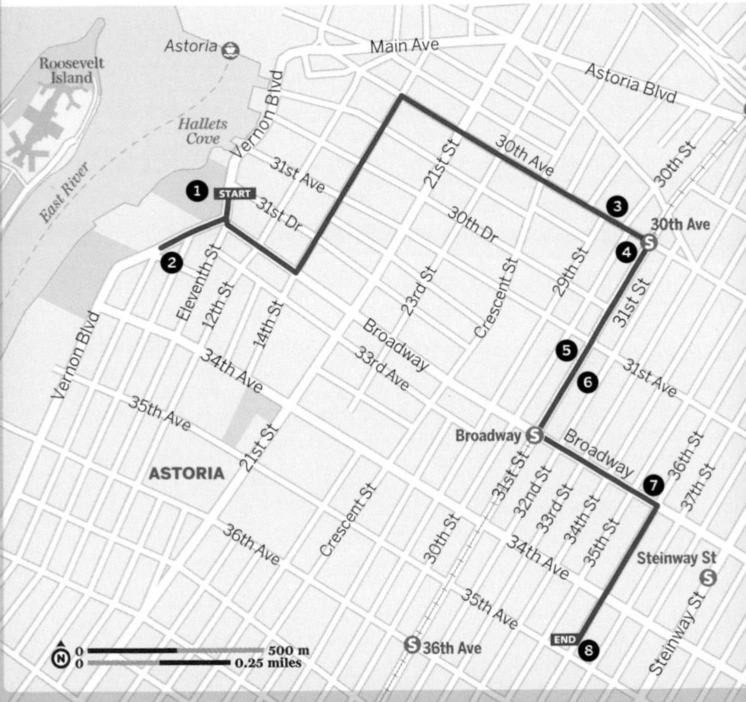

❶ Socrates Sculpture Park

In 1986 sculptor Mark di Suvero led a team of artists who salvaged this serene waterfront from its use as an illegal dump site, and now it's a proper **city park** (www.socratessculpturepark.org) with a lively spring-to-fall schedule of free art installations and events. Summer weekends look out for kayaking in Hallets Cove, just north.

❷ Noguchi Museum

This ex-factory was minimalist designer Isamu Noguchi's studio until his death in 1988. As a **museum** (www.noguchi.org), it's worth a visit as much for the artist's iconic paper lamps and stone sculptures as for the serene interior garden.

❸ Athens Square Park

Astoria is known as a Greek neighborhood, but that's just one layer. Small Athens Square hosts Greek, Italian and Egyptian dance nights in summer. In the next block, at El Athens Grill, Mexicans adapted a Greek restaurant, and near that, Athena's nail salon is Korean-run and staffed by the world.

❹ Trade Fair

Astoria's diverse home cooks demand an awe-inspiring variety of groceries: **Trade Fair** (www.tradefairny.com) is just one temple to tastes. In the labyrinthine aisles, you'll find imports from Brazil, Turkey, India, Peru and beyond; a halal butcher; and produce like bitter melon and cactus paddles.

❺ King Souvlaki

Follow the plumes of smoke to this celebrated Greek **food truck** (www.kingsouvlakinyc.com), one of Astoria's best. The meat, grilled over charcoal, is served on skewers or rolled in pita sandwiches, with fries (fried in olive oil) tucked in.

❻ Astoria Bookshop

Open since 2013, this much-loved indie **bookstore** (www.astoriabookshop.com) dedicates ample shelf space to local writers. Pick up a title on the Queens dining scene or the borough's heritage, or catch an author reading.

❼ Pye Boat Noodle

This excellent **Thai restaurant** (www.facebook.com/pyeboatnoodle) decked out like an old-fashioned country house serves, among other street-food classics, star-anise-laced boat noodles, topped with crispy pork crackling. Humid nights conjure Bangkok.

❽ Museum of the Moving Image

One jewel at **MoMI** (www.movingimage.us) is a wonderful exhibit about Muppets creator Jim Henson, but you'll also find 19th-century optical toys, vintage arcade games and the puffy shirt from *Seinfeld*.

Check the screening schedule; a film might be a great way to rest after your walk.

Explore Upper East Side

A manicured residential neighborhood beloved by NYC's upper crust, the Upper East Side is unsurprisingly home to some of the city's most expensive boutiques, which line Madison Ave. Architecturally magnificent Fifth Ave, running parallel to the leafy realms of Central Park, offers the 'Museum Mile' – one of the most cultured strips in New York.

The Short List

- ***Metropolitan Museum of Art (p184)*** *Wandering amid the priceless treasures, from mesmerizing Egyptian artifacts to Renaissance masterpieces.*
- ***Classic New York Cuisine (p192)*** *Visiting venerated neighborhood eateries for a slice of NYC flavor.*
- ***Guggenheim Museum (p189)*** *Walking the spiral ramp of Frank Lloyd Wright's iconic architecture.*
- ***Neue Galerie (p190)*** *Gazing at the lush, gilded paintings of Gustav Klimt, followed by a leisurely lunch at the museum's elegant cafe.*
- ***Bemelmans Bar (p195)*** *Sipping cocktails at this elegant bar, which hearkens back to the Jazz Age.*

Getting There & Around

S The 4/5/6 trains travel along Lexington Ave; the Q runs up Second Ave to 72nd, 86th and 96th Sts.

M1, M2, M3 and M4 buses run down Fifth Ave and up Madison Ave. Crosstown buses at 66th, 72nd, 79th, 86th and 96th Sts head through Central Park to the Upper West Side.

Neighborhood Map on p188

Metropolitan Museum of Art

Top Experience

Dive into World Culture at the Metropolitan Museum of Art

This palatial museum, founded in 1870, houses one of the world's largest and most important art collections. You'll find over two million paintings, sculptures, textiles and artifacts from around the globe here – even an Egyptian temple straight from the banks of the Nile. Wear comfy shoes and plan on spending some time.

MAP P188, A3

www.metmuseum.org

1000 5th Ave, at E 82nd St

adult/senior/child $30/$22/free

10am-5:30pm Sun-Thu, to 9pm Fri & Sat

Egyptian Art

The museum has an unrivaled collection of ancient Egyptian art, some of which dates back to the Paleolithic era. Located to the north of the Great Hall, the 38 Egyptian galleries open dramatically with one of the Met's prized pieces: the **Tomb of Perneb** (c 2300 BCE), an Old Kingdom burial chamber crafted from limestone.

From here, a web of rooms is cluttered with funerary stelae, carved reliefs and fragments of pyramids. In Gallery 105 don't miss the intriguing models from the **Tomb of Meketre**; these clay figurines were meant to help in the afterlife. These rooms eventually lead to the **Temple of Dendur** (Gallery 131), a sandstone temple to the goddess Isis given to the US by Egypt in 1965. It resides in a sunny atrium gallery with a reflecting pool – a must-see for the first-time visitor.

European Paintings

Want Renaissance? The Met's got it. On the museum's 2nd floor, the European Paintings galleries display a stunning collection of masterworks. This includes more than 1700 canvases from a 500-year period starting in the 13th century, with pieces by every important painter from Duccio to Rembrandt.

After admiring the classics, skip south to see 19th and early 20th-century paintings like Vincent Van Gogh's sweeping *White Field with Cypresses* (Gallery 822) and self-taught artist Henri Rousseau's *The Repast of the Lion* (Gallery 825).

Art of the Arab Lands

In the southeastern corner of the 2nd floor you'll find the Islamic galleries, with 15 incredible rooms showcasing the museum's extensive collection of art from the Middle East and Central and South Asia. In addition

★ Top Tips

- Don't try to see everything – pick a few collections and immerse yourself.
- Stream the Met's free audioguide via smartphone by visiting www.metmuseum.org/audio-guide.
- Docents offer guided tours of specific galleries (free with admission). Check the website or information desk for details.

✕ Take a Break

The museum's ground-floor **American Wing Cafe** sells coffee, wine, beer and light snacks – all served under the vaulted ceiling of the statue-sprinkled Charles Engelhard Court.

For an inexpensive meal with NYC old-fashioned character, head to nearby Lexington Candy Shop (p194) for a burger and an egg-cream soda.

to garments, secular decorative objects and manuscripts, you'll find a magnificent 14th-century mihrab (prayer niche) from Iran, lined with elaborately patterned blue, white and yellow ceramic tile work (Gallery 455).

There's also a superb array of Ottoman textiles (Gallery 459), a medieval-style **Moroccan court** (Gallery 456) and the 18th-century **Damascus Room** (Gallery 461).

American Wing

In the northwestern corner, the two-floor American Wing showcases a wide variety of decorative and fine art from throughout the history of the United States.

These include everything from colonial portraiture to Hudson River School art – not to mention Emanuel Leutze's massive canvas of *Washington Crossing the Delaware* (Gallery 760).

Greek & Roman Art

The 27 galleries devoted to classical antiquity are another Met doozy. From the Great Hall, a passageway takes you through a barrel-vaulted room flanked by the chiseled torsos of Greek figures.

This spills right into one of the Met's loveliest spaces: the airy **Greek and Roman sculpture court** (Gallery 162), full of marble carvings of gods and historical figures. The statue of a bearded Hercules from 68–98 CE, with a lion's skin draped about him, is particularly awe-inspiring.

The Greek and Roman sculpture court

Modern & Contemporary Art

The rooms in the far southwestern corner of the 1st and 2nd floors feature art from the early 20th century onward. All the rock stars of modern art are represented here. Notable names include Spanish masters Picasso (whose 'high' cubist *Still Life with a Bottle of Rum* hangs in Gallery 905), Dalí and Miró, as well as American painters Georgia O'Keeffe and Edward Hopper. Thomas Hart Benton's magnificent 1930s 10-panel mural *America Today* takes up an entire room in Gallery 909.

The Roof Garden

One of the best spots in the entire museum is the roof garden, which features rotating sculpture installations by contemporary and 20th-century artists. (Jeff Koons, Andy Goldsworthy and Imran Qureshi have all shown here.) Best of all are the views it offers of the city and Central Park.

It's also home to the Cantor Roof Garden Bar (p195), an ideal spot for a drink – especially at sunset. It's normally open from April to October.

***Self Portrait with a Straw Hat*, Van Gogh**

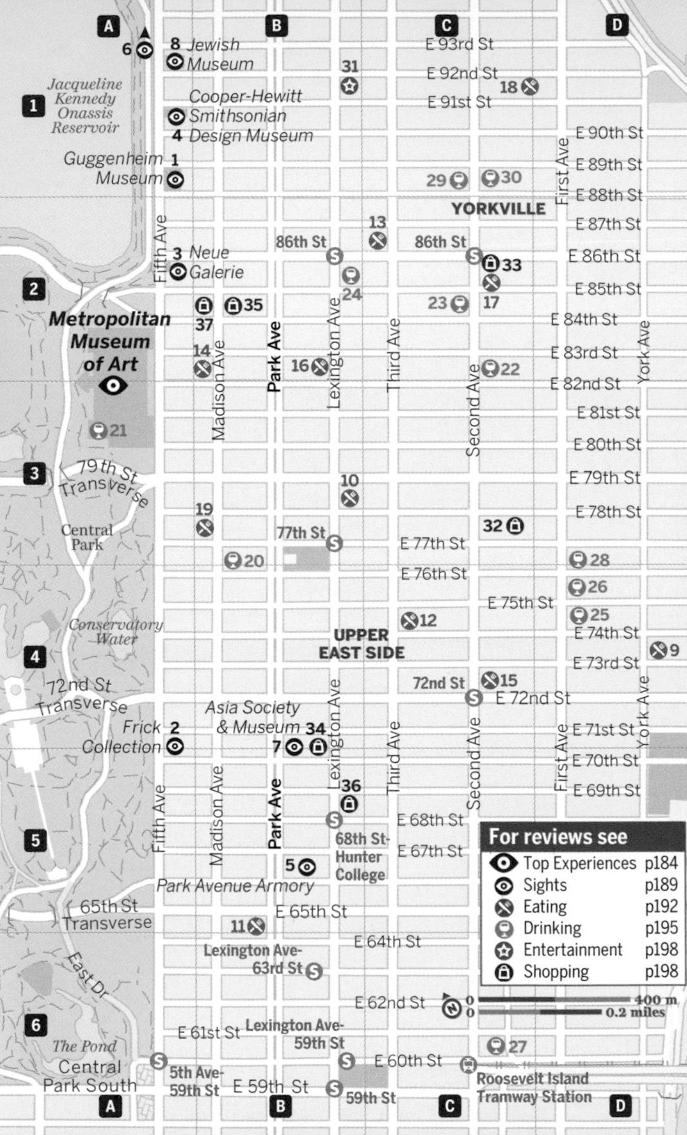
A
B
C
D
1
2
3
4
5
6
8 Jewish Museum
6
E 93rd St
E 92nd St
E 91st St
31
18
Jacqueline Kennedy Onassis Reservoir
Cooper-Hewitt Smithsonian
4 Design Museum
Guggenheim Museum
1
E 90th St
E 89th St
E 88th St
E 87th St
E 86th St
E 85th St
E 84th St
E 83rd St
E 82nd St
E 81st St
E 80th St
E 79th St
E 78th St
29
30
YORKVILLE
First Ave
13
86th St
86th St
33
3 Neue Galerie
Fifth Ave
24
23
17
35
37
Metropolitan Museum of Art
14
16
22
Madison Ave
Park Ave
Lexington Ave
Third Ave
Second Ave
York Ave
21
79th St Transverse
10
19
Central Park
77th St
32
E 77th St
20
E 76th St
28
26
E 75th St
25
E 74th St
E 73rd St
12
9
Conservatory Water
UPPER EAST SIDE
72nd St
15
E 72nd St
72nd St Transverse
Asia Society & Museum
34
7
Frick Collection
2
E 71st St
E 70th St
E 69th St
36
E 68th St
68th St-Hunter College
E 67th St
5
Park Avenue Armory
65th St Transverse
E 65th St
11
E 64th St
Lexington Ave-63rd St
East Dr
E 62nd St
E 61st St
Lexington Ave-59th St
27
The Pond
Central Park South
5th Ave-59th St
E 59th St
59th St
E 60th St
Roosevelt Island Tramway Station
400 m
0.2 miles
For reviews see
Top Experiences p184
Sights p189
Eating p192
Drinking p195
Entertainment p198
Shopping p198

Sights

Guggenheim Museum MUSEUM

1 MAP P188, A1

A New York icon, architect Frank Lloyd Wright's conical white spiral is probably more famous than the art inside, which includes works by Kandinsky, Picasso, Pollock, Monet, Van Gogh and Degas, photographs by Mapplethorpe, and a huge collection of important surrealist pieces.

But temporary exhibitions climbing the much-photographed central rotunda are the real draw. Download the Guggenheim app for information about the exhibits and its architecture. (www.guggenheim.org)

Frick Collection GALLERY

2 MAP P188, A4

This historic mansion was built by steel magnate Henry Clay Frick, one of the many such residences lining a section of Fifth Ave once called 'Millionaire's Row.'

While undergoing renovations, the Frick's spectacular art collection can be found several blocks northeast at the Frick Madison, housed inside the modernist Breuer building (945 Madison Ave).

The Frick collection features masterpieces by Titian, Vermeer, Gilbert Stuart, El Greco, Joshua Reynolds, Goya and Rembrandt. Sculpture, ceramics, antique furniture and clocks are also on display. (www.frick.org)

Frick Collection

TRAVELVIEW/SHUTTERSTOCK ©

The Second Avenue Subway

The idea was born in 1919 and construction began in 1972, but the Second Avenue Subway didn't open to the public until January 1, 2017... well, the first phase of it, anyway. Two new miles of track – which took 10 years to build and cost $4.5 billion – connect an extended Q line to the F train at 63rd St and Lexington Ave, then continue up Second Ave for stops at 72nd, 86th and 96th Sts. With an airy feel and broad, open platforms, the three gleaming stations feature permanent tile and mosaic installations by artists Chuck Close, Jean Shin, Vik Muniz and Sarah Sze.

All the trouble seems to have been worth it: a once-sleepy section of Second Ave (especially between 82nd and 86th Sts) is now a hotbed of worthwhile bars and restaurants with appeal that reaches far beyond the neighborhood.

East Harlem residents are still waiting for Phase Two (expected in 2029, for a whopping cost of over $6 billion), which will bring new stations to 103rd, 116th and 125th Sts.

Pity the downtown crowd, though: there's no proposed timeline for Phases Three and Four, which will extend south to Houston St and then Hanover Sq. Until then, the fastest way to zip down Second Ave? Probably the bike lane.

Neue Galerie

MUSEUM

3 MAP P188, A2

This restored Carrère and Hastings mansion from 1914 is a resplendent showcase for Austrian and German art, featuring works by Alfred Kubin and Ernst Ludwig Kirchner, and incredible collections of Gustav Klimt and Egon Schiele. In pride of place on the 2nd floor is Klimt's golden 1907 *Portrait of Adele Bloch-Bauer I* – acquired for the museum by cosmetics magnate Ronald Lauder for a whopping $135 million. The fascinating story of the painting's history is told in the 2015 film *Woman in Gold*. (www.neuegalerie.org)

Cooper-Hewitt Smithsonian Design Museum

MUSEUM

4 MAP P188, A1

Part of the Smithsonian Institution in Washington DC, this is the only US museum dedicated to both historic and contemporary design.

Housed in the 64-room mansion built for billionaire Andrew Carnegie between 1899 and 1902, the roughly 215,000-piece collection offers artful displays spanning 3000 years over the building's three floors.

Admire the Gilded Age architecture from the garden, which is free to the public and accessible from 90th St or from inside the museum itself. (www.cooperhewitt.org)

Park Avenue Armory THEATER

5 MAP P188, B5

This Gothic brick behemoth from the 19th century was originally a military facility and social club for New York's Seventh Regiment of the National Guard – a group of Gilded Age royals including the Vanderbilts and Roosevelts.

Today, plays, concerts and art installations transform the former drill hall's 55,000-sq-ft space with giant sets unlike anything else you'll find in Manhattan.

Book a guided tour to admire interiors conceptualized by bigwig designers like Stanford White and Louis Comfort Tiffany. (www.armoryonpark.org)

Museum of the City of New York MUSEUM

6 MAP P188, A1

Situated in a Georgian Colonial Revival-style building at the top end of Museum Mile, this local museum focuses solely on New York City's past, present and its constantly evolving future.

Don't miss the 28-minute film *Timescapes* (on the ground floor), which charts New York City's growth from a tiny trading post for Native Americans to the burgeoning metropolis that it is today. (www.mcny.org)

Asia Society & Museum MUSEUM

7 MAP P188, B4

Founded in 1956 by John D Rockefeller III (an avid collector of Asian art), this cultural center hosts fascinating exhibits (retrospectives of leading Chinese artists, contemporary Southeast Asian art, etc), and boasts an awe-worthy collection dating back to the 11th century BCE.

There's also abundant cultural fare: concerts, film screenings, lectures and culinary events. Search the small museum shop for souvenirs like silk scarves, delicate jewelry, children's books and home decor, each selected to showcase the modern Asian lifestyle. (www.asiasociety.org)

(Almost) Free Museums

The Upper East Side is blessed with many of the finest museums in New York City, but visiting them all can be extremely pricey – unless you know how to game the system. Many museums offer specific hours once per week where you can pay whatever admission price you wish, so plan to visit at those times to save some cash. Two notable examples are the Neue Galerie (first Friday evening of each month, 4pm to 7pm) and the Guggenheim (pay what you wish on Saturday, 6pm to 8pm).

Jewish Museum

MUSEUM

8  MAP P188, A1

This gem occupies a French-Gothic mansion from 1908, housing 30,000 items of Judaica including Torah shields and Hanukkah lamps, as well as sculpture, painting and decorative arts. It does not, however, include any historical exhibitions relating to the Jewish community in New York. Temporary exhibits are often excellent, featuring retrospectives on influential figures such as Art Spiegelman or Leonard Cohen, as well as world-class shows on luminaries like Chagall and Modigliani. (www.thejewishmuseum.org)

Eating

Tanoshi

SUSHI **$$$**

9 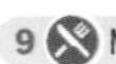 MAP P188, D4

It's not easy to snag a chef-facing stool at Tanoshi, a wildly popular, pocket-sized sushi spot. The setting may be humble, but the flavors are simply magnificent. Only sushi is on offer and only *omakase* (chef's selection) – which might include Hokkaido scallops, kelp-cured flake or mouthwatering *uni* (sea urchin). BYO beer, sake or whatnot. (www.tanoshisushinyc.com)

Pastrami Queen

DELI **$$**

10 MAP P188, B3

The pastrami sandwich is an NYC icon, and according to late culinary king Anthony Bourdain, this no-frills kosher deli makes one of the city's best. Sure, you could order the egg salad or matzo ball soup, but this institution is famous for one reason: pastrami stacked skyscraper-high between slices of Dijon-coated rye bread. If one's not enough, walk to the Upper West Side, where another Pastrami Queen reigns supreme. (www.pastramiqueen.com)

Daniel

FRENCH **$$$**

11 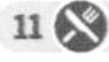 MAP P188, B5

Well-heeled gourmands gather under the coffered ceiling of star chef Daniel Boulud's eponymous French restaurant for one of Manhattan's best (and most expensive) fine-dining experiences. If you want to save a buck, skip the seven-course tasting menu ($275) and dip into the mahogany-covered lounge to dine on dishes like lamb chops and foie gras while sipping Old World wines from an impressive collection. (www.danielnyc.com)

JG Melon

PUB FOOD **$**

12 MAP P188, C4

JG's is a loud neighborhood pub that has been serving reasonably priced drinks and coveted, old-school juicy burgers ($12.50) on tea plates since 1972. It's a local favorite for both eating and drinking (the Bloody Marys are excellent) and it gets crowded in the after-work hours. Cash only. (www.jgmelon-nyc.com)

Café Sabarsky

AUSTRIAN $$

The lines can get long at this popular cafe evoking an opulent, turn-of-the-century Vienna coffeehouse (see 4 map p188, E2). The Austrian specialties, courtesy of Michelin-starred chef Christopher Engel, include crepes with apricot confiture, goulash soup and roasted bratwurst – all beautifully presented. There's also a mouth-watering list of specialty sweets, including a divine Sacher torte (dark chocolate cake with apricot). (www.neuegalerie.org/cafes/sabarsky)

Papaya King

HOT DOGS $

13 MAP P188, C2

The *original* hot-dog-and-papaya-juice shop from 1932, over 40 years before crosstown rival Gray's Papaya (p215) opened, Papaya King has lured many a New Yorker to its neon-lit corner for a cheap and tasty snack of hot dogs and fresh-squeezed papaya juice. (Why papaya? The informative wall signs will explain all.) Try the Homerun, with sauerkraut and New York onion relish. (www.papayaking.com)

William Greenberg Desserts

BAKERY $

14 MAP P188, B2

Stop in at this Manhattan institution for its signature New York–style black-and-white cookies – soft, cakey discs dipped in vanilla and chocolate glazes (grab a box of minis for the trip home). Bite-size rugulach come in four flavors, and the brownies are divine, too.

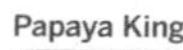
Papaya King

Takeout only. A second location in Hudson Yards also offers sugary temptations. (www.wmgreenberg desserts.com)

Mission Ceviche

PERUVIAN $$$

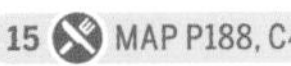

If it's really true that drinking *leche de tigre* (leftover ceviche juice) is an aphrodisiac, this Peruvian restaurant should top your list for date-night dining. Fresh seafood is the menu's star, and many of the meals come bathed in magical tiger's milk. Grab a table for two in the plant-happy interior and nurse pisco sours as the ceviche works its wonders. (https://missionceviche.com)

Lexington Candy Shop

DINER $$

16 MAP P188, B2

Founded in 1925, this picture-perfect diner is a tasty reminder of old New York. Sadly it's more a tourist attraction than a neighborhood favorite these days. Slip into a booth or sit at the long counter for reliable standards like burgers, tuna melts and milkshakes – plus egg creams made fresh from the old-fashioned soda fountain. (www.lexingtoncandyshop.net)

Heidelberg

GERMAN $$

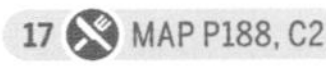

This family-run Yorkville holdout from 1936 recalls a time when E 86th St was better known as Sauerkraut Blvd due to its booming

Mission Ceviche

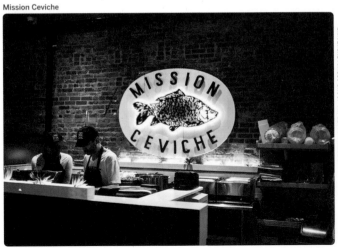

German population. Overflowing with Oktoberfest oom-pah-pah, it's hard to believe much has changed. Gobble up München-style staples like *schweinshaxe* (pork shank) and *käsespätzle* (Emmenthaler mac 'n' cheese), then raise a boot-shaped glass to Bavaria's beermakers. *Prost*! (www.heidelberg-nyc.com)

Drunken Munkey

INDIAN $$

18 MAP P188, C1

This lively lounge channels colonial-era Bombay with vintage wallpaper, cricket-ball door handles and jauntily attired waitstaff. The monkey chandeliers may be pure whimsy, but the craft cocktails (favoring gin, not surprisingly) and tasty curries are serious business. Expect a good level of spice in Anglo-Indian dishes like masala Bombay lamb chops; portions tend to be large. Book ahead. (www.drunkenmunkeynyc.com)

Sant Ambroeus

ITALIAN $$$

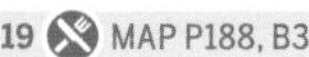
19 MAP P188, B3

Behind the demure facade of this beloved mini-chain lies a dressy Milanese bistro and cafe that oozes Upper East Side sophistication. The long granite counter up front dispenses rich cappuccinos, pastries and panini (grilled with the likes of *cotto* ham and San Daniele prosciutto DOP); the elegant dining room behind dishes up northern Italian specialties, such as branzino, risotto and lasagna verde. (www.santambroeus.com)

Cheaper Eats

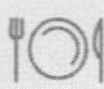

The Upper East Side is the epitome of old-guard opulence, especially the area that covers the blocks from 60th to 86th Sts between Park and Fifth Aves. If you're looking for eating and drinking spots that are easier on the wallet, head east of Lexington Ave. Third, Second and First Aves are lined with less pricey neighborhood venues.

Drinking

Bemelmans Bar

LOUNGE

20 MAP P188, B3

This atmospheric bar from 1947 is now a Gen-Z TikTok mecca. Sink into a chocolate-leather banquette and you'll understand why: bartenders in red smoking jackets mix dry martinis as a pianist tickles the ivories under a 24-karat gold-leaf ceiling. What's more, the walls are covered in whimsical murals by the bar's namesake Ludwig Bemelmans (creator of the *Madeline* books). It's a quintessential splash of New York history. (www.thecarlyle.com)

Cantor Roof Garden Bar

ROOFTOP BAR

21 MAP P188, A3

The sort of setting you can't get enough of (even if you are a jaded local).

Located atop the Met, this rooftop bar sits right above Central Park's tree canopy, allowing for splendid views of the park and the city skyline all around. Sunset is when you'll find fools in love... then again, it could all be those martinis.(www.metmuseum.org/visit/dining)

Penrose

BAR

22 MAP P188, C2

The Penrose, famous for its dirty pickle martinis and beer-battered pickles, brings a dose of style to the UES, with craft beers, exposed brick walls, vintage mirrors, reclaimed-wood details and friendly bartenders.

It's packed with a young neighborhood crowd on weekends, but you can usually get a seat along the wall or in the back. (www.penrosebar.com)

Ethyl's Alcohol & Food

BAR

23 MAP P188, C2

This funky, divey 1970s-themed bar harks back to the gritty, artsy NYC of yore, before famed punk club CBGB became a fashion boutique.

(The $14 cocktails make it decidedly modern.) There's '60s/'70s music nightly from bands or DJs, plus go-go dancers and occasional burlesque shows. Also offers a famed *Fi'Dolla'* ($5.99) burger. (http://ethylsalcohol.com)

Variety Coffee Roasters

COFFEE

24 MAP P188, B2

The UES outlet of this Brooklyn-based mini-chain makes a strong case for 'wfcs' (working from coffee shop): there are smooth brews, delectable pastries, and floor-to-ceiling windows that give the wood-slatted interior a bright and airy feel. But good luck finding a table – laptop-laden freelancers regularly fill up this classy cafe. (https://varietycoffeeroasters.com)

2nd Floor Bar & Essen

BAR

25 MAP P188, D4

The dimly lit staircase to this 2nd-floor annex above a kosher deli is like a time portal to a 1920s speakeasy.

Worn wood floors, tufted leather booths and vintage Yiddish posters might confirm suspicions, but this cocktail joint is actually a 2017 invention from the matzo ball mavericks below, featuring creative cocktails, Israeli wines and shtetl-style bar bites. (https://2ndfloor.com)

Pony Bar

CRAFT BEER

26 MAP P188, D4

The best craft-beer destination in Upper Manhattan, Pony Bar pours exclusively American craft (including cask-conditioned ales) with a near total devotion to New York State breweries. You'll find 20 rotating taps and a whole lot of rustic hardwoods (the bar, the seating, the barrels, the canoe...). If you're in pursuit of a locally devout hoptopia in the UES, then look no further than Pony Bar. (www.theponybar.com)

Jeffrey

CRAFT BEER

27 MAP P188, C6

In the shadow of the Queensboro Bridge, under the Roosevelt Island Tramway, this unpretentious craftbeer and cocktail hub attracts hordes of post-work hops pursuers with its custom-built draft system, which spits brews from over 30 rotating taps.

Park yourself at the tin-topped bar, relax in the outdoor beer garden or check out the connected espresso-and-cocktail lab. (www.thejeffreynyc.com)

Hex & Co

CAFE

28 MAP P188, D3

Board games and beer go hand-in-hand at this relaxed cafe. Choose from roughly 1000 games ($10 per player), including classics like Guess Who and strategy-based Carcassonne, then tuck into a menu of greasy feel-good grub with mozzarella sticks, tuna melts, pizza tots etc.

The atmosphere skews more 'mom's basement' than 'happening bar' – a welcome respite from loud NYC nightlife. (www.hexnyc.com)

UES NYC

COCKTAIL BAR

29 MAP P188, C1

Scooping delicious ice cream by day, this kitschy candy-colored

Ethyl's Alcohol & Food

ROBERT K CHIN/ALAMY STOCK PHOTO ©

Top Shopping for Less

Madison Ave isn't for amateurs. Some of the globe's glitziest shops line the stretch from 60th St to 72nd St, with flagship boutiques from the world's top designers, including Chanel, Michael Kors and Prada.

A handful of consignment stores offer preloved designer deals; for gently worn top brands such as Louboutin, Fendi, and Dior try Michael's or La Boutique Resale..

parlor lets rip as a speakeasy by night. Cocktails ($15 to $25) are named after Upper East Side landmarks, such as 'Meet Me at the Met' and '2nd Avenue Subway.'

Beware: there's a dress code, so no sneakers, flip-flops, ripped jeans or T-shirts. (www.theuesnyc.com)

Auction House BAR

30 MAP P188, C1

Dark maroon doors lead into a candlelit hangout that's perfect for a relaxing drink. Victorian-style couches and fat, overstuffed easy chairs are strewn about the wood-floored rooms.

Take your well-mixed cocktail to a seat by the fireplace and admire the scene reflected in the gilt-edged mirrors propped up on the walls. (www.theauctionhousenyc.com)

Entertainment

Café Carlyle LIVE MUSIC

This swanky spot at the Carlyle Hotel (see 20 map p188, B3) draws top-shelf talent from Michael Feinstein to Kylie Minogue. Bring mucho bucks: the cover charge doesn't include food or drinks, and there's a minimum spend. The dress code is 'chic' – so gentlemen, please wear a jacket. (www.thecarlyle.com)

92nd Street Y ARTS CENTER

31 MAP P188, B1

In addition to its wide spectrum of concerts, dance performances, literary readings and family-friendly events, this nonprofit cultural center hosts an excellent lecture and conversation series. Filmmaker Ken Burns, cellist Yo-Yo Ma, comedian Steve Martin and novelist Salman Rushdie have all taken the stage here. (www.92y.org)

Shopping

Tiny Doll House ARTS & CRAFTS

32 MAP P188, C3

If the Carrie Stettheimer dollhouse at the Museum of the City of New York (p191) turned you on or you're otherwise in the market for a dream dollhouse, this fascinating shop is NYC's only store dedicated to dollhouses and miniature accessories. The tiny worlds offered here come in a variety of styles (Victorian, Chippendale, contemporary) and are rendered in stunning detail. (www.tinydollhouse newyorkcity.com)

Schaller & Weber

FOOD & DRINKS

33 MAP P188, C2

This award-winning charcuterie and delicatessen is a holdover from Yorkville's days as a German enclave.

It sells over 15 varieties of sausage made at its factory in Pennsylvania, including German classics such as *bauernwurst* and *weisswurst,* chicken bratwurst, cheddar-stuffed brat', plus Irish bangers, Polish kielbasa and more. It also stocks lots of imported European goodies such as cheese, pickles, wine and beer. (www. schallerweber.com)

Creel & Gow

GIFTS & SOUVENIRS

34 MAP P188, B4

Step into this eclectic cabinet of curios to eyeball one-of-a-kind objects sourced internationally by Jamie Creel and his team of world adventurers.

Taxidermied peacocks, silver-plated shells and centuries-old sketches are some of the gems you might find in this wonderfully wacky collection housed in a 19th-century town house. (https:// creelandgow.com)

Michael's

CLOTHING

35 MAP P188, B2

In operation since the 1950s, this vaunted Upper East Side resale store features high-end labels, including Chanel, Gucci, Prada and Jimmy Choo.Almost everything on display is less than two years old. It's pricey but cheaper than shopping on Madison Ave. (www. michaelsconsignment.com)

Shakespeare & Co

BOOKS

36 MAP P188, B5

No relation to the Paris seller, this popular bookstore with two locations is one of NYC's great indie options.

It has a wide array of contemporary fiction and nonfiction, and art and local history books, plus a small but unique collection of periodicals, while an Espresso book machine churns out print-on-demand titles.

A small cafe serves coffee, tea and light meals. (www.shakeandco. com)

La Boutique Resale

CLOTHING

37 MAP P188, B2

Upper East Side fashionistas had been emptying out their closets at the pioneering consignment and resale shop known as Encore since 1954 (even Jacqueline Kennedy Onassis sold her clothes here), but Encore took its final bow in 2019.

La Boutique Resale took over the space and kept the fire alive for its customers. Head upstairs to find the very best discounts. (www. laboutiqueresale.com)

Walking Tour

Feel the Pulse of Harlem Soul

Harlem: where Billie Holiday crooned; where acclaimed artist Romare Bearden pieced together his first collages; where Ralph Ellison penned Invisible Man, *his epic novel on truth and intolerance. Walk past elegant town houses, groove to sounds of African drums and feast on Southern-fried staples with Manhattan style. Vibrant and effusive, brooding and melancholy, this neighborhood is the deepest recess of New York's soul.*

Getting There

Harlem is north of Central Park in Manhattan.

S 2/3 to 125th St

❶ Malcolm Shabazz Harlem Market

Trawl this low-key, semi-enclosed market for a colorful array of African textiles, jewelry, drums, leather goods and oils.

❷ Sylvia's

Founded by Sylvia Woods in 1962, this Harlem icon has drawn locals, celebrities and even a few presidents with its lip-smackingly good down-home Southern cooking. (www.sylviasrestaurant.com)

❸ National Jazz Museum in Harlem

This small, Smithsonian-affiliated museum is a love letter to Harlem's Jazz Age, featuring important memorabilia like Duke Ellington's cream-white baby grand piano. Entrance is free with a $10 suggested donation. (www.jazzmuseuminharlem.org)

❹ Strivers' Row

The blocks of 138th and 139th Sts, also known as the the St Nicholas Historic District, are graced with 1890s town houses, once home to some of Harlem's greatest luminaries, like blues veteran WC Handy and singer-dancer Bill 'Bojangles' Robinson.

❺ Shrine

This mainstay on Harlem's nightlife circuit hosts an incredible nightly lineup of music, from calypso, Afropunk and French electro to Latin jazz and straight-up soul. (www.shrinenyc.com)

❻ Apollo Theater

One of the best places to catch a concert (www.apollotheater.org) in Harlem. Ella Fitzgerald debuted here in 1934 at one of the theater's earliest Amateur Nights; they still take place every Wednesday (February to November), notoriously tough crowds and all.

❼ Flamekeepers Hat Club

Harlem's Gilded Age lives on at this friendly corner boutique lined with dapper hats and caps. Can't decide? Seek owner Marc Williamson's keen eye. (www.flamekeepershatclub.com)

❽ Minton's Playhouse

Bebop was incubated at this formal jazz-and-dinner club, where greats like Thelonious Monk, Dizzy Gillespie and Charlie Parker were all regulars. Dress to impress and savor sweet grooves over decadent Southern fare. (www.mintonsharlem.com)

Explore
Upper West Side & Central Park

The Upper West Side is a slice of old-school elegance sandwiched between sprawling green spaces. Cultural institutions like Lincoln Center and the American Museum of Natural History act as anchors, but residential side streets give the neighborhood its charm. Walk down brownstone-lined blocks linking Central Park to the Hudson River, and you may feel like you've stepped out of a movie.

The Short List

- ***Central Park (p204)*** *Escaping the city's frantic urban madness by picnicking, row-boating and strolling.*
- ***Lincoln Center (p219)*** *Plunging into the sheer depth of artistic choices at this first-class arts center.*
- ***American Museum of Natural History (p210)*** *Walking among some of the world's largest dinosaurs.*
- ***Nicholas Roerich Museum (p210)*** *Taking a pilgrimage to Tibet via a beautiful 19th-century town house.*
- ***Riverside Park (p210)*** *Ambling along the Hudson waterfront as the sun goes down over the far shore.*

Getting There & Around

S Use the 1, 2 and 3 lines for between Broadway and the river; the B and C are best for museums and Central Park.

The M104 runs up Broadway; the M10 up the park's western edge. Crosstown routes at 66th, 72nd, 79th, 86th and 96th Sts head to the Upper East Side.

Neighbourhood Map on p208

Central Park (p204) INGUS KRUKLITIS/SHUTTERSTOCK ©

Top Experience

Ramble Through Central Park

With more than 800 acres of picturesque meadows, ponds and woods, Central Park might seem to be Manhattan in its raw state. But the park, designed by Frederick Law Olmsted and Calvert Vaux, is the result of serious engineering: thousands of workers shifted 10 million cartloads of soil to transform swamp and rocky outcroppings into the 'people's park' of today.

MAP P208, E4

www.centralparknyc.org

59th to 110th Sts, btwn Central Park W & Fifth Ave

S A/C, B/D to any stop btwn 59th St-Columbus Circle & Cathedral Pkwy (110th St)

Strawberry Fields

This tear-shaped **garden** serves as a memorial to former Beatle John Lennon, who lived directly across the street in the **Dakota Building** and was fatally shot there. It contains a grove of stately elms and a tiled mosaic that says, simply, 'Imagine.' The spot is officially designated a quiet zone, but you wouldn't know it from the multitude of tour guides and buskers who come here to vocalize – it's a hugely popular area of the park.

Bethesda Terrace & the Mall

The arched walkways of **Bethesda Terrace**, crowned by the magnificent **Bethesda Fountain**, at 72nd St, have long been a gathering area for New Yorkers. To the south is the **Mall,** featured in movies like *Breakfast at Tiffany's* and *Kramer vs. Kramer*, and offers a promenade shrouded in mature North American elms. The southern stretch, known as **Literary Walk**, is flanked by statues of famous authors.

Great Lawn & the Ramble

The **Great Lawn** is a massive emerald carpet at the center of the park, surrounded by ball fields and London plane trees. (It's where Simon & Garfunkel played their famous 1981 concert.) Immediately to the southeast is Delacorte Theater (p220), home to an annual Shakespeare in the Park festival, as well as **Belvedere Castle**, a Victorian folly with scenic panoramas. Further south is the leafy Ramble, a popular birding destination that leads to **the Lake** (www.centralpark.com) – a 20-acre pool with rocky outcroppings, a romantic bridge and opportunities for rowboat rentals on the northeastern tip.

★ Top Tips

- Hit up Central Park Bike Tours (p213), just one block south of the park, for bike rentals and guided tours.
- Avoid the carriage rides. They're expensive and a bitter source of controversy between animal-rights activists and carriage drivers.

Take a Break

- Consider packing a picnic from the assortment of gourmet goodies at Zabar's (p214), a few blocks from the park.
- Inside the park you can dine alfresco at casual Le Pain Quotidien (www.lepainquotidien.com), or stop by a food cart for snacks and drinks (be prepared with cash).

Central Park Zoo

This small **zoo** (www.centralparkzoo.com), which gained fame for its part in the DreamWorks animated movie *Madagascar*, is home to penguins, snow leopards and lemurs. Feeding times in the sea lion and penguin tanks make for a rowdy spectacle. The attached petting zoo, **Tisch Children's Zoo**, has baby doll sheep and mini-Nubian goats; it's perfect for small children.

Jacqueline Kennedy Onassis Reservoir

Don't miss your chance to walk or run around this 1.58-mile track near 90th St, which draws a slew of joggers in warmer months.

The 106-acre reservoir no longer distributes drinking water to residents, but serves as a gorgeous reflecting pool for the city skyline and flowering trees.

Nearby, at Fifth Ave and 90th St, is a statue of NYC Marathon founder Fred Lebow.

Conservatory Garden

For a little peace and quiet (as in no runners, cyclists or singing buskers), visit this 6-acre, formal garden – one of the park's official quiet zones. And it's beautiful to boot. Its three sections are designed in French, English and Italian styles, each with its own fountain.

It's bursting with crabapple trees, meandering boxwood and, in spring, offers a riot of flowers.

Conservatory Gardens

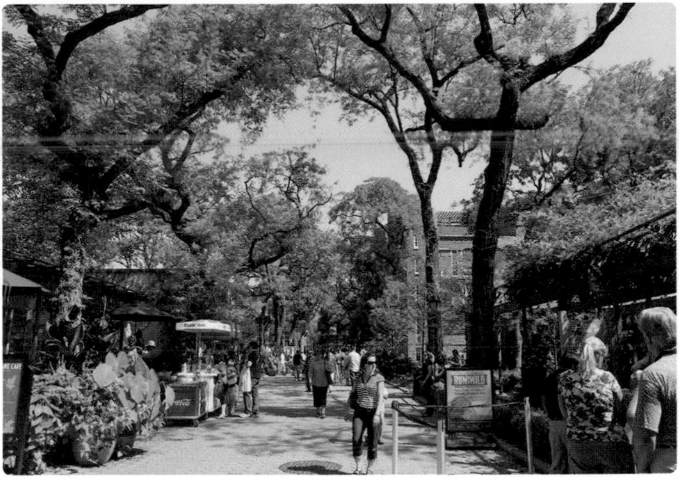

Central Park Zoo

Summer Happenings

During the warm months, Central Park is home to countless cultural events, many of which are free. The two most popular are Shakespeare in the Park (p220), which is managed by the Public Theater, and **SummerStage** (www.cityparksfoundation.org/summerstage), a series of free concerts.

Central Park Then & Now

In the 1850s this area of Manhattan was occupied by pig farms, a garbage dump, a bone-boiling operation and Seneca Village – the largest community of free African American property owners in pre–Civil War New York. After the city displaced the area's roughly 1600 residents, it took 20,000 laborers two decades to transform this terrain into a park. Today, Central Park has over 18,000 trees, 136 acres of woodland, 21 playgrounds and seven bodies of water – and more than 40 million visitors a year.

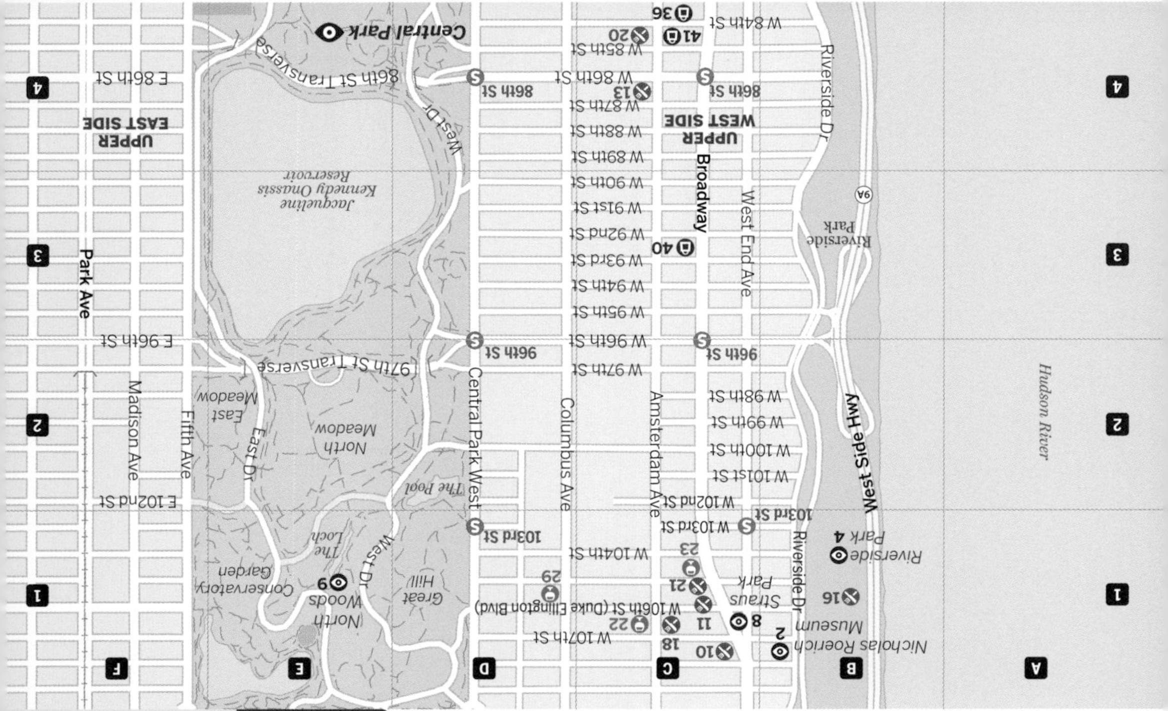

Hudson River

West Side Hwy

9A

Riverside Park

Riverside Park 4

Nicholas Roerich Museum 2

16

Riverside Dr

Straus Park

8

10

11

18

21

22

23

29

W 107th St

W 106th St (Duke Ellington Blvd)

W 104th St

W 103rd St

103rd St

W 102nd St

W 101st St

W 100th St

W 99th St

W 98th St

W 97th St

W 96th St

96th St

W 95th St

W 94th St

W 93rd St

W 92nd St

W 91st St

W 90th St

W 89th St

W 88th St

W 87th St

W 86th St

86th St

W 85th St

W 84th St

13

20

36

40

41

West End Ave

Broadway

Amsterdam Ave

Columbus Ave

Central Park West

UPPER WEST SIDE

Great Hill

The Pool

North Woods

9

The Loch

West Dr

Conservatory Garden

North Meadow

East Meadow

East Dr

97th St Transverse

Jacqueline Kennedy Onassis Reservoir

86th St Transverse

Central Park

Fifth Ave

Madison Ave

Park Ave

E 102nd St

E 96th St

E 86th St

UPPER EAST SIDE

A B C D E F

1 2 3 4

For reviews see
Top Experiences p204
Sights p210
Eating p212
Drinking p216
Entertainment p219
Shopping p220
500 m
0.25 miles
A
B
C
D
E
F
5
6
7
8
Hudson River
West Side Hwy
9A
Pier 1
Riverside Park South
Toga Bike Shop
West End Ave
Amsterdam Ave
Broadway
Columbus Ave
Central Park West
Fifth Ave
Madison Ave
Park Ave
W 82nd St
W 81st St
W 80th St
W 79th St
79th St
W 78th St
W 77th St
W 76th St
W 75th St
W 74th St
W 73rd St
W 72nd St
72nd St
W 71st St
W 70th St
W 69th St
W 68th St
W 67th St
W 66th St
66th St-Lincoln Center
W 65th St
W 64th St
W 62nd St
W 61st St
W 60th St
W 59th St
Lincoln Center
Columbus Circle
59th St-Columbus Circle
American Museum of Natural History
81st St-Museum of Natural History
New-York Historical Society
5 American Folk Art Museum
Great Lawn
Turtle Pond
Metropolitan Museum of Art
East Dr
79th St Transverse
The Ramble
The Lake
Bow Bridge
Conservatory Water
72nd St Transverse
The Mall
Sheep Meadow
West Dr
Center Dr
Literary Walk
65th St Transverse
Wollman Skating Rink
The Pond
6 Central Park Conservancy
5th Ave-59th St
Central Park South
E 79th St
E 72nd St
E 65th St
E 59th St
1
3
7
12
14
15
17
19
24
25
26
27
28
30
31
32
33
34
35
37
38
39

Sights

American Museum of Natural History

MUSEUM

1 MAP P208, D5

Founded in 1869, this classic museum contains a veritable wonderland of more than 34 million artifacts – including lots of menacing dinosaur skeletons – as well as the **Rose Center for Earth & Space**, which has a cutting-edge planetarium. From October through May, the museum is home to the **Butterfly Conservatory**, a vivarium featuring 500-plus butterflies from all over the world that will flutter about and land on your outstretched arm. (www.amnh.org)

Nicholas Roerich Museum

MUSEUM

2 MAP P208, B1

This compelling little collection, housed in a three-story town home from 1898, is a divine departure from megasized museums. It displays 150 paintings by the prolific Nicholas Konstantinovich Roerich (1874–1947), a Russian-born poet, philosopher and painter. His most remarkable works are his depictions of the Himalayas, where he and his family settled in 1928. Indeed, his mountainscapes are a wonder to behold: icy Tibetan peaks in bright swaths of blue, white, green and purple paint – similar in style to Georgia O'Keeffe and Rockwell Kent. (www.roerich.org)

New-York Historical Society

MUSEUM

3 MAP P208, D6

As the antiquated hyphenated name implies, the Historical Society is the city's oldest museum, founded in 1804 to preserve historical and cultural artifacts. Its collection of more than 60,000 objects is quirky and fascinating and includes everything from George Washington's inauguration chair to a 19th-century Tiffany ice-cream dish (gilded, of course). However, it's far from stodgy, having moved into the 21st century with renewed vigor and purpose. (www.nyhistory.org)

Riverside Park

PARK

4 MAP P208, B1

A classic beauty designed by Central Park creators Frederick Law Olmsted and Calvert Vaux, this waterside spot, running north on the Upper West Side and banked by the Hudson River from W 59th to 155th Sts, is lusciously leafy. Plenty of bike paths, playgrounds and dog runs make it a family favorite. Take to the trails at sunset, when nature's spectacular light show dips below Jersey's side of the Hudson. (www.riversideparknyc.org)

American Folk Art Museum

MUSEUM

5 MAP P208, D7

Admission is free at this tiny treasure trove of self-taught artistry featuring three small galleries with rotating exhibits. Kaleidoscopic quilts, hand-carved decoy ducks, whimsical sculptures and centuries-old sketchbooks are some of the works you might find inside. The gift shop is an equally unique assemblage of art: books, jewelry, accessories, scarves, home decor etc. (www.folkartmuseum.org)

Central Park Conservancy

WALKING

6 MAP P208, F8

The nonprofit organization that supports Central Park maintenance also offers year-round tours covering everything from woodland ecology to little-known park histories. Family-geared tours (including the Turtle Pond Tour) cost $5, but most tours cost $25, last roughly 90 minutes, and require advance booking. Tours start from various park locations; check the website for schedules and pricing. (www.centralparknyc.org/tours)

Wollman Skating Rink

SKATING

7 MAP P208, E8

Rent a set of skates to glide around this rink at the southeastern edge of Central Park. The rink is much larger than the one at Rockefeller Center, and views of Midtown's skyscrapers shooting above the treeline make for a magical experience. Once you've worked up an appetite, head to the rinkside cafe for soul food from Melba's. (www.wollmanskatingrink.com)

American Folk Art Museum

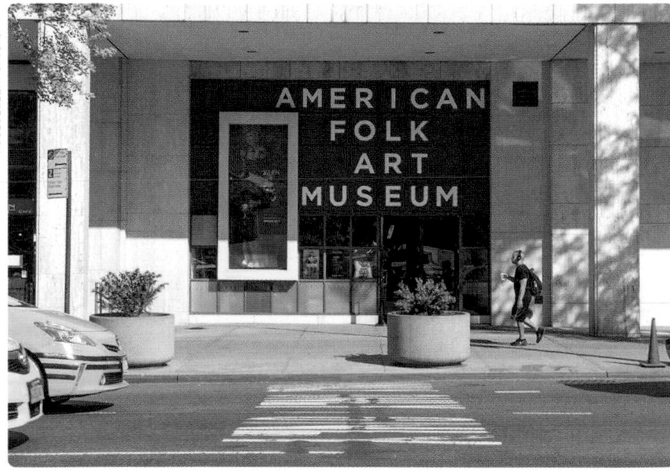

PIO3/SHUTTERSTOCK

Straus Park PARK

8 MAP P208, C1

This leafy little triangle is dedicated to the memory of Ida and Isidor Straus, a wealthy couple (Isidor owned Macy's) who died together in 1912 on the *Titanic*, when Ida insisted on staying with her husband of 41 years instead of boarding a lifeboat. A curving granite exedra bears a fitting biblical quote: 'Lovely and pleasant were they in their lives and in their death they were not divided.' (www.nycgovparks.org)

North Woods AREA

9 MAP P208, E1

This 40-acre arcadia on the upper reaches of Central Park feels more like the Adirondacks than the heart of Manhattan. Amble along the waterfall-linked **Loch**, a gentle tree-hugged stream, to spot scampering chipmunks, sunning turtles and the occasional raccoon.

Pause at the **Blockhouse**, the park's oldest-surviving structure, built as a military defense during the War of 1812. If you wander deep enough, skyscrapers disappear and traffic becomes but a murmur. (www.centralparknyc.org)

Eating

Absolute Bagels BAGELS $

10 MAP P208, C1

A bagel shop run by Thai immigrants might be puzzling to connoisseurs, but one thing's for sure: many folks – most of whom wait in

Levain

a line down the block – agree this is the city's best. With a degree in look-away decor and appalling coffee, it's all about the bagels: heft and crunch on point, perfectly boiled and wonderfully satisfying.

Mama's TOO! PIZZA $

11 MAP P208, C1

You'll understand why locals line up outside this bite-sized pizza shop once you tear into the Angry Nonna – a thick, square slab topped with crisped *soppressata cups*, melted mozzarella, Calabrian chili oil and hot honey. With pizza this good, the only reason to be angry is if you limit yourself to one slice. Seating is limited, but benches in Riverside Park (p210) are only two blocks away. (www.mamastoo.com)

Levain BAKERY $

12 MAP P208, C6

The original location of this national cookie chain remains its most charming. Descend the steep steps into its butter-scented basement, where fresh cookies cool on baking trays. Each dough ball is a 6oz lesson in decadence, but the chocolate-chip walnut earns highest marks: crunchy and gooey and a meal unto itself. (https://levainbakery.com)

Barney Greengrass DELI $$

13 MAP P208, C4

This Jewish-style deli still serves the same heaping dishes of eggs and salty lox, luxuriant caviar and melt-in-your-mouth chocolate babkas that first made it famous in 1908.

Eat breakfast at the casual tables amid crowded produce counters, or take lunch at the cafe in an adjoining room.

Order the smoked white fish and you'll see that the self-proclaimed 'Sturgeon King' more than lives up to the name. (www.barneygreengrass.com)

Cycling Central Park

The best way to cover Central Park's 840 acres is by bicycle. A full ride of the Central Park loop is 6.2 miles long, and takes in both hilly and flat terrain (the northern half is generally hillier than the south). Find more information and a map of the park's paths at the Central Park Conservancy website (www.centralparknyc.org).

For rentals try **Central Park Bike Tours** (www.centralparkbiketours.com) and **Toga Bike Shop** (Map p208, C7; www.togabikes.com). It's also possible to cycle the loop with Citi Bike, NYC's ubiquitous bike share program, though the program's docking system makes it more difficult to park bikes and explore along the way.

Bagel with a Schmear, Please

A bastion of gourmet kosher foodie-ism, sprawling local market **Zabar's** (www.zabars.com; 2245 Broadway, at W 80th St) has been a neighborhood fixture since the 1930s. And what a fixture it is!

It features a heavenly array of cheeses, meats, olives, caviar, smoked fish, pickles, dried fruits, nuts and baked goods, including pillowy, fresh-out-of-the-oven knishes (Eastern European–style potato dumplings wrapped in dough).

Cafe Luxembourg

BRASSERIE $$$

14 MAP P208, C7

It's no mystery why upper-crust locals have been knocking back cocktails at this French bistro since the 1980s: the setting is understatedly elegant, the staff are genuinely friendly and there's an outstanding food menu to boot.

The classics – steak tartare, *moules frites* (mussels and fries), seasonal roast chicken – are all deftly executed, and the proximity to the Lincoln Center makes it a perfect preshow destination to refuel and prepare for the packed night ahead. (www.cafeluxembourg.com)

Jin Ramen

JAPANESE $$

15 MAP P208, C5

This buzzing little joint off Amsterdam Ave serves delectable bowls of piping hot ramen. *Tonkotsu* (pork broth) ramen is a favorite, though vegetarians also have tantalizing options.

Don't neglect the appetizers: *shishito* peppers, pork buns and *hijiki* salad. The mix of rustic wood elements, exposed bulbs and red industrial fixtures gives the place a cozy vibe. (www.jinramen.com)

Ellington in the Park

AMERICAN $$

16 MAP P208, B1

Grab an upper-level picnic table to gorge on burgers and beer at this two-tiered outdoor restaurant within Riverside Park.

The food is fine, but the ambience is fantastic. Gymnastic rings below and a dog run above make for captivating people-watching, and if you arrive before twilight, you can soak in the sun setting beyond the Hudson. Open April through October. (https://ellingtoninthepark.com)

Peacefood Cafe

VEGAN $$

17 MAP P208, C5

This bright and airy vegan haven dishes up a popular fried seitan panini (served on homemade focaccia and topped with cashew cheese, arugula, tomatoes and pesto), as well as pizzas, roasted-vegetable plates and an excellent quinoa salad.

There are daily raw specials, energy-fueling juices and rich desserts, plus a more substantial dinner menu served 5pm to 9:30pm. (www.peacefoodcafe.com)

Bánh

VIETNAMESE **$$**

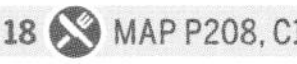
18 MAP P208, C1

Head to the Upper West Side's far reaches for home-style Vietnamese food so authentic you'll think you're in Hanoi.

Sticky mung-bean rice cakes (made with meat or mushrooms) and *bun cha* (a BBQ sampler with smoky pork skewers, lettuce wraps and noodles) are favorites, but the many variations of *banh mí*, served on toasty baguettes, make the trek worthwhile. (www.banhny.com)

Gray's Papaya

HOT DOGS **$**

19 MAP P208, C6

It doesn't get more New York than bellying up to this classic stand-up joint – founded by a former partner of crosstown rival Papaya King (p193) – in the wake of a beer bender. The lights are bright, the color palette is 1970s and the hot dogs are unpretentiously good. (www.grayspapayanyc.com)

Jacob's Pickles

AMERICAN **$$**

20 MAP P208, C4

Jacob's elevates the humble pickle to exalted status at this dark, loud and boisterous good-time eatery. Aside from briny cukes and other

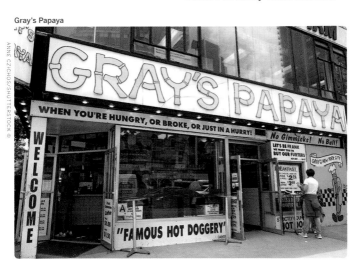

Gray's Papaya

preserves, you'll find heaping portions of upscale comfort food, such as catfish tacos, chicken and pancakes, and cheeseburger mac 'n' cheese.

The biscuits are top-notch. Two dozen or so draft craft beers showcase brews from coast to coast. (www.jacobspickles.com)

Silver Moon Bakery BAKERY $

21 MAP P208, C1

A small patisserie and boulangerie that brings a bit of Left Bank love to Morningside Heights.

Folks line up in droves for the baked goods and sweet treats of Judith Norell, who decided to hang up her harpsichord and flee to baking school in Paris before opening Silver Moon. (www.silvermoonbakery.com)

Drinking

Nobody Told Me COCKTAIL BAR

22 MAP P208, C1

Be thankful you got the memo: this casual bar is the coolest cocktail joint within a 10-block radius.

Slink inside the floral-wallpapered interior for craft concoctions and shareable plates of elevated bar food, including berbere-spiced eggplant dip and a yummy burger hugged by a Hawaiian roll. Grab a front booth in warm weather – picture windows open to the street, making them the bar's best seats. (www.nobodytoldme.nyc)

Plowshares Coffee COFFEE

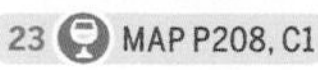

Plowshares got in the specialty coffee game way back in 2008, when this small-but-exquisite espresso spot opened in the Bloomingdale district of the UWS.

Your coffee is pulled from the Pagani of espresso machines: an $18,000 hand-built Slayer, of which just about as many exist as do the aforementioned made-to-order Italian car. It's a connoisseur's delight. (www.plowsharescoffee.com)

Empire Rooftop ROOFTOP BAR

24 MAP P208, D8

Sprawled across 8000 sq ft of the Empire Hotel's rooftop, this scenic bar is one of New York's most expansive drinking spaces in the sky. A bright, glass-roofed wing strewn with palms and sofas is perfect for winter and has a retractable roof for summer, and there's a handful of outdoor terraces.

Reserve a table or you might get turned away. (www.empirehotelnyc.com)

Gebhard's Beer Culture CRAFT BEER

25  MAP P208, C6

One of two locations in the city (the other is in Hell's Kitchen), cozy Gebhard's is one of the most serious hophead havens on the Upper West Side. You'll find 16 taps of New York–heavy craft, but brews can flow from anywhere, be

New York City on Page & Screen

New York has been the setting of countless works of literature, television and film. From critical commentaries on class and race to the lighter foibles of falling in love, these stories are not just entertainment, but carefully placed tiles in NYC's diverse mosaic of tales.

Books

A Tree Grows in Brooklyn (Betty Smith; 1943) An Irish American family living in the Williamsburg tenements of the 20th century.

Another Country (James Baldwin; 1962) Darts between Greenwich Village and Harlem, exploring race, sexuality and nationalism in the 1950s.

Down These Mean Streets (Piri Thomas; 1967) Memoirs of tough times growing up in Spanish Harlem.

The Amazing Adventures of Kavalier & Clay (Michael Chabon; 2000) Touches upon Brooklyn, escapism and the nuclear family.

Just Kids (Patti Smith; 2010) A real-life snapshot of bohemian Manhattan in the 1960s and '70s.

Vanishing New York (Jeremiah Moss; 2017) Non-fiction work exploring gentrification and 21st-century NYC policy.

Films

The Apartment (1960) Jack Lemmon stars in this rom-com where a clerk offers his apartment as a pad for philandering higher-ups.

Taxi Driver (1976) Martin Scorsese's story of a troubled Vietnam vet turned taxi driver.

Do the Right Thing (1989) Spike Lee's critically acclaimed comedy-drama probes the racial turmoil lurking beneath the surface.

Paris Is Burning (1991) A dazzling and intimate documentary about NYC's underground drag ball scene in the 1980s.

Angels in America (2003) Mike Nichols' movie version of Tony Kushner's Broadway play recalls the AIDS crisis in 1985 Manhattan.

West Side Story (2021) Stephen Spielberg's remake of the classic musical follows rival gangs fighting for space in a changing city.

it California or Canada. Wash it all down with burgers, nachos, hot dogs and other alcohol-absorbing pub grub. (www.beerculture.nyc/gebhards)

Dead Poet

BAR

26 MAP P208, C5

This narrow, mahogany-paneled pub is a neighborhood favorite. It takes its Guinness pours seriously, and features cocktails named after deceased local bards, including a Walt Whitman Long Island iced tea ($14) and an Edgar Allan Poe made with Misguided Spirits vodka ($15). Feeling adventurous? Order the signature cocktail ($16), a secret recipe of seven alcohols – you even get to keep the glass. (www.thedeadpoet.com)

Irving Farm Roasters

COFFEE

27 MAP P208, C5

Tucked into a little ground-floor shop, the Upper West Side branch of this popular local coffee chain is bigger on the inside – beyond the coffee counter the space opens up into a backroom with a sunny skylight. Enjoy a menu of light meals along with your freshly pulled espresso or on-tap cold brew. No wi-fi. (www.irvingfarm.com)

Owl's Tail

COCKTAIL BAR

28 MAP P208, C6

A snazzy cocktail bar that feels more downtown than UWS with its cozy banquet sofa seating, tiled flooring and industrial lighting. Owl art, from Northwest Coast style to wooden carvings to a stupendous

Lincoln Center

EILEEN_10/SHUTTERSTOCK ©

mural, peppers the place. The highly social L-shaped bar is your perfect perch for beat-the-heat cocktails like Bicycle Thief (Campari, gin, grapefruit, lemon, simple syrup and seltzer). (www.owlstail.com)

Bob's Your Uncle BAR

29 MAP P208, D1

This is the kind of friendly, easygoing neighborhood bar you wish was your local. (We do, anyway.) Beverages focus on craft brews (10 rotating selections on tap) and unfussy, inexpensive cocktails ($12). The exposed brick walls, industrial fixtures and lack of sport-playing TVs provide major Brooklyn vibes. Kudos if you can name all the famous Bobs adorning the walls: Marley, Hope, Dylan, Sponge... (www.bobsyouruncle.nyc)

Entertainment

Metropolitan Opera House OPERA

30 MAP P208, C8

New York's premier opera company is the place to see classics like *La Boheme*, *Madame Butterfly* and Wagner's epic *Ring* cycle. It also hosts premieres and revivals from contemporary composers like meditative minimalist Philip Glass and musical theater doyenne Jeanine Tesori. The season runs from September to June. Tickets start at $25 and can get close to $500. (www.metopera.org)

Lincoln Center

The stark arrangement of gleaming modernist temples that is **Lincoln Center** (Map p208, C8; www.lincolncenter.org) houses some of Manhattan's most important performance companies: the New York Philharmonic, the New York City Ballet and the Metropolitan Opera.

The lobby of the iconic Opera House is dressed with brightly saturated murals by painter Marc Chagall.

Various other venues are tucked in and around the 16-acre campus, including a theater, two film-screening centers and the renowned Juilliard School for performing arts.

New York City Ballet DANCE

31 MAP P208, C8

This prestigious company was first directed by the renowned Russian-born choreographer George Balanchine in the 1940s. Today, it's the largest dance organization in the US, performing from September through May at Lincoln Center's David H Koch Theater. Patrons ages 13 to 30 can nab $30 rush tickets. During the holidays the troupe is best known for its annual production of *The Nutcracker* (tickets go on sale in September; book early). (www.nycballet.com)

New York Philharmonic
CLASSICAL MUSIC

32 ✪ MAP P208, C7

The oldest professional orchestra in the US (dating to 1842) holds its season every year at David Geffen Hall – a concert space given a $550-million makeover in 2022. Internationally acclaimed music director Jaap van Zweden leads the orchestra, which plays a mix of classics (Tchaikovsky, Mahler, Haydn) and contemporary works, as well as concerts geared toward children. (www.nyphil.org)

Delacorte Theater
THEATER

33 ✪ MAP P208, E5

Every summer the Public Theater (p84) heads uptown to present its fabulous free productions of **Shakespeare in the Park**, which founder Joseph Papp began in 1954, before the lovely, leafy, open-air theater was even built. Productions are usually superb and the experience is magical. Waiting in line for tickets is a New Yorker rite of passage, though you can also try the digital lottery on the TodayTix app. (www.publictheater.org)

Film at Lincoln Center
CINEMA

34 ✪ MAP P208, C8

Film at Lincoln Center is one of New York's cinematic gems, providing an invaluable platform for a wide gamut of documentary, feature, independent, foreign and avant-garde art pictures. Films screen in one of two facilities at Lincoln Center: the Elinor Bunin Munroe Film Center, a more intimate, experimental venue, or the Walter Reade Theater with wonderfully wide, screening-room-style seats. (www.filmlinc.com)

Beacon Theatre
LIVE MUSIC

This historic 1928 theater is a perfect medium-sized venue with 2829 seats (not a terrible one in the house) and a constant flow of popular acts from Radiohead to the Dalai Lama (plus comedians like Jerry Seinfeld and Patton Oswalt). A 2009 restoration left the gilded interiors – a mix of Greek, Roman, Renaissance and rococo design elements – totally sparkling. (www.beacontheatre.com)

Shopping

Magpie
ARTS & CRAFTS

36 MAP P208, C4

This charming little shop carries a wide range of ecofriendly objects: elegant stationery, beeswax candles, hand-painted mugs, organic-cotton scarves, recycled-resin necklaces, hand-dyed felt journals and wooden earth puzzles are a few things that may catch your eye.

Most products are fair-trade, made of sustainable materials or locally designed and made. (www.magpienewyork.com)

Grand Bazaar NYC

MARKET

37 MAP P208, C6

One of the oldest open-air shopping spots in the city, this friendly, well-stocked flea market is a perfect spot to browse away a lazy Upper West Side Sunday morning. You'll find a little bit of everything here, including vintage and contemporary furnishings, antique maps, custom eyewear, hand-woven scarves, handmade jewelry and so much more. (www.grandbazaarnyc.org)

Icon Style

VINTAGE

38 MAP P208, C7

This tiny gem of a vintage shop specializes in antique, fine and costume jewelry dating from the 1700s to present day, but also stocks carefully curated dresses, gloves, bags and hats. Half of the shop is covered in strikingly restored apothecary units, with the goods displayed in open drawers. Stop by and indulge your inner Grace Kelly. (www.iconstyle.net)

Westsider Books

BOOKS

39 MAP P208, C5

This great little shop is packed to the gills with rare and used books, including a good selection of fiction and illustrated tomes. There are even some first editions available. It has a smattering of vintage vinyl, but most of its collection can be found about eight blocks south at Westsider Records. (www.westsiderbooks.com)

Shishi

FASHION & ACCESSORIES

40 MAP P208, C3

Shishi is a delightful Israeli-owned boutique stocking a constantly changing selection of stylish, affordable apparel: elegant sweaters, sleeveless shift dresses and eye-catching jewelry from Brazilian designers, among others. (All its clothes are wash-and-dry friendly, too.) It's fun for browsing, and with the enthusiastic staff kitting you out in the glamorous changing area, you'll feel like you have your own personal stylist. (www.shishiboutique.com)

West Side Kids

TOYS

41 MAP P208, C4

A great place to pick up a gift for that little someone special, no matter their age. In stock are lots of hands-on activities and fun educational games, as well as puzzles, mini musical instruments, science kits, magic sets, old-fashioned wooden trains and New York–themed kids' books. (www.westsidekidsnyc.com)

Explore Brooklyn: Williamsburg & Bushwick

Brooklyn's image as the global epicenter of 'cool' is most apparent in Williamsburg, with blocks of buzzy bars, restaurants and boutiques. Head east for Bushwick, an industrial neighborhood dipped in street art and colonized by a cutting-edge crew. Once up-and-coming, both of these neighborhoods have undoubtedly arrived.

The Short List

- ***House of Yes (p229)*** *Dancing till dawn at Bushwick's most funky and fabulous nightlife venue.*
- ***McCarren Park (p226)*** *People-watching in this sprawling green space while enjoying a summer picnic.*
- ***Eclectic Shopping (p232)*** *Rummaging through racks for vintage clothes and unique souvenirs at spots like Brooklyn Artists & Fleas.*
- ***Bushwick Collective (p227)*** *Admiring building-sized murals on blocks painted by international artists.*
- ***Craft Beer (p230)*** *Tasting what's on tap in NYC's microbrew mecca.*

Getting There & Around

S L and J/M/Z trains run through Williamsburg and Bushwick. Take the G to connect to South Brooklyn and Queens.

The B60 runs through Williamsburg and Bushwick, the B62 connects Williamsburg to Greenpoint and the B52 connects Bushwick to Bed-Stuy.

Neighborhood Map on p224

The House of Yes (p229) GUILLAUME GAUDET/LONELY PLANET ©

For reviews see

Sights	p226
Eating	p227
Drinking	p229
Entertainment	p232
Shopping	p232

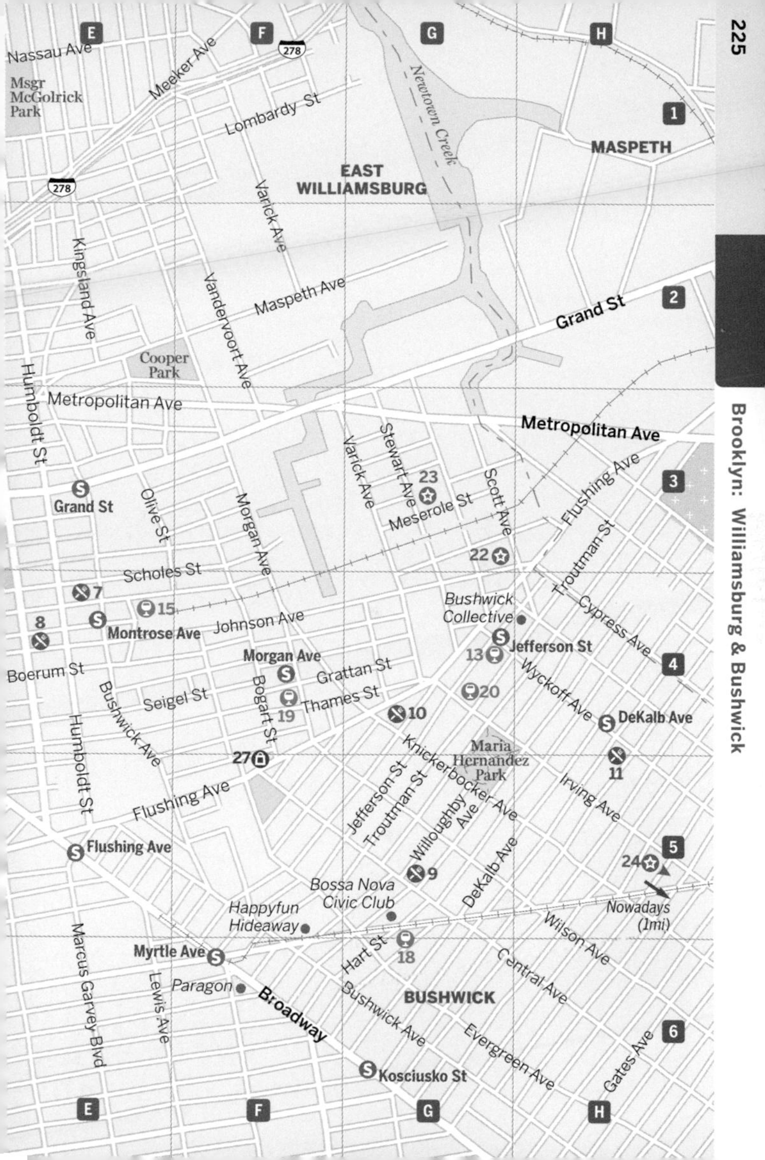
E
F
G
H
278
Nassau Ave
Msgr McGolrick Park
Meeker Ave
Lombardy St
Newtown Creek
1
MASPETH
EAST WILLIAMSBURG
Varick Ave
Kingsland Ave
Vandervoort Ave
Maspeth Ave
2
Grand St
Cooper Park
Humboldt St
Metropolitan Ave
Metropolitan Ave
Stewart Ave
Varick Ave
23
Scott Ave
Flushing Ave
3
Grand St
Olive St
Morgan Ave
Meserole St
22
Troutman St
Scholes St
7
15
Bushwick Collective
Cypress Ave
8
Montrose Ave
Johnson Ave
Jefferson St
13
4
Boerum St
Morgan Ave
Grattan St
Wyckoff Ave
Bushwick Ave
Seigel St
Bogart St
Thames St
19
20
DeKalb Ave
10
Humboldt St
27
Knickerbocker Ave
Maria Hernandez Park
11
Irving Ave
Flushing Ave
Jefferson St
Troutman St
Willoughby Ave
DeKalb Ave
Flushing Ave
5
24
9
Bossa Nova Civic Club
Nowadays (1mi)
Happyfun Hideaway
Wilson Ave
Myrtle Ave
Hart St
18
Central Ave
Marcus Garvey Blvd
Lewis Ave
Paragon
Broadway
BUSHWICK
Bushwick Ave
Evergreen Ave
Gates Ave
6
Kosciusko St

Sights

McCarren Park

PARK

1 MAP P224, D2

Brooklynites cram into this 35-acre park connecting Williamsburg and Greenpoint on summer weekends for all-day fun. Splash in the public pool, crash a family picnic or catch an acoustic jam session before refueling at McCarren Park House – a high-quality concession stand with ice cream, frozen margaritas and coffee from local start-up Blank Street. (www.nycgovparks.org/parks/mccarren-park)

City Reliquary

MUSEUM

2 MAP P224, C3

Walk through an antique subway turnstile into this tiny museum dedicated to Big Apple ephemera. The three-room collection contains an oddball mix of memorabilia like Lady Liberty figurines, chunks from landmark buildings and a shrine honoring Brooklyn Dodgers star Jackie Robinson. Check the website's event calendar to catch occasional readings, burlesque shows and lectures in the art-filled backyard. (www.cityreliquary.org)

Williamsburg Bridge

BRIDGE

3 MAP P224, A3

Pause at Bedford Ave and Broadway to admire this steel suspension bridge built in 1903, then take the mile-plus trek linking its namesake Brooklyn neighborhood to the Lower East Side. Flanked by bubblegum-pink fencing and

Williamsburg Bridge

littered with graffiti, the industrial pedestrian-and-cyclist path leads to impressive East River views, including the Empire State Building and Manhattan and Brooklyn Bridges.

Brooklyn Brewery

BREWERY

4 MAP P224, C1

Open since 1996, this brewery housed in a former matzo factory is the big daddy of Brooklyn's contemporary craft-beer boom. Soak up tasty local suds in the taproom, or book a 45-minute tour of its facilities. Tours from Monday to Friday include tastings of three experimental beers, plus history and insight into the brewery; reserve a spot online. Shorter tours on Sunday don't include tastings but come gratis. Note: sandals and high-heeled shoes aren't allowed on tours. (www.brooklynbrewery.com)

Marsha P Johnson State Park

PARK

5 MAP P224, B1

The first New York State Park named after a groundbreaking LGBTIQ+ icon has many reasons to be proud: an unobstructed panorama of Manhattan's steely skyline, 19th-century remnants from its cargo-handling past and green spaces perfect for waterfront picnics. Visit on summer Saturdays for the Smorgasburg (p228) food fest, and your cup will runneth over. (www.parks.ny.gov/parks/155)

Art Outdoors

Bushwick is the center of New York's prolific street-art scene, with blocks of buildings covered in murals.

Much of this is thanks to the **Bushwick Collective** (Map p224, H4; http://thebushwickcollective.com), an outdoor gallery curated by neighborhood native Joe Ficalora, who invites some of the world's most talented wall-scrawlers to create new works every year. Walk along Jefferson and Troutman Sts between Cypress and Knickerbocker Aves to admire the collection; more art – including graffiti and paste-ups – can be found near the Morgan Ave L stop, particularly on Seigel and Grattan Sts.

Eating

Lilia

ITALIAN $$$

6 MAP P224, C2

This pasta restaurant in a former auto shop cranks out handmade noodles tastier than an Italian *nonna*'s. Take a bite of the *cacio e pepe* (cheese and pepper) fritters before diving fork-first into a plate of carbohydrate heaven. True divinity comes in the form of sheep's milk cheese agnolotti, bathed in a buttery honey sauce. An adjoining cafe serves espresso, sandwiches and sweets. (www.lilianewyork.com)

Smash a Smorgasburg

Every Saturday from April to October, foodies file into Marsha P Johnson State Park to sample hand-held treats at this open-air culinary bazaar (www.smorgasburg.com). Expect an array of goodies sold by dozens of local vendors: Mexican ice pops, spaghetti donuts, rainbow-colored grilled cheese, vegan plantain bowls and craft cocktails just scratch the surface. Sister Smorg events pop up in downtown Manhattan and Brooklyn's Prospect Park on Friday and Sunday, respectively.

Champs Diner

VEGAN **$**

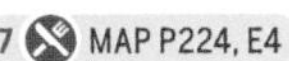

7 MAP P224, E4

Retro diner style gets the vegan treatment at this outpost for plant-based comfort food. Plop into a 1950s black booth to gorge on classics like chicken and waffles, Philly cheese steaks, and piles of pancakes. The jumbo-size portions put most NYC diners to shame. Weekend brunch sees lines out the door – if you don't want to wait, head around the corner and try the brunch at local bar Tradesman (www.champsdiner.com)

Win Son Bakery

TAIWANESE **$$**

8 MAP P224, E4

Stop by this counter-service cafe for Taiwanese takes on pastries and sandwiches. Mochi donuts and *bolo bao* (pineapple buns) make sweet morning treats, while crispy fried chicken and scallion pancakes give good reason to return for lunch or dinner. Taiwanese devotees can continue their bao binge by skipping across the street to Win Son, the bakery's popular sit-down mother restaurant. (www.winsonbrooklyn.com)

Le Garage

FRENCH **$$**

9 MAP P224, G5

The mother-daughter duo behind this classy-casual French bistro brings Parisian panache to a quiet corner of Bushwick. Nab a seat by the yolk-yellow accent wall to feast on mussels *marinière,* duck breast or a roast chicken for two, while sipping fizzy cocktails named after famous French dames like Coco Chanel and Marie Antoinette. (www.legaragebrooklyn.com)

Bunna Cafe

ETHIOPIAN **$$**

10 MAP P224, G4

Forget utensils at this cozy veggie restaurant. Ethiopian is best when scooped by hand with strips of tangy *injera,* a pancake-style sourdough.

Sample the menu by ordering a shareable platter with dollops of classic dishes like gingery collard greens and red lentils in berbere sauce, then wash it down with *bunna* (Ethiopian coffee spiced with cardamom and cloves). (https://bunnaethiopia.net)

Taqueria Al Pastor MEXICAN $

11 MAP P224, H5

Bushwick is chockablock with mouthwatering Mexican joints, but this no-frills taco counter earns the highest praise. Its eponymous taco, a made-to-order corn tortilla topped with thinly sliced pork and cubed pineapple, makes a satisfying light snack. To go whole hog, try the *volcane* – a crunchy tortilla bursting with cheese, salsa, onions, cilantro and guacamole. (www.taqueriaalpastor.nyc)

Diner AMERICAN $$$

12 MAP P224, A3

When this hipster haven started serving locally sourced, seasonal eats from an antique dining car in 1999, it was one of a kind. Since then, Brooklyn has birthed countless restaurants copying its retro vibe and new-American menu. Although the neighborhood has gentrified over the years, this eatery's trendsetting appeal remains. You can't beat friendly service and a juicy burger. (www.dinernyc.com)

Drinking

House of Yes CLUB

13 MAP P224, G4

Burlesque performers, drag artists and circus acts set the stage at this hedonistic warehouse venue with Burning Man flair. Join the eclectic crowd of outrageously costumed attendees by wearing something adventurous and stepping to everything from disco to house music. (www.houseofyes.org)

Maison Premiere COCKTAIL BAR

14 MAP P224, B3

Visit the green fairy at this oyster-and-cocktail bar and you might feel transported to 19th-century New Orleans. Absinthe flows from a marble fountain, soft jazz bounces off fleur-de-lis adorned walls and vintage pulleys are used for flushing the loo. Grab a seat on the plant-fringed patio or slurp down shellfish from the raw bar in back. (www.maisonpremiere.com)

3 Dollar Bill GAY

15 MAP P224, E4

This historic brewery-turned-club might date back to 1860, but there's nothing old about Brooklyn's biggest self-proclaimed 'queer bar'. Popular DJs and drag queens regularly pack the 10,000-sq-ft space with the borough's most colorful residents. See big-name performers strut their stuff, twirl on the industrial outdoor dance floor or keep it low-key at the bar near the entrance. Check the website for upcoming events. (www.3dollarbillbk.com)

Four Horsemen WINE BAR

16 MAP P224, C3

LCD Soundsystem frontman James Murphy is the owner behind this Michelin-starred natural wine bar with an exceptional food

Brooklyn's Craft-Beer Revolution

Before Brooklyn was synonymous with Biggie Smalls hip-hop and Lena Dunham hipsters, it was known for something headier: hops. As German immigrants flooded New York in the 19th century, breweries sprang up around the borough, turning Kings County into a lager Elysium.

By the turn of the century, it seemed like the tap would run forever. Brooklyn was home to nearly 50 breweries, and a 12-block stretch linking Williamsburg and Bushwick earned the nickname 'Brewer's Row' thanks to its near-dozen suds-focused establishments. But as the 20th century marched forward, the businesses dried up. By 1976, all of Brooklyn's beer makers were gone, leaving behind only shells of the former factories.

It took over a decade to turn the tap back on, starting with Brooklyn Brewery (p227), and now the borough is at the forefront of yet another pint-sized revolution. While most of America's microbrew scene struggles with identity (favoring makers who are white and male), Brooklyn's craft chemists are increasingly diverse. Women-owned Talea, Black-owned Daleview Biscuits and Beer (located in Prospect Lefferts Gardens) and LGBTIQ+-founded distribution companies Dyke Beer and Gay Beer make space at the bar for all people and palates. And that's just a short list of what Brooklyn's got on tap.

menu. The vino list of more than 40 pages might feel overwhelming, but with knowledgeable staff, you don't need to be an oenophile to find a palate pleaser. Order half glasses to take advantage of the expansive selection. (www.fourhorsemenbk.com)

Talea BREWERY

17 MAP P224, D2

New York's first women-owned brewery is a refreshing take on the city's craft-suds scene. Order a flight of fruit-forward beers while lounging in the roomy pastel-tiled interior, or nab a four-pack to crack open in nearby McCarren Park (p226). If beer isn't your thing, consider joining type-happy freelancers sipping coffee and kombucha in the morning. (www.taleabeer.com)

Mood Ring BAR

18 MAP P224, G6

Tattooed 20-somethings with a zeal for the zodiac get sweaty on the dance floor at this ultrainclusive, astrology-themed cocktail club. Order sign-specific drinks from the bar ($11 to $12) before floating away to electronic music in the room's celestial pink haze. (www.instagram.com/moodringnyc)

SEY Coffee

COFFEE

19 MAP P224, F4

If you think of good coffee like a glass of fine wine, the baristas at this Nordic-style roaster will gladly serve as your sommeliers. Sey's mad-scientist attention to detail ensures impeccable brews, plus the presentation is artful and the atrium-style setting is awash in natural light. (www.seycoffee.com)

Nook

CAFE

Find a bookshelf-carved cranny and curl up in an armchair at this friendly coffee-and-craft-beer 'parlour.' Laptops take over the large communal table for the nine-to-five slog, while tipsy troops tumble barside for evening events like trivia, comedy and jazz. A yummy spot for a morning pick-me-up. (https://nookbk.com)

Westlight

ROOFTOP BAR

21 MAP P224, C1

Views from the William Vale hotel's 22nd-floor terrace don't quit. Manhattan sparkles westward, Queens glitters up north, and bits of Brooklyn ring the rest. Vistas inside remain spectacular, thanks to floor-to-ceiling windows and a design that knows it's second fiddle to the panorama. (www.westlightnyc.com)

Brooklyn Flea Market (p20)

GABRIEL12/SHUTTERSTOCK ©

Entertainment

Elsewhere
LIVE MUSIC

22 MAP P224, G3

Rap, rock and rave music are just a few styles you'll hear inside this furniture-factory-turned-concert-venue in East Williamsburg. Float around the three-floor maze of concert halls, each with a different stage, or head to the rooftop in summer to catch indie and emerging artists serenading crowds as the sun sets. (www.elsewherebrooklyn.com)

Avant Gardner
CONCERT VENUE

23 MAP P224, G3

Dust off your dance shoes before seeing a show at East Williamsburg's 80,000-sq-ft electronic dance music palace. A diverse lineup of DJs and singers grace three indoor stages year-round, but seasonal concert hall Brooklyn Mirage is the complex's crowning achievement. This open-air space features massive projection screens and catwalks with Manhattan skyline views. (www.avant-gardner.com)

Bushwick Starr
THEATER

24 MAP P224, H5

This innovative Off-Off Broadway theater company transformed a former dairy factory into a home for New York's brightest stage stars of tomorrow. Big-name creatives like Jeremy O'Harris (author of *Slave Play*) occasionally present new works, but don't mistake this neighborhood black box for Great White Way glitz. The 90-seat theater isn't a commercial venue – it's a refuge for the avant-garde. (www.thebushwickstarr.org)

Shopping

Artists & Fleas
MARKET

25 MAP P224, B2

Every weekend, local artists and designers assemble at this indoor market near Marsha P Johnson State Park (p227) to sell a well-curated mix of goods like handcrafted jewelry, used vinyl, art prints and a museum-worthy selection of vintage clothes. DJ tunes set the mood. Chelsea Market houses a separate location with different vendors, open daily. (www.artistsandfleas.com)

Spoonbill & Sugartown
BOOKS

26 MAP P224, B2

Leaf through piles of new and used books at this independent outpost for everything from eye-popping art tomes to recently released bestsellers. Magazine lovers can pore over pages from rare publications, and there's a small children's lit section tucked in a back corner. (www.spoonbillbooks.com)

Catland
GIFTS & SOUVENIRS

27 MAP P224, F5

The neon sign proclaiming this a 'witch shop' might inspire images of a green-skinned sorceress, but

Up All Night in Brooklyn

A small community of up-and-coming artists run Bushwick's night-life scene; the DJs you hear today might be traveling internationally tomorrow. Here are my favorite spots for drinking and dancing.

Paragon (Map p224, F6; www.instagram.com/paragonbroadway) This three-floor discotheque is like dance-club church.

Nowadays (https://nowadays.nyc) The massive outdoor space makes for lively summer dance parties.

Pokito (Map p224, B3; www.pokito.nyc) A tiny bar with quirky decor and tasty cocktails.

Bossa Nova Civic Club (Map p224, G5; http://bossanovacivicclub.com) This intimate techno club is a beloved neighborhood mainstay.

Happyfun Hideaway (Map p224, F5; www.facebook.com/happyfun-hideaway) A LGBTIQ+-friendly tropical-themed bar that served as inspiration for Mood Ring.

Recommended by Bowen Goh
co-owner of the Bushwick-based bar Mood Ring (p231) with Vanessi Li

this lair is more pagan palace than silver-screen camp. Crystals, tarot cards and astrology books share shelves with sage bundles and pheasant feet. (www.catlandbooks.com)

BEAM

DESIGN

28 MAP P224, A2

This quirky home-goods collection near the Brooklyn waterfront is artsy-fartsy, fresh and fun. Browse a colorful assortment of accessories like pillows, vases, glassware and art before eyeing flamboyant furniture ideal for a creative's loft in Williamsburg. (https://beambk.com)

DS & Durga

PERFUME

29 MAP P224, B2

An olfactory tour of this petite Brooklyn-made fragrance shop is like traveling the world through scents. Cowboy Grass plants itself in the Wild West with smoky sage-brush; Jazmin Yucatán, a melange of sweet passion fruit and flower. Perfumes, candles, lotions and soaps. (www.dsanddurga.com)

Walking Tour

Time Travel in Brooklyn Heights

Ogle stately brownstones and wood-frame row houses around this neighborhood's leafy streets for a snapshot of bygone Brooklyn. With over 600 homes predating the Civil War, Brooklyn Heights is Kings County's crowning achievement in historic preservation. Discover stories behind the eye-catching architecture before imbibing at a retro cocktail club or perusing local boutiques on Montague and Atlantic Aves.

Getting There

Brooklyn Heights is located in South Brooklyn, across the Brooklyn Bridge from Lower Manhattan.

S 2/3 from Midtown to Clark St.

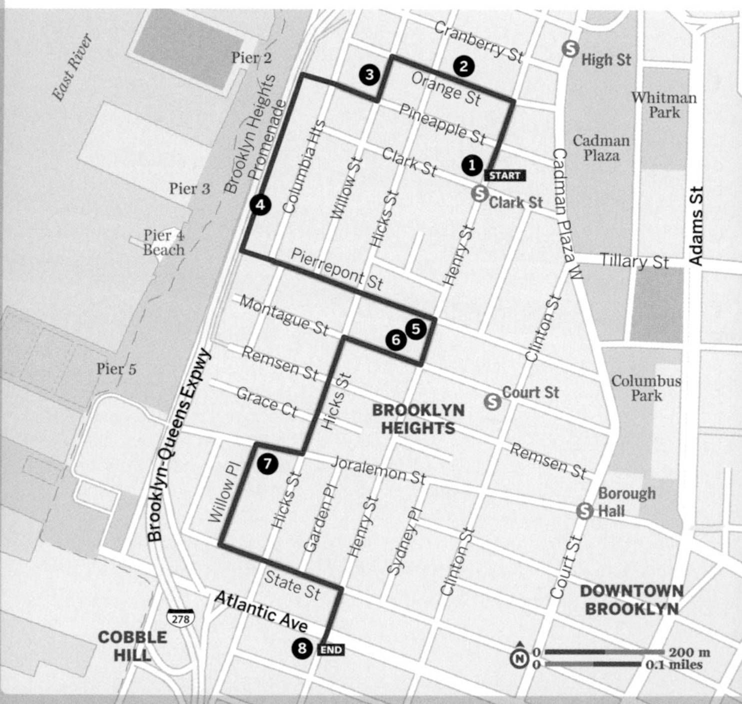

❶ Drip Coffee Makers

Start with a hand-brewed pour-over from **Drip**, housed in the Clark St subway station underneath the former Hotel St George.

❷ Plymouth Church

In the 1850s and '60s, Minister Henry Ward Beecher held mock slave auctions to purchase the freedom of actual enslaved people at this church, which also served as a station on the Underground Railroad. A plaque in pew 89 memorializes a visit from presidential candidate Abraham Lincoln in 1860. (www.plymouthchurch.org)

❸ 70 Willow Street

You'll want to read Truman Capote's *Brooklyn: A Personal Memoir*, his valentine to the neighborhood, after walking past *70 Willow Street*, where the acclaimed author wrote *In Cold Blood* and *Breakfast at Tiffany's* in the 1950s.

❹ Brooklyn Heights Promenade

Snag a bench to admire East River views from this eight-block esplanade perched atop the three-tiered Brooklyn-Queens Expressway. Manhattan's skyline shimmers across the tidal strait, while 19th-century homes overlook the park in Brooklyn Heights. (www.nycgovparks.org)

❺ Herman Behr Mansion

If the terra-cotta ornaments on this 1888 Romanesque Revival beauty could talk, they'd tell secrets from its days as a merchant's mansion, hotel, brothel and sleeping pad for Franciscan monks. Today, the building is divided into one-bedroom apartment rentals.

❻ L'Appartement 4F

The couple behind this sunny bakery live in neighboring Cobble Hill, but the pastries taste like they're straight from Paris. Locals queue up early for the coveted croissants; if they're gone, try a melt-in-your-mouth chocolate-chip cookie. (https://lappartement4f.com)

❼ 58 Joralemon Street

This Greek Revival building isn't a typical town house – it's an artfully disguised exterior for an MTA subway vent. The red-brick facade and ominous black windows follow laws protecting the neighborhood's historic landmark status.

❽ Long Island Bar

Slide into a red vinyl booth at this cool-cat juice joint dating back to 1951. With its easy-breezy atmosphere and cocktails crafted by Toby Cecchini (inventor of the Cosmo), it's easy to see why hip locals keep this bar abuzz. (http://thelongislandbar.com)

Worth a Trip

Spend a Day at Coney Island

Tattooed mermaids, vintage roller coasters and greasy-food stands await at this gritty-glamorous escape along the Brooklyn waterfront. A one-hour trip from Midtown, Coney Island became a democratized day-tripper destination in turn-of-the-20th-century New York, enticing locals with its promise of sugar-sand beaches and cotton-candy clouds. Spend a day admiring its old-world charms with childlike wonder.

Coney Island is around 14 miles southeast of Times Sq.

S D/F or N/Q to Coney Island-Stillwell Ave (last stop).

Strut Your Stuff

Walk down **Riegelmann Boardwalk** – a 2.5-mile waterfront promenade dating back to 1923 – to pass the area's top sights and spot a sea of colorful characters, including the Steeplechase Funny Face.

This smirking cartoon started as a logo for the now-demolished Steeplechase Park; it's become a Coney Island mascot, symbolizing the merry and maniacal sides of Brooklyn's historic 'riviera.'

Get Topsy-Turvy

Fancy getting flung into the air at 90 miles per hour? The Sling Shot awaits at **Luna Park** (www.lunaparknyc.com). Perhaps the 56mph race around the 2233ft-long Thunderbolt is more your speed. Or you can go old-school: New Yorkers started shrieking down the 85ft plunge of the wooden Cyclone in 1927, and the drop still thrills riders a century later.

But you don't have to be an adrenaline junkie to enjoy the fun. For an alternative to wild whirligigs, hop on the Wonder Wheel (white cars are stationary; red and blue cars swing) at Deno's Wonder Wheel Park (www.denoswonderwheel.com). Around since 1920, Coney Island's oldest-operating ride is also its most romantic: sweeping views from 150ft above the ground are bound to make your heart pitter-pat.

A Taste of Tradition

In 1916, Polish immigrant Nathan Handwerker started selling wieners for a nickel on the corner of Surf and Stillwell. Nowadays, **Nathan's Famous** (www.nathansfamous.com) is an international chain with a flagship eatery at Handwerker's original haunt.

The beefy frank – snuggled in a toasted bun, smothered with ketchup and mustard – is a Coney cuisine classic.

★ Top Tips

- There are two amusement parks with separate fees. Luna Park is bigger, with options to pay per ride or purchase an all-inclusive wristband that's good for four hours ($62). Deno's Wonder Wheel Park is a must-visit for its namesake Ferris wheel ($10).
- The official season runs Memorial Day to Labor Day. Go weekdays to avoid crowds.
- Experience Coney Island at its wackiest during the Mermaid Parade (June), Nathan's Famous Hot Dog Eating Contest (July) or Polar Bear Plunge (January).

Take a Break

For a refreshing reprieve from amusement-park mayhem, stop by **Coney Island Brewery** to sample local suds like the kölsch-style Beach Beer or summery Mermaid Pilsner.

citi bike
citi bike
citi bike
citi bike
citi bike
citi bike
00250
02030